IS GOD DEAD?????

IS GOD DEAD?????

THE TRUTH ABOUT JAMMU & KASHMIR

RAGHUBIR LAL ANAND
And
ABHILASH

PARTRIDGE
A Penguin Random House Company

To order additional copies of this book, contact
Partridge India
000 800 10062 62
www.partridgepublishing.com/india
orders.india@partridgepublishing.com

CONTENTS

Dedicated To

My revered parents *Shri Malik Chand Anand* (father) and Smt. *Mayadevi* (mother), who left for their heavenly abodes long ago. Their teachings have always inspired my journey of life.

FOREWORD

Today the whole world brought together by social media is raising their eyebrows and demanding justification for the happenings in Kashmir without actually knowing the problem in Kashmir and its fundamental roots. Everybody has heard somewhere or the other that Kashmir is the only paradise on Earth, but nobody knows—how many Kashmirs exist within this paradise? And everyday this paradise inches towards new hellish depths. This book is going to present the facts that have been historically recorded. With the sole purpose of raising the awareness level of students, teachers, politicians, corporations and in general every global citizen who is interested in justice, we strongly recommend the inclusion of this book in the curricullumn of all major Universities. Since Jammu and Kashmir has big potential for tourism (being the only paradise on Earth) this book should be placed in every room of all the 3 star and 5 star hotels around the world. The writers also invite the Police, Military, Intelligence agencies and other security establishments to read this book and send comments to the writers through publishers.

INTRODUCTION

The State of Jammu and Kashmir is in constant turmoil. Many a times people outside of this State and outside India do not make an effort to uncover the truth behind this tragedy. How is reading a three hundred page book on the plight of a community alien to the reader any different from the vast swarms of newspaper headlines, detailed editorials and documentaries that have scrutinized the Kashmir issue? The pages that follow this introduction have been written dispassionately and will arouse a heightened sense of rationale in the reader. What is Kashmir? Where is Kashmir? Who is a Kashmiri? An answer to all these and a reason as to *"Why only Kashmir?"* lies ahead for the reader. So embrace yourself for a walk in the paradise.

Until the mid 19th century, the term Kashmir geographically denoted only the valley between the Great Himalayas and the *Pir Panjal* mountain range. However today Kashmir denotes a larger area that includes the Indian administrated state of Jammu and Kashmir (the Kashmir Valley, Jammu and Ladakh), the Pakistan Occupied and administrated (*Gilgit Baltistan*), the so called—"*Azad*" (free) Kashmir Provinces, and the Chinese administrated regions of Aksai Chin and Trans Karakoram Tract.

In the first half of the first millennium, the Kashmir valley served as a prominent centre of Hinduism, which later also integrated Buddhism. *Shahmir* became the first Muslim ruler of Kashmir & established the *Salatin-e-Kashmir* of *Swati* dynasty. For the next five centuries Muslim monarchs ruled Kashmir, this included the *Mughals* who ruled from 1526 to 1751 followed by the Afghan *Durrani* Empire that ruled for another seven decades. Maharaja Ranjeet Singh annexed Kashmir in 1821 and made it a part of the (then flourishing) Sikh empire. Once the British East India Company had brought a sufficient number of princely states to submission, via the false pretext of commerce, they marched on to conquer the Sikh army of Punjab. The victory came finally in 1846 and Gulab Singh, who was a former official at the court of Sikhs and had spied for the British in Anglo-Sikh wars, purchased the Kashmir region from the British. Under the newly signed treaty of Amritsar he was given the title of Maharaja of Kingdom of Jammu. In the year 1947-48 this region became a point of contention once again. The Himalayan kingdom was connected to India via Hardoyi a district of Punjab, but its population was 77% Muslim and it shared a boundary with Pavidhan, Pakistan. Hence it was anticipated that the Maharaja would accede to Pakistan once the British occupation ended. When he hesitated to do this, Pakistan launched a guerrilla onslaught meant to frighten its ruler into submission. Instead the Maharaja appealed to the governor general for assistance who agreed on the condition that Kashmir would have to become a part of Independent India. Indian soldiers drove out the Pakistan sponsored irregulars from all but small section of the state. The United Nations was then invited to mediate the quarrel. The U.N. mission insisted that the opinion of citizens of Kashmir must be taken into account. India insisted that no referendum could occur until the entire state had been cleared of irregulars. In the last few days of 1948, a ceasefire was agreed upon. But since the plebiscite demanded by the U.N. was never conducted, the Princely state became a contentious territory, now administrated by three countries India, Pakistan and the People's Republic of China.

We have put forward a brief explanation of the geographical, political and religious tangents that intersect and divide this land which was once known as *"The Paradise on Earth"*. These facts also lead to the only formidable solution not only for the Indian audience but also readers abroad.

THE GREAT HIMALAYAS

India is the most diverse nation in the world. It has one sixth of the world's population living on the seventh largest landmass. The present book mainly concerns itself with one of its states—the northernmost state of Jammu and Kashmir. This state comprises of three major regions Jammu, the Kashmir Valley and Ladakh. Encompassing the land between the Greater Himalayan Range (*Himadri*) and the northern limits of the Deccan Plateau, this state is an integral part of India as ratified by her constitution.

The state is located in the lap of the Himalayas—the highest and the youngest mountains in the world that stretch over a length of about 2500 km (1553 miles) along the Indian sub-continent's northern edge, separating it from Central Asia and the Tibetan Plateau. According to Geographers it was about 30 million years ago when the Himalayas came into being as a result of a shift in the Gowdwana Land towards the North and its subsequent collision with the Eurasian land mass. As a result of the push, earth's crust took the form of three parallel mountain ranges now known as the Himalayas. These mountains have 30 of the world's highest peaks.

As for the Indians, Mount Kailas—the abode of Lord Shiva, who is believed to be the Destroyer of the Universe—is the most important peak of the Himalayan ranges. It is fairly important to note here that although Mt. Everest, the highest peak in the world, has been scaled many a times in the past by numerous mountaineers (both male and female) but the holy mountain of Kailas is yet to be conquered and according to Indian mythology it is impossible to do so unless your soul is pure enough to be accepted by Lord Shiva himself. The state of Jammu and Kashmir lies across six major Himalayan ranges with an area of 222,000 square kilometres or 85,000 square miles. It is India's northernmost state bordering Pakistan and the Tibetan Plateau.

The Himalayas have captivated almost all the countries of the world and the state of Jammu and Kashmir forms the pivot of this fascination. Alberuni, the court historian of Mahmood of Ghazni who accompanied him in his raids on India, praised the newly conquered Kashmir in Persian-

"Agar firdaus bar roo-e-zameen ast
Hameen ast Hameen ast Hameen ast"

—If at all paradise occurs on the surface of this earth, it is here and here alone.

THE HIMALAYAN PEAKS

Fourteen peaks in the Himalayas tower above 8,000 metres. Mount Everest, the world's highest peak rising to a height of 8848 metres above the sea-level, is located in Nepal. The two highest Himalayan peaks in India are—*Kanchan Jungha* 8598 metres (28,209 feet) and *Nanda Devi* 7817 metres (25,646 feet). *Nanda Devi* is also the highest Himalayan peak in the Kashmir region. *Kedarnath Peak* is 6940 metres (22,769 feet) above sea level. It has special importance as it is regarded as Lord Shiva's sacred mountain by Indians and houses the famous *Kedarnath* temple. A cloud burst ravaged the state of *Uttarakhand* in the month of June 2013. However the initial relief efforts by the army revealed that though the entire town and its neighbouring village lay in debris the holy shrine and the ceremonial garlands that were offered by the pilgrims lay untouched upon the mountain. *Trishul* (Trident) is 7120 metres (23,360 feet) above sea level and is equally important as it is directly associated with Lord Shiva's preferred weapon—*Trishul*. *Bandar Punchh* (Monkey's Tail) is 6316 metres above sea level and attracts mountaineers from across the globe in large numbers as it is visible from *Dodital*.

MARINE FOSSILS

A large number of Marine fossils have been found in the Himalayan rocks at high altitudes. They testify the fact that the Himalayas have risen from the depths of an ocean floor which has been named Tetbys by the geographers.

FLORA AND FAUNA

The vegetation of the Himalayas includes sub-tropical forests, temperate coniferous tree lands and Alpine vegetation. They are a source of an abundant variety of useful plants, herbs and animal life. *Brahma Kamal* (*Sanssurea ovvallata*) is of great religious importance as it is considered to be the most sacred offering in the temples of this region. Deodar (*Cedrus deodars*) is a towering coniferous tree in the temperate zone of the Western Himalayas.

Bar-headed Geese (*Ancer indicus*) reside in attractive aquatic worlds that flourish in high-altitude lakes of Ladakh. Bharal (*Pseudois nayaur*) popularly called blue sheep because of the blue sheen on its grey court is a beautiful animal that inhabits the harsh stony slopes above the snowline. Snow leopard (*Crucia uncial*) is an endangered species that inhabits the slopes above the height of 4,000 metres (13,123 feet). It preys on wild sheep and hares. Yak is a domestic animal that gives milk and is used as a pack animal for rides and carrying loads in Ladakh

The Future of Himalayas

The Future of world's most famous mountain range could be endangered by a vast dam building project, as a risky regional race for water resources begins in Asia. New academic research shows that India, Nepal, Bhutan and Pakistan are engaged in a huge *"water grab"* in the Himalayas, as they seek new resources of electricity to power their economics. Taken together, these countries have plans of more than four hundred hydroelectric power projects which if built could provide more than 160,000MW of electricity. In addition, China has plans for around 100 dams to generate a similar amount of power from major rivers rising in Tibet. A further 60 or more dams are being planned for the Mekong River which also rises in Tibet and flows through south-east Asia. Most of the Himalayan Rivers have been relatively untouched by dams near their sources. Now India and China are rushing to harness them as they cut through some of the world's deepest valleys. Many of the proposed dams would be amongst the tallest in the world with the ability to generate more than 4,000MW of power individually. The result is that over the next 20 years the Himalayas could become the most dammed region in the world. India aims to construct 292 dams, thereby doubling the current hydropower capacity and increasing the share of hydro electric power to 6% of the total installed capacity of India. If all dams are constructed as proposed the Indian Himalayas would have one of the highest average dam densities in the world with one dam for every 32km of river channel. Every neighbour of India with undeveloped hydropower sites is building or planning to build multiple dams totalling a minimum 129 projects. China is building multiple dams on all the major rivers running off the Tibetan plateau and is likely to emerge as the ultimate controller of water for nearly 40% of the world's population. China is in a haste to gain control over the entire supply of water in Asia. Not only is it damming the rivers on the plateau but also financing and building mega dams in Pakistan, Laos, and Burma and elsewhere making agreements to take the power.

The Tibetan Plateau is the source of the single largest collection of International rivers in the world including the Mekong, Brahmaputra, Yangtse and the Yellow river. It is the head water of rivers on which nearly half the world depends. The net effect of the dam building could be disastrous. The landslides, cloud bursts and the recent tragedy at Lord *Kedarnath* temple in Uttarakhand are an eye opener because the devastation has happened primarily due to the construction of dams in the sacred valley of *Kedarnath* temple. We cannot imagine the irreversible consequences of this large scale exploitation of Mother Nature.

JAMMU REGION

The name of this region—*Jambu Dweep*—meaning *Jamun (Syzygium cumini)* shaped island comes from the old Hindu Scriptures belonging to the Vedic Times. This island is one of the nine islands mentioned in the *Puranas*. Jammu, the capital of this region is situated on the banks of river *Tawi*. This region borders the states of Punjab and Himachal Pradesh. Its capital is at a distance of 500 kilometres (311 miles) from Delhi, the national capital. Nestled in the foot-hills of the *Shivalak range* it overlooks the Great Northern Plain of India. *Shivalak* means the tresses of Lord Shiva. The capital of Jammu and Kashmir was shifted to Jammu during the intense winter months that enveloped the Kashmir valley by the end of November. Srinagar served as the summer capital. The Abdullah Family that has been in constant command of politics in the state of Jammu and Kashmir are natives of Jammu city.

Geography

Jammu borders Kashmir to the north, Ladakh to the east and Himachal Pradesh and Punjab to the south. In the west, the Line of Control separates Jammu from the Pakistan region called Azad Jammu and Kashmir. Sandwiched between the Valley of Kashmir to the north and the *Darran Koh* Plains to the south, the *Shivalak* Range dominates the topography of Jammu. The *Pir Panjal* Range, the *Trikuta* Hills and the low-lying *Tawi* River basin add beauty and diversity to Jammu. The *Pir Panjal* range separates Jammu from the Kashmir Valley.

The People

The people of Jammu are religious, peace loving, secular and broadminded in their day to day dealings. They are desirous of peace and prosperity not only for themselves but for the entire nation. At the same time they are extremely valiant and ever ready to face any impediment that may threaten their peaceful ways. Dogras are known for their bravery just like the *Rajputs* of Rajasthan. Hitler's army was defeated by the *Dogra* Soldiers in 1942 in Egypt during the Second World War, though they had to sacrifice an entire generation for this arduous task. The Hindus and Sikhs constitute a majority of Jammu's population, though Muslims are also there as an important community. The Sikhs probably migrated to this region during the reign of Maharaja Ranjeet Singh, whose general had conquered not only the Jammu Region but the Kashmir Valley and its neighbouring Ladakh region as well. The lifestyle of the people of Jammu region resembles that of the people of Punjab.

The Holy City

Jammu is known as the city of temples. An aura of spirituality surrounds the visitors. A particular sense of peace prevails as soon as one enters the precincts of this holy city and it will not be out of place to remark that blessings of Goddess *Vaishno* and Lord Shiva, the King of demigods, prevail in the entire state and especially in the Jammu region. Most of the prominent temples in Jammu were constructed by the *Dogra Kings* except the *Raghunath* temple which was built at the behest of Emperor *Jahangir* who had been blessed by a sage living at the place where this temple stands now. There is no denying the fact that the Vaishno Devi Cave Shrine, Amaranth Caves and several holy places of Muslims in Jammu and other parts of the state form the very basis of the state earnings through the tourism department. Apart from the *Raghunath* Temple, Amar Mahal Museum which was once the residence of Maharaja Amar Singh is another place of attraction. The magnificent museum is full of valuable artefacts of the past.

Jammu—The Lifeline

Jammu virtually forms the gateway to the state of Jammu and Kashmir. All the rail and road routes originate as well as terminate at this summer capital of the state. The State Police, Paramilitary Forces and the Army units responsible for the defence of the state against internal and external dangers have their bases located within this important city. The city has its own airport. Industries in Jammu reap ample benefits from the electricity produced here. Bari Brahman Industrial Area is an important industrial centre with a number of small and medium enterprises. These industries provide employment to a large number of people. In spite of the curse of militancy in the state of Jammu and Kashmir, Jammu is unquestionably a role model of our democratic and secular values.

Jammu serves as the green belt and the reservoir of goods and services for the entire state. Various fruits (green as well as dry), vegetables, condiments, worship materials, chemicals and herbal medicines, various types of vehicles, petro-products consumed by the people of the state are easily available in the markets of this grand city. That is why Jammu forms a base and a hub for the tourists visiting the state almost all the year around.

Economic Hub

Jammu is famous for the production of its superior variety Basmati rice, for which a big export market is located at *Ranbir Singh Pura*. All horticultural exports of the state of Jammu and Kashmir to other parts of India originate from this very market. Also Jammu is a major source of revenue generation and the Head Office of the State Department of Tourism. This department is responsible for the promotion of Tourism in the entire state, contributing a major share of the total revenue of the state which is then used for governmental expenditure elsewhere. The city of Jammu has developed a strong infrastructure to accommodate tourists in extremely large numbers and in the process attract huge sums of foreign exchange. The grandeur of its monuments and architectural splendour of its tourist lodges are often better than their global counterparts.

Refuge

Most of the poor Kashmiri pundits from the valley of Kashmir have been provided shelter in a big camp located in this grand city after their forcible exodus from the valley by extremists and separatist Muslim fanatics.

Maa Vaishno Devi Temple

Mythology

According to *Shikhir* (Hindu epic), *Maa Vaishno Devi* was born in the south of India in the home of *Ratnakar Sagar*. Her worldly parents had remained childless for a long time. *Ratnakar* had promised the night before the birth of the Divine child that he would not interfere with whatever his child desired. *Maa Vaishno Devi* was called *Trikuta* as a child. Later she was called *Vaishnavi* because of her birth from Lord Vishnu's lineage. When *Trikuta* was 9 years old, she sought her father's permission for doing penance on the seashore. *Trikuta* prayed to Lord Vishnu's incarnation in the form of Ram. During Shree Ram's search for Sita, he reached the seashore with his army. His eyes fell on this divine girl in deep meditation. *Trikuta* told Shree

Ram that she had accepted him as her husband. Lord Rama told her that he couldn't accept her, as he was obligate with one wife consort in this life but promised her to meet in Kaliyug. In the meantime Shree Ram asked *Trikuta* to meditate in the cave found in the *Trikuta* Range of *Manik* Mountains in northern India. Lord Ram gave her a bow and arrows, an army of monkeys and a lion for her protection. *Maa* observed the *Navratra* (nine nights) for the Victory of Shree Rama against *Ravana*, hence one reads the epic of Ramayana during the nine days of *Navratra*. Shree Rama promised that the whole world would sing *Maa Vaishno Devi's* praise. Lord Rama said *Trikuta* was to become famous as *Vaishno Devi* and would become immortal forever. The abode of *Maa Vaishno devi* has attained a primary status among other pilgrimages due to Lord Rama's blessings.

Story of Shreedhar

With the passage of time many more stories about the Mother Goddess emerged. One such story is about *Shreedhar*. *Shreedhar* was an ardent devotee of *Maa Vaishno Devi*. He resided in a village called *Hansali*, 2 km from the present *Katra* town. Once *Maa* appeared to him in the form of a girl, the girl asked the humble Pundit to hold a 'Bhandara' (a feast to feed the mendicants and devotees). The Pundit set out to invite people from the village and nearby places. He also invited *Bhairav Nath*, a selfish tantric. *Bhairav Nath* asked *Shreedhar* how he was going to provide for the feast. He reminded him of the bad consequences in case of failure. As Pundit ji was lost in worry, the divine girl appeared and told him not to be despondent as everything had been arranged. She asked that over 360 devotees be seated in the small hut. True to her word the *Bhandara* went smoothly with food and place to spare.

Bhairav Nath admitted that the girl had supernatural powers and decided to test her further. He followed the divine girl to *Trikuta* Hills. For nine months *Bhairav Nath* was searching for the mystic girl in the mountains, who he believed was an incarnation of the Mother Goddess. While running away from *Bhairav*, Devi shot an arrow into the Earth from which water gushed out. The resultant river is known as "Baanganga". It is believed that by taking a bath in *Baanganga* (baan: arrow), a believer of the Mother Goddess can wash away all his sins. The banks of the river, known as *Charan Paduka*, are marked by Devi's foot imprints, which remain intact till date. *Vaishno Devi* then took shelter in a cave known as *Garbh Joon* near *Adhkawari*, where she meditated for nine months attaining spiritual wisdom and powers. Her meditation was cut short when *Bhairav* located her. *Vaishno Devi* was then compelled to take the form of *Maha Kali* when *Bhairav* tried to kill her. The manifestation of the Mother Goddess took place at the mouth of the Holy cave at *Darbar*. The Goddess then beheaded *Bhairav* with such sheer force that his skull fell at a place known as *Bhairav Ghati*, 2.5 km from the Holy Cave.

In his dying moments, *Bhairav* pleaded for forgiveness. The Goddess knew that *Bhairav's* main intention in attacking her was to achieve salvation. She liberated Bhairav from the cycle of reincarnation and ordained that every devotee had to visit the nearby temple of Bhairav Nath (after visiting the Holy cave) to ensure the completion of his pilgrimage. Meanwhile *Vaishno Devi* assumed the shape of a rock with three *Pindis* (heads) and immersed herself into meditation forever.

Meanwhile, Pundit *Shreedhar* became impatient. He started to march towards *Trikuta* Mountain on the same path that he had been shown in a dream. He ultimately reached the cave mouth. He made a daily routine of worshiping the *Pindis* in several ways. His worship pleased the Goddess. She appeared in front of him and blessed him. Since that day, *Shreedhar* and his descendants have been worshiping the Mother Goddess *Vaishno Devi*.

Geography

Vaishno Devi Temple is near the town of Katra, in the Reasi district of Jammu and Kashmir, India. It is one of the most revered places of worship in India. The shrine is at an altitude of 5300 feet and a distance of approximately 12 kilometres (7.5 mi) from Katra. About 8 million pilgrims visit the temple every year and it is the second most visited religious shrine in India. The Sri Mata Vaishno Devi Shrine Board maintains the shrine. A rail link from Udhampur to Katra has been recently completed to facilitate the pilgrimage. The nearest airport is Jammu Airport which has very high flight frequency, and is served by all leading domestic airlines. This place contains three idols of *Maha Saraswati, Maha Lakshmi,* and *Maha Kali,* which are all images of *Vaishno Devi.* The shrine is worshiped as a *Shakti Peetha* which believes its association towards the mythology of *Daksha yajna and Sati's* self immolation as its origin. *Shakti Peethas* are shrines sanctified with the presence of *Shakti* (primordial cosmic energy) due to the falling of body parts of the corpse of Sati Devi, when Lord Shiva carried her dead body and wandered throughout in sorrow. There are 51 *Shakti Peetha* linked to the 51 alphabets of Sanskrit language.

Travel

Maa Vaishno Devi temple can be reached from Katra. Katra is a small but bustling town around 45 km from Jammu. From Katra, after getting the 'Yatra Parchi' (Journey Slip) for *darshan* (visit), devotees can proceed to the *Bhavan* (temple complex). The way to the *Bhavan* is steep and requires a long walk uphill. Alternatively ponies and palanquins are also available. Helicopter service can also be taken for a large part of the trip. The Trust offers comfortable stay for pilgrims. Indian Railways have started rail services up to Katra from July 1st 2013. They are negotiating with the Jammu and Kashmir Government to integrate permit slips for Vaishno Devi Darshan with the train ticket. The passenger can get permit slips while booking the train ticket.

DOGRAS

The origins of the name "Jammu" are shrouded in mystery, as is the history of the people inhabiting the territory. Popularly known as *Duggar*, the towns of the region with their fortresses stand testimony to a distinct cultural and linguistic identity. Some try to trace the origin of the name to the word—"*Jambudvipchandraa*", a combination of the words *Jambu* and *dwipa* (island). According to Sir Walter Hamilton (Description of Hindustan), *"It is possible that an ocean may at one time have reached the base of these mountains forming high table lands into islands."* The famous Chinese traveller

Xuanzang describes the valley of *Pamir* as "the centre of *Jambudwipa*." Some attribute the name to *Jambavantha* or *Jamwant*, the *Riksharaja* (the king of the bears in the army of King Sugriva in the Ramayana), who is said to have meditated in the *Peer Kho* Cave on the banks of the *Tawi* River. Another popular belief is that Jammu owes its name to Raja *Jambulochan*, and the city remains significant since the 14th century BC. According to the Imperial Gazetteer of India, the origin of the word "Dogra" is accredited to the fact that the cradle of the Dogra people lies between the two lakes of *Sruinsar* and *Mansar*. *Dwigart Desh* (meaning country of two hollows) was converted into *Duggar* and *Dugra*, which then became "Dogra".

Demogarphics

Dogras are an Indo-Aryan ethnic group native of South Asia. The Dogras include both *Savarnas* such as Rajputs and Brahmins as well as *non Savarnas*. The Dogras also include some mercantile classes (Vaishyas) such as *Mahajans, Suds Guptas* and *Aggarwals* etc.

Rajput Dogras are believed to be *Suryavanshi* sharing their lineage with *Chandervanshi Rajputs* of *Schattari*. They migrated many centuries ago from *Rajputana* (now called Rajasthan) to the hilly areas of Himachal Pradesh in (*Una, Kangra, Mandi, Bilaspur, Hamirpur*). They live predominantly in the Jammu region of the state of Jammu and Kashmir with some scattered population extending to adjoining areas of Punjab, Himachal and North-Eastern Pakistan. They speak their own language, *Dogri,* which was recognized as one of the national languages of India in 2003. Most Dogras are Hindus, but some are Sikhs and Muslims.

The Jammu Dogras traditionally inhabited the slopes of *Shivalak* range of mountains, between the sacred lakes of *Saroien sar* and *Mannsar,* but gradually over a period of several centuries they spread to other parts of Jammu region as well. They generally speak *Dogri* and some dialects which also have similarity with *Dogri*. Majority of them have faith in Hinduism. The Dogra Culture has been derived from the same Indo-Aryan branch which migrated to and settled in Gangatic plains. Dogras are divided into castes on the same lines as Hindus in other parts of India, but have local variations. In the sixteenth and seventeenth centuries some Dogras embraced Islam. Hence a good number of Dogras in Jammu and Kashmir believe in other religions also. Moreover large scale immigration in this region resulted in the amalgamation of all major religions within the Jammu and Kashmir *Dogra* population.

DOGRA ART

According to *Kurl Khaddalwal*, Raja Kirpal of *Basholi* was the first to patronize artists in his court. In 1875 *Pahari* School came into being. The earliest paintings in *Pahari* Style originated in *Basohli*. The first mention of *Basohli* paintings is in the annual report of the archaeological Survey of India for the year 1918-1919 published in 1921. Subsequently, this style spread to the Hill States of *Maknkot, Nurpur Kullu Mandi, Suket Bilaspur, Nalagaph chamba, Guler and Kangra.* Raja Sandra Chand, Raja Balwant Singh and other *Pahari* rulers, further nurtured generations of proficient artists in their courts.

FOLK DANCES

KUD

It is basically a ritual dance performed in honour of Local deities. This dance is performed mostly during nights. It is a spontaneous dance and people of all ages participate in this folk dance. Instruments used during the dance are *Narshimgha, Chhaina*, Flute, drums etc. It is the rhythm of music which controls the movement of participants. This dance continues for the whole night. Members of both genders participate in numbers ranging from 20 to 30.

HEREN

It is a traditional dance form performed during *Lohri* festival by 10-15 member troupes. This style is mostly performed in hilly regions of Jammu.

FUMENIE AND JAGRATA

This dance style is performed by the ladies on the eve of groom's departure to in-law's house. Both the songs are by a group of females consisting of 15-20 members. The traditional dance form depicts the feelings and emotions of women folk.

BAKH/GWATRI/KARK/MASADE

It is a chorus narrative sung by a group of 10 singers without the accompaniment of any musical instruments.

GWATRI

It is a song and dance tradition in which the singers narrate some text while the *Gwatri* dancers enact it simultaneously.

KARAK

A Ballet sung by a community called *Jogis*. The three member group narrates a popular folk tale and dance to the music of a typical folk instrument called *Rabab*.

BENTHE

This is a chorus singing tradition performed specifically by a tribal community called Gujjar.

DOGRI FOLK LITERATURE

Dogri folk literature is rich in both prose and verse.

LYRICS

They are vast and varied ranging from love lyricism, ceremonial lyrics, and dance lyrics to Dogri folk songs. Some tell tales of heroism and sacrifice while others explore human reactions to ceremonies. *Biayian* are sung to celebrate the birth of child. *Dogri* also has a rich collection of Ballads—*Baran, Kaarkan*, and Devotional.

RELIGION

The mountains of Jammu and Kashmir are sacred for Hindus all over the world as it has many famous temples.

MATA VAISHNO DEVI SHRINE

This is the most pious and famous of Hindu Religious places. The holy cave of the Mother Goddess is situated at an altitude of 5200 ft. atop the *Shivalik* Mountains. The devotees undertake a 12 km uphill trek from the base camp at *Katra*. Three natural rock formations called *Pindies* represent the mother, the woman, the female fountainhead of all creations.

AMARNATH CAVE

The shrine of *Amarnath ji* is one of the four principal Hindu pilgrimages. It is located in a narrow gorge at the farther end of *Lidder* valley. The devotees travel a distance of nearly 100 km and ascend to an altitude of 3,888m above sea level to reach the holy cave within a period of 2 days. The sanctum enshrines an ice lingam which is formed naturally every year.

RAGHUNATH TEMPLE

Raghunath temple is a spectacle of Hindu temple architecture. It is situated in *Raghunath* bazaar, Jammu. Dedicated to Lord Rama, the temple was constructed by the *Dogra* Kings of Jammu region.

MARRIAGE CUSTOMS AMONG DOGRAS

Some Dogras still follow a special type of marriage which is called 'Dohry'. According to this tradition families unite by virtue of two marriages. One boy and one girl from each family marry his/her respective partner from the other family. This was usually the case when brother and sisters would get married in the same ceremony. The ingenuity of this idea curtailed several social evils like dowry. 'Chadar pana', or marrying the brother's widow is also prevalent in Jammu. Child marriage was rampant until Maharaja Hari Singh banned it in 1940 and raised the age of marriage for girls to 16 years and boys to 18 years. In the hilly areas of *Udhampur, Kathua and Doda* people also take concubines termed as 'Duals'. Some Dogras take their surname from their sub-caste which is useful when traditional families are looking to arrange marriages for their children.

DOGRA CUISINE

Breads made from wheat, maize and barley are the staple assortments of everyday cuisine. Rice, cereals and a tangy preparation made from either mango or tamarind (also popularly known as *Maani*) is savoured together as a complete meal famously known as *Dal Puth Manni*. *Mitha Madra* is a favourite and is cooked from milk, dry fruits and semolina. Preparations of *Rajmosh* (a special variety of red kidney beans), *Auria* a dish of curd fermented by rye, *Ambal* made from pumpkin, jaggery and tamarind are favourites especially during ceremonial cooking. The expert cooks are called *Siyans* who are usually Brahmins.

Non-vegetarian food was limited to Rajputs and Vaishyas *(Mahajans)*. *Khatta Meat*—mutton cooked with sour pomegranate seeds or lime juice and flavoured with fumes of a burning charcoal soaked in mustard-oil. *Keur* is one of the famous foods of Dogras. It is prepared from flour, butter and is served with sugar and curd. Mostly, it is served to bridegroom at the time of marriage by the in-laws. *Kalari* is also one of the favourite foods of Dogras in the rainy season. It is prepared by mixing flour with cottage cheese and milk cream *(malai)* with water in a small pot. *Kalari* is served with milk. *Kalari* cheese is also popular in the Jammu region. *Babbru or Pathoru* is prepared from flour and fried in mustard oil. Babbru is served with curd. *Kheer* is a dish prepared from milk by adding some rice and dry fruit in it. It is a special dessert and served in almost all the special occasions and festivals. Another popular exotic dish is *Guchiyyan* (dried mushroom—black morel), usually added as an ingredient in rice. As it grows naturally in forests and cannot be cultivated, it is a priced commodity and makes an excellent dish with mountain potatoes. Saffron or *Kesar* is extensively used to flavour sweet dishes and for its anti-oxidant benefits.

THE MARTIAL TRADITION OF THE DOGRAS

The Dogras are known for their valour. The Dogras Regiment was one of the prominent regiments of the British Indian Army, which made significant contributions in both the World Wars on all fronts from the Far East to Europe and North Africa. After Independence, it became an infantry regiment of the Indian Army composed largely but not exclusively of the Dogras. The Jammu and Kashmir Rifles, another regiment of the Indian Army, consisting of mainly Dogras was formed out of the former army of the Kingdom of Jammu and Kashmir after it was absorbed into the Indian Army.

NOTABLE DOGRAS

1. Adarsh Sein Anand, Padma Vibhushan Awardee, the Chief Justice of the Supreme Court of India.
2. Banda Singh Bahadur, Sikh warrior and martyr.

3. Bansi Lal Sharma, a Geo-Scientist from Jammu who was a member of the 9th Indian Expedition to Antarctica.
4. Chaman Lal Gupta Politician, BJP leader Ex-Minister Union of India.
5. General Zorawar Singh, general of Maharaja Gulab Singh.
6. Hari Singh (1895-1961) last ruling Maharaja of the princely state/ Kingdom of Jammu and Kashmir in India.
7. Karan Singh, son of Hari Singh and distinguished diplomat.
8. Kundan Lal Saigal, Hindi movie singer and actor.
9. Maharaja Gulab Singh, general of Mahraja Ranjit Singh and later Maharaja of the Dogra Kingdom of Jammu and Kashmir.
10. Malika Pukhrakj, Renowned singer.
11. Mukesh Rishi, Bollywood actor.
12. Om Prakash, vetran bollywood actor.
13. Paras Dogra, Cricketer, Plays for Rajasthan Royals in IPL.
14. Premchand Dogra, bodybuilder, Mr. India (9 times) Mr. Asia (8 times) and IFBB Mr Universe 1988.
15. Shesh Pail Vaid, IPS officer.
16. Som Nath Sharma, first recipient of the Param Vir Chakra.
17. Shivkumar Sharma, renowned *santoor* player.
18. Ustad Alla Rakha, Padama Shri Awardee, Tabla player.
19. Girdhari Lal Dogra, Freedom Fighter, former MLA and former Member of Parliament Jammu (*Udhampur*) from partition till death.
20. Krishan Kumar Sharma, Journalist and Hindi poet.
21. Bhavan Singh, Vedic vision.

ROYAL HOUSE OF JAMMU AND KASHMIR

According to Legend, the Dogras trace their ancestry to the *Ikshvaku* (Solar) Dynasty of Northern India (The same clan in which Lord Rama was born). Lord Ram is therefore the *Kuldevta* (family deity) of the Dogras. A *Raghuvanshi* descendant, *Agni Garba,* who was living as a recluse, came to *Nagakote* (Kangra) in the *Shivalak* Hills. When the Raja of *Kangra* (Himachal Pradesh) came to know about his ancestry he offered him the hand of his daughter and a part of the Kingdom. The river Ravi was then the boundary of *Nagarkote. Agni Garba* crossed it and captured some villages in *Kathua* area and declared himself as a sovereign King. His son *Bayusharva* (B.C. 1530-1500) married the princess of *Parole* (*Kathua*). The princess was known as *Erwan* and she died young. The Raja founded a city near *Parole* in her memory. Though now the city has been reduced to a small village, her tomb is still the centre of an annual festival which is held every year on the auspicious day of *Baisakhi* (13th or 14th April). *Bayusharva* extended the boundaries up to the river *Ujh*. *Bayusharva's* great grandson, *Bahulocha* was enthroned after his death. He migrated from *Erwan* (the city) and built his fort on the banks of River *Tawi*. *Bahulochan* died in a bloody battle with *Chjadaras*, Raja of *Sialkot* and his younger brother *Jambulochan* (B.C. 1320-1289) ascended the throne. In those days the area beyond *Tawi*—the present city of Jammu—was used for hunting. History states that one day *Jambulochan* came to the area and while he was sitting behind a bush to ambush some animal, he saw a lion (a tiger in some accounts) and a goat drinking water from the same pond. The miraculous sight encouraged him to lay the foundation of the city of Jammu, which some say is named after him. One of his descendents, *Raja Shakti Karan* (B.C. 1200-1177) introduced the *Dogri* Script. Their successors are primarily responsible for developing Jammu in to a major city of North India. *Raja Jasdev* and *Raja Karan Dev* *famously* founded the cities along the banks of river *Ujh* and *Basantar* respectively. In the early centuries of the first millennium this area was conquered by Indo-Greeks who ruled from the capital city of *Sakala (Sialkot)*.

Establishing the Modern Rule

The *Duggar* Raj was established as a regional domain with Maharaja Gulab Singh emerging as a warrior and the subjects in his domain getting special martial recognition by the British Empire. Gulab Singh's reign extended over the entire Jammu Region and large parts of Ladakh region by March 1846 and was popularly known as Dogra Raj. An extensive part of Punjab (now Himachal Pradesh) too was traditionally a part of Dogra clan irrespective of the religious faith one held. The treaty of Lahore signed on 9th March 1846 ceded Kashmir (and some other territories) to the British Empire, who then handed it over to Gulab Singh. Under the Treaty of Amritsar, the Dogra king of Jammu was thereafter known as the Maharaja of Jammu and Kashmir Raj (state), also referred to as Kashmir State thereafter. The term Dogra hence is akin to the subjects of Himachal Pradesh, some areas of Punjab and whole region of Jammu that was ruled by Raja Gulab Singh as part of Dogra Raj irrespective of the religion one practiced.

Prominent Rulers

Among the prominent rulers of Jammu was *Raja Ranjit Dev*, (1728-1780) who introduced certain social reforms such as a ban on Sati (immolation of the wife on the Pyre of the husband) and female infanticide.

The Sikh dynasty was at its pinnacle under Maharaja Ranjeet Singh, who annexed Jammu and Kashmir. Under his rule this state was governed by one of his generals, Maharaja Gulab Singh Jamwal, who belonged to the Jamwal Rajput clan that ruled Jammu. He extended the boundaries of Jammu to western Tibet with the help of General Zorawar Singh. The Sikh Empire extended beyond Jammu region and the Kashmir Valley to the Tibetan Buddhist Kingdom of Ladakh and the emirate of *Hunza, Gilgit* and *Nagar*. After the first Anglo—Sikh War in 1846, British gave Kashmir and the title of Maharaja to Gulab Sigh as a reward for his treachery against the Sikhs.

Pratap Singh (enthroned in 1855) saw the construction of *Bahihal Cart Road* (B.C. Road) mainly to facilitate telegraph Services. The last kings of Rajput Kingdom of Jammu and Kashmir ceded their kingdom to the Indian Union in 1947. The last ruler of Jammu and Kashmir was Maharaja Hari Singh, who ascended the throne in 1925. He made primary education compulsory in the state, introduced laws prohibiting child marriage and threw open places of worship for low caste. Singh's reign saw the accession of Jammu and Kashmir to the newly independent Indian Union in 1947. He originally manoeuvred to maintain his independence by playing off India and Pakistan against each other however, following an incursion by Pakistan in October 1947. Singh appealed to India for its help and acceded to India. These events triggered the first Indo-Pakistan War. Singh retreated to Jammu and eventually left the State. In 1951 Singh's rule was terminated by the State Government of Indian Kashmir. His son Prince Karan Singh was elected *Sadre-e-Riyasat* (President of Province) and Governor of the state in 1964. His Highness Dr. Karan Singh is the present titular Maharaja of Jammu and Kashmir.

LIST OF MAHARAJA OF JAMMU AND KASHMIR

Gulab Singh (1846-1857)
Ranbir Singh (1857-1885)

Pratap Singh (1885-1925)
Hari Singh (1925-1949)
Hari Singh (Title only) (1949-1961)
Karan Singh (Title only) (1961-Present)

Maharaja Hari Singh

Maharaja Hari Singh (21st September 1895-26th April 1961) was the last ruling Maharaja of the princely state of Jammu and Kashmir in India.

EARLY LIFE

Hari Singh was born on 23 September 1895 at the palace of *Amar Mahal*, Jammu. He was the only surviving son of General Raja Sir Amar Singh, who was the younger son of General *Maharajadhiraj Sri Sir Ranbir Singh* and the brother of Lieutenant-General *Maharajadiraj Sri Sir Pratap Singh*, the then Maharaja of Jammu and Kashmir.

EDUCATION AND PREPARATION FOR THE THRONE

In 1903, *Hari Singh* served as a page of Honour to Lord Curzon at the grand Delhi Durbar. At the age of 13, *Hari Singh* was dispatched to Mayo College in Ajmer. A year later in 1909, when his father died, the British took a personal interest in his education and appointed Major *H.K. Brar* as his guardian. After Mayo College the ruler-in-waiting went to the Imperial Cadet corps at Dehradun for military training. As such he was conditioned to the British upper-crust atmosphere. By the age of 20 he had been appointed commander-in-chief of the Jammu and Kashmir state forces.

REIGN

Following the death of his uncle, *Sir Pratap Singh*, in 1975, *Sir Hari Singh* ascended the throne of Jammu and Kashmir. He made primary education compulsory in the State, introduced laws prohibiting child marriage and threw open places of worship for the low castes. Singh was hostile towards the Indian National Congress, in part because of the close friendship between Kashmir political activist sheikh Abdullah and Nehru. He also opposed the Muslim League and its member's communist outlook, illustrated in their two-nation theory. During the Second World War, from 1944-1946 *Sir Hari Singh* was a member of the Imperial War Cabinet. In 1947, after India gained independence from British rule, Jammu and Kashmir had the option to join either India or Pakistan or to remain independent. He originally tried to maintain his independence by avoiding commitment to either of the two. There was a widespread belief that rulers of the princely states, in deciding to accede to India or Pakistan, should respect the wishes of the population. But few rulers took any steps to consult the public on such decisions. Jammu and Kashmir was a Muslim majority state, and a mutiny of Muslim regiments in *Gilgit* occurred in October 1947. *Hari Singh* appealed to India for help. India refused to come to his aid unless he acceded to India. *Hari Singh* signed the instrument of accession on October 26, 1947, according to which the princely state (including Jammu, Kashmir, Northern Areas of Ladakh, Trans-Karakoram Tract and Aksai Chin) became a part of India. These events triggered the first Indo-Pakistan War.

Pressure from Pundit Jawaharlal Nehru and Sardar Vallabh Bhai Patel compelled *Hari Singh* to appoint his son and heir Karan Singh, as the regent of Jammu and Kashmir in 1949. Hari Singh remained the titular Maharaja of the state until 1952, when the monarchy was abolished. Hari Singh retried to Bombay (Mumbai) where he died on 26 April 1961 of a heart attack.

FAMILY

Singh married four times in all:—

1. Dharampur Rani Sri Lal Kunverba Sahiba married at Rajkot 7 may 1913, died during pregnancy in 1915. No Issue.
2. Chamba Rani Sahiba married at Chamba 8 November 1915, died 31 January 1920. No issue.
3. Maharani Dhanvat Kunveri Baiji Sahiba (1910-19) married at Dharampur 30 April 1923. No issue.
4. Maharani Tara Devi Sahiba of Kangra (1910-1967) married 1928, separated 1950, one son.
5. Yuvaraj (Crown Prince), i.e. heir-apparent Karan Singh (9 March 1931).

TITLES

- 1895-1916 Sri Hari Singh.
- 1916-1918 Raja Sri Hari Singh.
- 1918-1922 Captain Raja Sri Sir Hari Singh, KCIE.
- 1922-1925 Captain Raja Sri Sir Hari singh, KCIE, KCVO.
- 1925-1926 Captain His Highness Shriman Rajarajeshwar Maharaja Adhiraj Sri Sir Hari Singh Indar Mahinder Bhadur Sipar-i-Sultanat Maharaja of Jammu and Kashmir, GCIE, KVCO.
- 1933-1935 Colonel His Highness Shriman Rajrajeshwar Mahraja Adhiraj Sri Sir Hari Singh Indar Mahinder Bahadur Sipar-i-sultanat Maharaja of Jammu and Kashmir, GCIE, GCIE, KCVO
- 1935-1941 Major-General His Highness Shriman Rajarajeshwar Maharajadhiraj Sri Sir Hari Singh Indar Mahinder Bahdur Sipar-i-Sultanat Maharaja of Jammu and Kashmir, GCSI, GCIE, KCVO.
- 1941-1946 Lieutenant-General His Highness Shriman Rajarajeshwar Maharajaadhiraj Sri Sir Hari Singh Indar Mahinder Bahadur Sipar-i-Sultanat Maharaja of Jammu and Kashmir, GSCI, GCIE, GCVO.

HONOURS

- Delhi Durbar Medal-1903
- Delhi Durbar Medal-1911
- Prince of Wales Visit Medal-1922
- Knight Grand Commander of the Order of the Indian Empire (GVIE)-1929 (KCIE-1918)
- Grand Cross of the Order of the Crown of Italy-1930
- Knight Grand commander of the Order of the Star of India (GCSI)-1933
- King George V. Silver Jubilee Medal-1935
- King George VI Coronation Medal-1937
- Hon. L.L.D. from Punjab University-1938
- Grand Officer of the Legion of Honmeur-1938
- Africa Star-1945
- War Medal 1939-1945-1945
- India Service Medal-1945

- Knight Grand Cross of the Royal Victorian Order (GCVO)-1946 (KCVO-1922)
- Indian Independence Medal-1947.

Maharaja Karan Singh

Karan Singh is a member of India's Upper House of Parliament, the *Rajya Sabha*. He holds the ostensible royal seat of Jammu and Kashmir and has served successively as *Sadr-i-Riyasat* and Governor of Jammu and Kashmir. He is a senior member of the ruling Indian National Congress (INC) Party. Singh (born 1931) is the son of the last ruler of the princely state of Jammu and Kashmir, Maharaja Hari Singh. In the 26th constitution of India, promulgated in 1971, the Government of India abolished all official symbols of princely India, including titles, privileges and remuneration (privy purses). Singh received the *Padma Vibhushan* in 2005.

EARLY LIFE AND EDUCATION

Maharaja Karan Singh was born on March 9, 1931, in Cannes, France, in the Royal Dogra Rajput family to the last ruler of the princely state of Jammu and Kashmir, *Hari Singh* and his wife *Tara Devi*. He was educated at Doon School, Dehra Dun and received a B.A. from Srinagar which was later followed by a PhD. from Delhi University.

POLITICAL CAREER

In 1949, at age of eighteen, Singh was appointed as the regent of Jammu and Kashmir after his father stepped down as the ruler, following the state's accession to India. He served successively as the first and last *Sadr-i-Riyasat* and the governor of the state of Jammu and Kashmir from

1965 to 1967. In 1967, he resigned as Governor of Jammu and Kashmir and became the youngest ever member of the Union Cabinet holding the portfolios of Tourism and Civil Aviation. Two years later, he voluntarily surrendered his privy purse, which he had been entitled to since the death of his father in 1961. He placed the entire sum into a charitable trust named after his parents. In 1971, he was sent as an envoy to the Eastern Bloc Nations to explain India's position with regard to East Pakistan. He attempted to resign following an aircraft crash in 1973, but the resignation was not accepted. The same year, he became the Minister for Health and Family planning, serving in this post until 1977. Following the Emergency, Singh was elected to the *Lok Sabha* from *Udhampur* in 1977, becoming Minister of Education and Culture in 1979. He resigned from this post as well as from the INC in mid 80s to sit as an independent legislator in the *Lok Sabha*. In 1989-1990, he served as India's Ambassador to the US. This experience became the subject of his book. Since 1996, he has been a Member of Parliament in the *Rajya Sabha*. He served as the Chancellor of Banaras Hindu University, Jammu and Kashmir University and Jawaharlal Nehru University.

LADAKH REGION

Thinly populated Ladakh, which covers two-thirds of the entire area of the state of Jammu and Kashmir, is a high altitude cold desert. The harsh climate is mellowed to some extent by its lush green village oasis. The crystal clear light of its cloudless sky complements the serenity of its Buddhist monasteries as well as nourishes rare species of flora and fauna that are the main tourist attractions.

LEH

Leh is the principal town of Ladakh situated at a distance of 1077 kilometres north of Delhi, the capital of India. Since the 17th century right up to the middle of the 20th century, Ladakh had been an important economic centre along the ancient trade route between Central Asia and Punjab as well as between the Kashmir Valley and Tibet. The main bazaar of Leh was designed with broad curves to facilitate the passage of horses, mules, donkeys and camels and to provide room for the display of merchandise of various varieties.

The most prominent building of this town is the Nine-storied Leh Palace built in the year 1630 by *King Senzee Nangyal,* who took keen interest in construction of monasteries and forts. The inner walls of this palace follow the same architectural tradition as the *Potala Palace* in *Lassa.* It was built about 500 years ago, but sadly the palace is suffering dilapidation in spite of the repair work that is being carried out. The visitors can go up to the open terrace of the palace built above the main entrance. Much of Leh's charm lies in the pleasant strolls that one can take in the main bazaar and *Chang Gali.* Shops on either side lined with eateries serving local cuisine and shops selling curios, precious statues, prayer wheels and various objects linked to religious rituals. Women of the nearby villages sit on the curves of the bazaar with fresh vegetables and spindles for spinning wool. They carry on brisk sales of their wares and take time out to exchange lively chatters during intervals.

The *Jokhang*, a modern Buddhist establishment and the town mosque built in the late seventeenth century are quite close to this bazaar. The old Leh town lies to the East, between the bazaar and the Polo ground. It comprises of a maze of fascinating narrow alleys, dotted with chortens and clusters of flat-roofed houses built from dried mud bricks. On the peak above the town are the small fort and monastery complex of *Namgayal Tasemo* (mid 16th century) which is believed to be the earliest royal lodge in Leh. Next to it lie the ruins of the fort *Gonkhkhank* (temple of Guardian Deities) and a temple to *Maitreya* (the future Buddha). Both of these structures have vibrant murals that include a court scene and a portrait believed to be of King *Tashi Namgayal.*

At the Western edge of Leh is the ecological centre which manages developmental projects in agriculture, solar energy, health and environmental awareness in the surrounding villages. This centre also houses a library and shop selling local handicrafts. The gleaming white *Shanti Stupa* (Peace Pagoda) founded in the 1980's under the sponsorship of Japanese Buddhists is situated on a hilltop west of the city. Just a 10 minute walk in any direction away from the heart of the town leads one to barley fields, green or gold according to the season. Down the hill is the village of *Skara* where the massive mud walls of the nineteenth century *Zoravar* Fort catch the eye. Another lovely sight awaits one after a short and steep walk past the Moravian Church to the serene village of *Chandspa* and its ancient Chorten. From here a road turns towards the beautifully maintained nineteenth century Shankar Monastery with its impressive images of *Avlokitesvara* of *Bajra Bhairav*, guardian of the *Gelugpa* order.

Choglamsar is 7 kilometres to the south of Leh. It serves as the main Tibetan refugee settlement in Ladakh. The complex contains Dalai Lama's prayer ground known as *Shanti Sthal*, a S.O.S. children's village, the Central Institute of Buddhist studies, a hospital fitted with solar thermostats for keeping the whole building warm and workshops that promote colourful Tibetan Handicrafts. Dramatically situated on a hill top quiet close to the airport is the 15th century *Spituk* monastery, the oldest establishment of the *Gelugpa* sect of Ladakh. It houses the library of *Tsongkappa*, the founder of the sect and a shrine devoted to Goddess Tara with striking images of her various manifestations. Situated in one of Ladakh's most charming villages is *Phiyang* monastery, which is one of the only two that represent the *Drigungpa* sect. It was founded by *Tashi Namgayal* in 16th century, supposedly as an act of atonement for the violence and treachery by which he came to the throne. Among its many treasures is a large and interesting collection of Kashmiri bronze idols dating back to the 13th century.

The tourists can pay a visit daily to Leh Palace, *Namgayal, Tsemo, Jokhang Sankar, Monastry, Spituk Monastry*. But the ecological centre opens for the tourists from Monday to Friday only.

FESTIVALS

Hemis festival is celebrated in the month of June in all the monasteries across Ladakh. *Hemis* festival is most famous for its spectacular dance-drama with coloured masks and costumes. It offers a wonderfully authentic experience of Ladakh's culture.

Sindhu Darshan is celebrated from 1st of June to the 3rd of June and is a recent introduction. This festival is homage to the Indus and is celebrated on its banks. It is famous for exhibitions, polo matches and archery contests.

Ladakh festival is celebrated during the month of September. The fortnightly celebrations commence on 1st September and conclude on the 15th of the same month. It is held in the Leh polo grounds and some selected villages. Apart from the traditional mask dances, the events include polo matches and archery contests—both being popular traditional sports of the region. A handicraft exhibition is also held. This whole event is sponsored by the Ladakh tourist cell.

Thikse festival is the annual festival of the *Gelugpa* sect. The precise dates of the monastery festivals are fixed according to the Tibetan lunar calendar and fall mostly in the month of October and November.

BUDDHISTS SECTS IN LADAKH

Five sects of Tibetan Buddhism coexist in Ladakh. The Lamas of all these sects wear red hats on ceremonial occasions. Those who wear yellow hats belong to the reformist *Gelugpa* sect headed by the Dalai Lama, who exercised political control over Tibet until 1959. The *Drugpa* and *Drigungpa* sects are based on the teachings of a line of Indian masters from the Eleventh Century. All the monasteries in Ladakh belong either to the *Drugpa* or the *Gelugpa* sect of Buddhism. The only two exceptions are *Thak-Thok* and *Matho.* The former belongs to the *Nyingmapa* sect, which is based on the teachings of the 8th century saint *Padmasambhava* and the latter with its oracle monks belongs to the *Sakyapa* sect.

BUDDHIST MONASTERIES AND PALACES ALONG THE INDUS

Indus Valley is the historical and cultural heartland of Ladakh. All the world famous monasteries are situated along this river. Typically a monastery or *Gompa* stands on a hill or a ridge above the village that adjoins it. Its upper part consists of the temples (*iba khang*) and assembly halls (*Dukhang*) together with the *Gonkhang*, the temple of fearsome guardian deities. The residential monks are allocated dormitories down the hill-side. The monasteries are still active centres of worship so the tourists approach them respectfully.

ALCHY MONASTRY

Founded in the early 20th century, the religious enclave of *Alchy* is the jewel among Ladakh monasteries because *Alchy* was abandoned as a site of active worship for reasons unknown as early as the 16th century. The 12th and 13th century paintings in its temples have remained remarkably well-preserved undimmed by soot from butter lamps and incense sticks. Of the five temples in this enclave the finest murals are in the two oldest ones—the

Dukhans and the *Sumtsek*. These murals have been skilfully crafted by master painters who were probably from Kashmir.

EXPLORATION OF ALCHY MONASTERY

Alchy is an exceptional piece of Buddhist art in Ladakh. Unknown to the outside world till 1974, (the year Ladakh was opened to tourists) it soon gained recognition the world over. It was built as a tribute to the second spreading or the revival of Buddhism that took place in Tibet in the 11th century, based on the religious texts brought from Kashmir. The entire treasure of Mahayana sect of Buddhism is preserved in its five temples complemented by the superb paintings of court light, battles and pilgrimages depicting the historic costumes, architecture and customs. The assembly hall, known as *Dukhang*, is the oldest of the five temples and it holds some of *Alchy's* greatest treasures. The beautiful central image of *Vairochna*, the main Buddha of Meditation, is surrounded by a wooden frame exuberantly carved with dancers, musicians, elephants and mythical animals. *Vairochna* is flanked by four other Buddha of meditation. Even more impressive are the six elaborate *mandals* painted on the walls together with small scenes of contemporary life. The decorative details have an unexpectedly Rococo appearance.

SUMSTEK

Sumtek is the second oldest temple. It also houses spectacular images and paintings. Its distinguishing feature is undoubtedly the gigantic images of *Avlokiteshvara, Manjushri* and *Maitreya* that stand in special alcoves made in three of its walls. Only their legs and torsos are visible from the ground floor while their heads protrude into the upper story. From waist to the knees they are draped in *dhoti-like* garments covered with remarkably animate and sophisticated miniature paintings. It is advisable to have a torch and examine these credible details. The *Avlokiteshvara's* image is covered with shrines, pieces and vignettes of contemporary life. The *Maitreya's* image has scenes from Buddha's life painted within its roundels and the *Manjushri's* image depicts the eighty four masters of the *Tantra*.

The three other temples, probably dating back to the late 12th century to the early 13th century, look faded when compared with the *Dukhang* of the *Sumstek;* though they would win acclaim in any other setting. The *Manjushri Lakhang* has murals of a thousand buddhas and an enormous recently repainted image of *Manjushri*. The *Lotsawa Lakhang* has costlier paintings. It is dedicated to the saint *Rinchen Zangpo* who was also closely associated with *Thiksey* and *To Bo* monasteries.

The *Lakhang Soma* was the last temple to be built at *Alchy*. It has a profusion of fierce looking deities on its walls and scenes showing the Buddha in the act of preaching.

LIKIR

It was founded in the 12th century and it houses a fine collection of *Thangka* or images that are nicely carved into wooden frames.

RI-DZONG

It was built atop a ridge of glacial debris which blocks a winding gorge. It was founded in the 1840's by the *Gelugpa* sect and its monks follow a particularly austere regime.

LAMA YURU

It is situated on a high spot overlooking an eroded tract of land. Believed to be dating back to the 11th century, its oldest temple has a famous image of *Vairocama*, the Central Buddha of Meditation. *Lama Yuru* also has a beautiful collection of *Thangkas*.

BASGO

It was founded in the sixteenth century and has beautiful murals in its fort. The temple is dedicated to *Maitreya*, the future Buddha. It was the capital of Lower Ladakh in the fourteenth and fifteenth centuries.

STAKNA

It was built in the early 17th century and it has exquisite silver *Chorten* in its *Dukhang* surrounded by vividly coloured murals.

THIKSE

It was founded in the 15th century. The *Gelugpa* monastery is an architectural gem crowning the crest of a hill. The temple complex has a modern *Maitreya* Temple also. This temple was consecrated by Dalai Lama.

CHEMREY

It is perched on a hill-top and dates back to the 1640's. It houses Buddhist Scriptures with silver covers and gold lettering.

THAK THOK MONASTERY

This monastery belonging to the *Nyingmapa* sect was built around a cave which Guru *Padmasambhava*, the 8th century saint, is believed to have used for his daily meditation.

MATHO MONASTERY

This monastery is located in the Leh District at a distance of 30 kilometres south-east of the city of Leh. It is the only monastery of the sixteenth century that belongs to *Sakyapa* sect. The monastery continues to attract numerous new devotees even till this date. Its main importance however lies in its oracles—two monks who observe fast and meditate there months together in order to purify their souls. They are believed to be possessed by a deity. This event of fasting takes place during the *Matho* annual festival held between February and March. The anticipation of this occasion rises tremendously as people flock to see the oracles traverse the topmost parapet of the monastery blind-folded. The oracles answer questions put to them about public and private affairs. People repose with great faith in their predictions. *Matho* also has a small museum with a rare collection of the 16th century *Thangkhas* and costumes.

HEMIS MONASTERY

It is located 43 kilometres south-east of Leh city. It is trapped way up in a winding glen for five months during the winter. *Hemis* is the largest and richest of the Central Ladakh monasteries. It was founded in the 1630's as a *Drugpa* establishment by *King Sengse Namgyal* and continued to be the most favoured monastery of the *Namgyal* dynasty. Of its several temples the most revered is the *Tshog-Khang,* which has a secondary assembly hall containing a live image of the Buddha in front of a huge silver chorten set in place with flawless turquoises.

Hemis is also renowned for its spectacular annual festival dedicated to *Guru Padmasambhav*, the 8th century Indian apostle who took Buddhism to Tibet. A unique feature of this festival, which is held in summer, is that once every twelve years the monastery unveils its greatest treasure for the public eye. Huge crowds of devotees throng the monastery to behold the enormous three storeys high *Thangka* of *Padmasambhav* which is embroidered and studded with pearls and semiprecious stones. The next unveiling ceremony of this *Thangka* is due in 2016.

STALK PALACE

It is located at a distance of 17 kilometres south of Leh and it can be visited through May to October. This palace has been the residence of the *Namgyal* dynasty, the former rulers of Ladakh, since its independence in the year 1843. A part of the palace has been converted into a live museum of the dynasty and its history. Its collections include a set of 35 *Thangkas* representing the life of Buddha, said to have been commissioned by the 16th century king *Tashi Nangyal*. Images of rituals and religious objects lie in the hall. Secular objects include fine jade cups, the queen's jewellery (including a spectacular headdress), the king's turban, strapped crown and ceremonial robes. There is also a sword along with its blade twisted into a knot said to have been distorted by the enormous strength of *Tashi Nangyal*.

SHEY PALACE

It is situated at a distance of 15 kilometres south-east of Leh. It was the ancient capital of Ladakh. The palace contains a temple with a gigantic lake and 17th century Buddha Image surrounded by murals of deities painted in rich colours and gold. Another beautiful Buddha image is housed in a nearby temple. Just below the palace are huge 11th century rock carvings of five buddhas in meditation.

MONASTIC DANCE DRAMA

The dance-dramas performed at various monasteries in Ladakh during the annual festivals are immensely popular. They constitute a link between the popular and esoteric Buddhism. Attended by high lamas and novice monks in their ceremonial robes and hats as well as by local families in their splendid traditional costumes, these events are a vibrant expression of the age-old cultural and religious values. The dancers representing divine and mythological figures wear coloured brocade robes and heavy masks as they perform ceremonial dances around the monastery courtyard. The solemnity of the occasion is laced with interludes of light hearted gymnastic performances. The dancers dressed as skeletons bounce into the arena and entertain the crowds with caricatures specially prepared for the festival. In the climax scene, the mask figures ritually dismember a doll moulded from barley-flour dough (perhaps symbolising the human soul) and scatter its fragment in all directions. Besides, attracting large number of tourists, these monastery festivals also provide the people from far flung Ladakh villages an eagerly awaited opportunity to meet one another and exchange news and views.

BUDDHIST ICONOGRAPHY

The external manifestations of Buddhism are ubiquitous in Leh district and *Zansker*—Prayer Flags fluttering along the breeze, prayer-wheels turning in the hands of the elderly, walls inset with stone carvings of sacred invocations *Om Mani Padmey Bum* (hail to the Jewel in Lotus). Inside the monasteries the iconography is more complex. Each divinity of the Mahayana Buddhist Pantheon is depicted in several different manifestations together with a host of saints, teachers and mythical figures.

THE BODHISATVAS

A person who attains divine enlightenment and attains Nirvana is called a Buddha. The *Bodhisattvas* on the other hand are supremely compassionate (almost Buddha) who have attained enlightenment but are willing to forgo Nirvana so that they can help others achieve liberation from the endless cycles of rebirths.

Akasagarbha is the Bodhisattva of infinite happiness generated by helping countless numbers of sentient beings.

Avalokitesvara, is the bodhisattva of compassion. The listener of the world's cries who uses skilful means to come to their aid. He is also the most universally acknowledged Bodhisattva in Mahayana Buddhism. *Tara* is the female form of *Avalokitesvara* and is depicted in 21 different forms. *Avalokitesvara* is often shown with eleven heads and multiple arms symbolizing his benign omnipresence.

Ksitigarbha is the bodhisattva of the beings suffering in hellish realms, or the bodhisattva of great vows.

Mahasthamaprapta represents the power of wisdom.

Maitreya is the bodhisattva to be reborn and to become enlightened, thus succeeding Gautama Buddha in the future.

Manjushri, the bodhisattva of wisdom, bears a flaming sword in his hand to cut through the fog of ignorance.

Nagarjuna is the founder of the *Madhyamaka* (Middle Path) school of Mahayana Buddhism.

Nio are the two strong guardians of the Buddha, standing at the entrance of many Buddhist temples under the appearance of frightening wrestler like statues. They are manifestations of the Bodhisattva *Vajrapani*.

Padmasambhava is most associated with Tibetan Buddhism and Bhutanese Buddhism.

Samantabhadra represents the practice and meditation of all buddhas.

Sitatapatra is the goddess of the White Parasol and protector against supernatural danger.

Skanda is a *Dharmapala* who guards the Dharma. With links to *Vajrapani,* he is somewhat similar to *Murugan,* a Hindu deity.

Vajrapani is an early bodhisattva in Mahayana and the Chief Protector of the Buddha and earthly bodhisattvas

Vasudhara is the Bodhisattva of abundance and fertility.

Guardian deities are usually represented in fierce forms with skull headdresses, wicked fangs and flames in hair. Most commonly seen is *Mavakala* usually above the main door of a temple.

THE WHEEL OF LIFE

The wheel of life depicts animate human and animal figures. It is mostly painted on temple verandas. It shows the temptations and sins that make life on the earth an endless misery.

The lords of the four quarters guard the four cardinal directions. And so we see that the monasteries in Ladakh are a testament to the once flourishing Buddhist culture of the valley. Even though they occupy only the hard to reach tracts of the Ladakh region, they have a profound presence. "A simple life with elaborate customs" that has been passed down from generation to generation gives a unique charm to this part of the country. The patronizing dynasties as well as the local population have kept this common consciousness alive which echoes with the Buddhist philosophy of "Live and Let Live". Amongst these monasteries also we see a wide variety of sects and philosophies. Thus Buddhism of Jammu and Kashmir is a thriving example of cultural evolution which began at the time of *Mauryan* King Asoka and is continuing till date.

SOUTH-EAST LADAKH

Pang-Gong Tso falls in Leh district 150 kilometres to its east. *Tso Moriri* is 220 kilometres south-east of Leh. A special travel permit is required for any visitor and can be obtained from the Deputy Commissioner of Leh in advance. South-east Ladakh lies on the sensitive international border with Tibet. It is a region with a series of spectacular lakes. The two major lakes *Pang-Gong Tso* and *Tso Moriri* are accessible by roads although there are no scheduled bus services. The biggest of the lakes is the long and narrow *Pang-Gong Tso* which is located at an altitude of 4420 metres above sea level. It is 130 kilometres long and extends far into Western Tibet. The visitors may go as far as *Spangmik* along the lakes southern bank which offers spectacular views to the north of the *Changchenmo* Range. The lake shimmers in the sunlight reflecting ever changing shades of blue and green. Further up along the same road one can find the glaciers and snow capped peaks of the *Tso Moriri*. Thirty kilometres to the south of *Pang-Gong Tso* is a one hundred and forty square kilometres expanse of intense blue water. At an altitude of 4600 metres above sea level, it is set among rocks behind which lie snow covered mountains. The region's only permanent settlement is on the lakes Western shore.

Karzo consists of a handful of houses and a monastery with barley fields around it. These are perhaps the highest cultivated areas in the world. The lake and its fresh water inlets are breeding areas for many species of migratory birds such as the rare black necked crane and great crusted grebe.

The only human settlers in south-east Ladakh are the nomadic herders known as *Chang-pa* who brave extreme cold in winter and freezing nights even in summer, living in there black yak hair tents. They raise yaks and sheep but their main wealth is the *Pashmina goat*. The severe cold of winter stimulates the goats to grow an undercoat of soft warm fibres which they shed at the beginning of summer. This fibre known as *Pashm* is the raw material for Kashmir's renowned shawl industry and is in fact the unprocessed form of the world famous pashmina wool. The lucrative trade in *Pashm* from Ladakh's high altitude pastures attracted *Maharaja Ranjeet Singh* of Kashmir who conquered the Ladakh region and the Western Tibet in 1834.

The twin lakes of *Tso-kar* and *Startsapuk* Tso are located 80 kilometres north of *Tso Muriri* on the road to Leh. While *Startsapuk Tso* has fresh waters, the *Tso-kar* is so briny that the *Chang-pa* herders regularly collect salt deposits from its banks.

NUBRA VALLEY REGION

The *Nubra* region starts from Leh and follows the old caravan trade route to Central Asia. It used to be a feeder of the famous silk route that connected China with Central Asia and further with Europe. One has to traverse the world's highest motorable road—the *Khardungla* pass—in order to reach the *Nubra* valley. Pretty wild flowers surround the villages amidst strands of willow and poplar trees. The vast stretches of sand dunes are covered with Sea-buckthorn shrubs where double humped Bactrian camels graze. Remote monasteries and medicinal hot springs charm any and every tourist who happens to visit this region.

KARGIL

Kargil is a district 230 kilometres north-west of Leh. It connects Leh with Srinagar. For the travellers between Leh and Srinagar, Kargil town is a good place to stop for the night. Being the second largest urban centre in Ladakh, Kargil was an important trading centre before the partition of India when the road to *Skardu* in *Baltistan* (Pakistan) was still open. The majority of Kargil's population is *Shia* Muslim (an Islamic sect that regards *Hazrat Mohammad's* cousin and son-in-law Ali as his successor and the true first Imam). Kargil is famous for apricots and its hill side orchards are an enchanting site in the month of May, when the trees are in full bloom and in July when they are laden with ripe fruits. This town also serves as the base for expeditions to *Suru Valley, Zanskar* and *Nunkun. Kargil* region was one of the main battlefields during the failed Pakistani invasion of 1999.

MULBEKH

From *Kargil* at a distance of 90 kilometres north-west of Leh is a pretty village in the *Kargil* district. *Mulbekh*, spread over the broad green valley of the *Wakha* River, is the point at which the earliest tide of Islam spreading towards Central Ladakh lost its impetus. As a consequence, *Mulbekh* has a mixed population of Buddhists and Muslims and has a mosque as well as a monastery perched on a crag above the village. Its main attraction however is a giant engraving of *Maitreya*, the future Buddha, on a large free standing rock by the roadside. It dates back to the 8th century.

SURU VALLEY

Suru valley lies at a distance of 19 kilometres south of *Kargil*. It is connected with bus service up to *Sankhu*. The *Suru* Valley starts from *Kargil* and runs across hundreds of kilometres towards the south-east. It is one of Ladakh's most fertile regions and boasts of rolling alpine pastures, mud walled villages and views of majestic snow capped peaks. Abundant water from melting snow gives the *Suru* Valley rich harvests of barley and plantations of willow and poplar trees, especially around *Sankhu* village. Close to this village are the ruins of ancient forts together with rock-engravings of *Maitreya* and *Avlokiteshvara* belonging to the valley's pre-Islamic past. The upper valley is dominated by peaks, ridges and glaciers of the 7135 metre-high *Nunkun Massif*. Expeditions to the monasteries are organized from the picturesque village of *Panikhar,* where pastures are covered with alpine flowers during June and July.

DARDS

A conspicuous site in the bazaars of *Kargil* and Leh are the *Dards*. They roam the streets proudly dressed in their colourful caps which are decorated with flowers. Their aquiline features and complexion give them a unique identity amongst the natives of Ladakh. A stark novelty is also observed in their costumes and traditions. There are several theories about the origin of this small community. One of them is that they are descendents of Greek soldiers who invaded India as a part of Alexander's army. Anthropological research however indicated that their ancestors migrated from *Gilgit* (Pakistan) before it came under the influence of Islam. There are *Dard* villages at *Dha-hanu,* east of *Kargil* on the Indus close to where this river leaves Ladakh for *Baltistan.*

RANGDUM

It is located at a distance of 110 kilometres south-east of *Kargil.* This village serves as a night halt between *Kargil* and *Zanskar,* though geographically a part of *Suru* Valley it has a predominantly Buddhist population. The flourishing monasteries incline it culturally towards *Zanskar.* Situated on a wide flat plateau at a height of 3800 metres above sea level, it is crisscrossed by water courses and framed by snow peaks and hills of curiously striated rocks, *Randum* has white desolate beauty. The fortress like 18th century *Selugpa* Monastery is built on a hillock and a small temple in the complex has fine wall paintings of a battle scene with warriors sporting Mongolian looking armours and battle dresses.

ZANSKAR

It is located at a distance of 230 kilometres south-east of Kargil towards *Padum*. There is an undoubted air of mysticism about *Zanskar* due to its remoteness and high altitudes (3350 m to 4400 m) and the fact that the region is difficult to access. The only motorable road into the valley is usually open from early June to mid October but Zanskar's reputation as a Shangri-la also derives from the grandeur of its landscape, the simplicity of life in its villages and serene ambience of its *Gompas* often built around ancient cliff top meditation caves.

Zanskar is also called the valley of two rivers—the *Stowed* and the *Lunak* which flow towards each other along the northern flank of the *Sreaeer* Himalayas and later join to become the *Zanskar* River. It continues northwards through a gorge in the Zanskar Range to join the mighty Indus.

The western arm of Zanskar, the Stowed Valley, and its Central plain are fertile. The well watered villages along with its green pockets and virtual absence of trees contribute to an extraordinary sense of light and space. The inhabitants of this region are mostly farmers growing barley and wheat in the low lying villages and raising livestock—yaks, *sheep* and *dzos* (a hybrid animal between cows and yaks)—in the upper reaches.

In winter many of these farmers take the only route out of the area trekking for six gruelling days across the frozen Zanskar River to sell their highly prized yak butter in Leh. In contrast to the fertile western arm and central plain, the eastern arm of the Zanskar—the Lunak Valley—is a forbidden stony gorge with few villages to be seen in the vicinity.

The main gateway to Zanskar is the *Pensi-la* (4400 m high) located about 130 kilometres south-east of Kargil. This pass offers a spectacular view of the impressive *Drang-drung* glacier which is the source of the *Stowed* River. The road then continues down to *Tadum*. Located at 230 kilometres south-east of *Kargil* and at an altitude of 3500 metres is the main village and administrative headquarter of Zanskar. This is the only place in the region with basic facilities including accommodation, transport and a few rudimentary shops. It is also the starting point for a number of treks in the region. *Padum* itself has few sites of interest except for a rock engraving of the five *Dhayani buddhas* in the centre of the village but there are a number of interesting sites to explore in the vicinity. The Muslims have built a mosque to offer prayers. The village of *Pipiting* has a temple and a *Chorten* atop the mount of glacial debris. There is a pavilion which was specially constructed for Dalai Lama's prayer assemblies.

A short distance away is the village of *Sani*, North-West of *Padum*, which is one of the oldest religious sites in the western Himalayas. Inside the monastery walls stands the *Kanika Chorten* which is probably linked to the *Poshana* Ruler *Kanishka*, whose empire stretched from Afghanistan to Varanasi in the first and second centuries A.D. The monastery itself is set to have been founded by *Padmsambhav* in the 8th century and its main temple has some murals. Even more interesting is another small temple within the complex which has unique beautifully painted Stucco. *Sani* is conspicuously surrounded by a strand of poplar trees in this otherwise treeless landscape. The building of *Gelugpa* Monastery of *Karsha* is visible from *Padum*. It is ten kilometres north-east of *Padum*. It seems that the monastery spills down the mountain west of the main valley till they merge with the house and fields of the village. This site includes ancient rock engravings and murals of the *Avlokiteshvara* just outside the main complex, which seems to place it in the same period as *Alchy*. Tradition however attributes the monastery's foundation to the ubiquitous *Padmasambhava*. *Karsha* has a large community of resident monks and hold its colourful annual festival between July and August.

Spongde, from the opposite side of the valley 12 kilometres away from Padum, is perched up on a ridge high above the mosaic of the village fields. Believed to have been founded in the 11th century it houses no fewer than seven well maintained temples, some of them containing exquisite murals.

The villages of *Sani*, *Karsha* and *Stongde* are connected by motor transport, though the monasteries in the *Lungnak* Valley are less accessible. The narrow footpath leading up to the valley winds along unstable slopes high above the river and the walk is strenuous. It takes a sharp climb on foot or on horseback to reach *Bardhan* and *Phugtal* monasteries.

Bardhan, 9 kilometres south-east of *Padum*, is spectacularly located atop a crag jutting out from the mountain and rising to about a hundred metres towards the river. It has five wall-paintings, dating back to the time of the monasteries foundation in the early 17th century. Out of all the monasteries in Ladakh *Phugtal* distinguishes itself by the sheer grandeur and charisma of its location. Its main temples are constructed inside a huge cave along the mountain side above the *Tsarap* River at a point where the drop of the river water is almost vertical. Yet below the temples, the monks' dwellings have somehow been built on or into the cliff face and the whole improbable complexity is linked by a puzzling system of ladders and walkways. There is no record of *Phugtal* Monastery's foundation but the style of the paintings, some of which are quite striking, link it with the *Tobo*. Monastery in *Spiti* and

the traditions established by the Tibetan saint *Rinchen Zangpo* in the 11th century. Its monks belong to the *Gelugpa* order. *Sani, Karsha, Stonged Bardhan* and *Phugtal* monasteries can be visited daily.

TREKKING IN LADAKH AND ZANSKAR

Trekking in the arid cold Trans Himalayan desert of Ladakh and Zanskar at an altitude that often exceeds 5000 metres can be a uniquely exhilarating experience. The terrain is astonishingly beautiful and just like any other highland setting in the world has a number of foot trails, many of which served as a part of the ancient trade routes to Central Asia. These include some spectacularly located remote mountain passes, which sometimes lead to staggering heights, steep gorges and lush green meadows and on other occasions to scattered remains of *chortens*. The best time to trek is between June and September. By this time the snow melts away so that the farmers can harvest their crop across the terraces specially graduated on the slopes.

OTHER OUTDOOR ACTIVITIES

White water rafting on the Indus and Zanskar rivers is a popular activity through July to mid-September. There are various options to consider on the Indus River. Either one can float leisurely from *Hemis* to *Choglamsar* or try a longer physically demanding route between *Spitok* and *Alchy*. Jeep safari to the lakes of *Tso-Kar* and *Tso-Muriri* take three days with tents pitched near *Karzok* village. The region's rich wild life includes bar-headed geese, black-necked cranes and the *Kaing* (Tibetan ass).

THE CARAVAN TRADE

For centuries Ladakh had been the route for busy trade between Punjab and Central Asia. The caravans halted at Leh, where a lot of business transactions occurred, before proceeding to the 5578 metre high *Karkoram* Pass. This is one of the highest points on any trade root in the world. In summer the caravans traversed Nubra Valley, while in winter they crossed the upper valley of *Shayok* River. Every year over 10,000 pack animals—horses, yaks, Bactrian camels and an especially sturdy breed of local sheep—traversed the Nubra region carrying Varanasi brocades, Chinese silk, pearls, spices, Indian tea, *Pashmina* wool, salt, indigo, opium, carpets and gold.

INDO CHINA BORDER ISSUES

The Indo-China border has become a very contentious territory. A grim future awaits the Line of actual control (L.A.C.) with reports of Chinese transgression in the *Daulet Beg Oldi* sector, *Depsang Bulge* and *Chumar*. The report says that the situation could become volatile at any time as the People's Liberation Army (PLA) of China has firmly trenched in their position in *Srijap* area. India is also concerned about a similar contravention of the international borders in *Chumar* where PLA have claimed 85 square kilometres of Indian Territory. India will have to be firm and deploy army in these sectors to avoid any further transgressions.

A BRIEF HISTORY OF KASHMIR

The history of Kashmir germinates from an ancient civilisation, Aryan culture and Vedic way of life. The word "Kashmir" has its origin in the primordial language of human race i.e. Sanskrit and literally means, "The Land of Sage *Kashyap*". *Kashyap Rishi* was a *Saraswat* Brahmin who formulised the ancient Vedic culture. The valley was named in his honour. Hindu temple of *Jyeshteswar* (Shankaracharya) on the Shankaracharya Hill near Srinagar is testament to this fact.

The unexcavated Buddhist Stupa near Baramula, with two figures standing on the summit and another at the base with measuring scales, was discovered by John Brute in 1868 and was later dated back to 500 A.D. The Mauryan Emperor *Asoka* who later adopted Buddhism and denounced violence is often credited with having laid the foundation of the old capital of Kashmir, *Shrinagari*, which now lies in ruins on the outskirts of modern Srinagar. Kashmir was a fertile ground for Buddhist philosophy for many centuries. As a Buddhist seat of learning, the *Sarasvativadan* School strongly influenced Kashmir. Buddhist monks from East and central Asia have several memoirs recollecting their visits to the holy Kingdom. In the late 4th century A.D. the famous *Kuchanese* monk *Kumarjiva*, born to an Indian noble family studied *Dirghagama* and *Madhyagama* in Kashmir under *Bandhudatta*. He later became a politico transfer who helped take Buddhism to china. His mother *Jiva* is thought to have refined Kashmiri *Vimalaksa*. A *Sarvastivadan* Buddhist monk travelled from Kashmir to *Kucha* and instructed *Kumaradiva* in the *Vinayapitaka*.

Adi *Shankara*, visited the Pre-existing *Sarvajanapita* (*Sharda Peeth*) in Kashmir somewhere between late 8th century and early 9th century A.D. The *Madhaviya Shankarvijayam* states that this temple had four doors representing four directions. The fourth scholar door representing South India had never been opened indicating that no scholar from south India had entered the *Sharda Peeth*. *Adi Shankara* opened the southern door by defeating all the scholars in debates encompassing various scholastic disciples such as *Mimamsa,* Vedanta and other branches of Hindu Philosophy. He ascended to the throne of Transcendent *Kirtans* of the Temple.

Abhinav Gupta (Approx. 950A.D.-1020 A.D.) was one of the greatest philosophers, mystics and aestheticians. He was also considered an important musician, poet, dramatist, exegete, theologian and logician, a polymath personality who exercised strong influences on Indian culture. He was born in the Valley of Kashmir to a family of scholars and mystics. He studied all the disciplines of Philosophy and art of his time under the guidance of as many as fifteen (or more) teachers. In his long life he completed over 35 works, the two most famous being—*Tantraloka and Abhinavabharati*. While the former is an encyclopaedic treatise on all the philosophical and principal aspects of *Trika* and *Kaula* (known today as Kashmir *Shaivism*), the latter is a commentary of *Natyasastra* by *Bharata Muni*, a very important contributions in the field of Philosophy of aesthetics.

In the 10th century A.D. *Mokosopaya Shastra* a philosophical text on salvation for the non-ascetic (*Moksa Upaya*: means to salvation) was written on the

Pradyumna hill in Srinagar. It has the form of a public sermon and claims human authorship. It contains about 30,000 hymns making it longer than the Ramayana. The main part of the text forms a dialogue between *Vasistha* and *Rama*, exchanging numerous short stories and anecdotes to illustrate the content. The text was later expanded on the basis of Vedas which resulted in the Yoga *Vashishta*.

Thus we see an epicentre of flourishing Vedic culture which gave birth to a prolific environment for human evolution in disciplines spanning the vast array of performing arts, philosophy, medicine, theology, grammatology, spirituality and all this was made possible only because of half a millennium of peaceful co existence amongst the various inhabitants and immigrants who travelled to this paradise in pursuit of eternal peace.

The last Hindu Ruler *Ramchandra* had appointed *Rinchan* as the administrator of Ladakh. *Rinchan* became ambitious and sent a force in the guise of traders and merchants, who took *Ramchandra's* men by surprise. *Ramchandra* was killed and his family was imprisoned.

To earn local support, *Rinchan* appointed *Rawanchandra* the son of *Ramchandra* as the administrator of Leh and Ladakh. He married his sister *Kota Rani*. She employed Shah Mir as a trusted courtier, who had entered Kashmir earlier and had been given an appointment in the Government. *Rinchan's* rule was short lived due to his authoritarian stance and finally he was assassinated for his strictness after ruling only for three years.

Kota Rani was first appointed as a guardian for *Rinchan's* young son. She was persuaded to marry *Udayanandeya* by elders. *Udayanadeya* died in 1338. *Kota Rani* had two sons. *Rinchan's* son was under the charge of Shah Mir and *Udayanadeva's* son was taught by *Bhaha Bhikshana*. Soon *Kota Rani* became the ruler and appointed *Bhaha Bhikshana* as her Prime Minister.

Shah Mir pretended to be sick and when *Bhatta Bhikshana* visited him, Shah Mir jumped out his bed to assassinate him. He asked *Kota Rani* to marry him but she refused to marry a coward. Shah Mir then attacked to force her to marry him. According to a prominent historian of that period, Jonaraja, she committed suicide and offered her intestines to him as the wedding gift. History is unaware about the fate of her sons.

Kota Rani was a very great thinker. She saved the city of Srinagar from frequent floods by commissioning a canal which is still named after her, *Kute Kol*. This canal gets water from the river Jhelum at the entry point of the city and again merges with river Jhelum beyond city limits.

With her death the Hindu rule in Kashmir was lost forever. Kashmir state has been an integral part of India right from the very beginning of the Vedic period. Foreign forces invaded Kashmir time and again. Even now a large chunk of Jammu and Kashmir has been occupied by Pakistan and China. India has been struggling to preserve its religion, culture and philosophy, an age old civilization inherited thousands and thousands of years ago from *Rishi-Muni*.

Change is the law of nature, but the invaders and Jihadists are imposing their religion on India by means of violence and dishonesty. In the name of their God they instigate large scale genocides, destroy the historical places of worship, and deface the sacred relics preserved in the temples and monasteries, compelling the non-Muslims to leave their homes through sadistic means. God knows when love, peace and prosperity will return in this land of Rama-Krishna, Buddha and Guru Nanak, when the abode of Lord Shiva will be freed from forces of terror?

The Mughals had a deep influence on this land and imposed various restrictions in the form of new laws governing revenue, land ownership and industry, which added to the hardships of the citizens. In 1820 Maharaja Gulab Singh got the Jagir of Jammu from *Maharaja Ranjeet Singh*. He is said to have laid the foundation of the Dogra Dynasty. In 1846 Kashmir was sold to Maharaja Gulab Singh. Thus the areas of Kashmir and Jammu were integrated into a single political unit. A few Chieftains who formed part of the administration were of the *Hunza, Kishtwar, Gilgit*, and Ladakh. During the Dogra rule trade improved along with the preservation and promotion of forestry.

MUSLIM RULE

The Muslims and Hindus of Kashmir lived in perfect harmony since the Sufi Islamic way of life that Muslims followed in Kashmir complimented the *rishi* (sage) tradition of Kashmiri *pundits*. Sufi Saints such as *Sheikh Noor-ud-din Wali* were thought of as Muslim *rishis*. This led to a syncretic culture where in the Hindus and Muslims revered the same local faith and prayed at the same shrines. Famous Sufi saint *Bulbul Shah* was able to convert *Rinchan Shah,* the prince of Ladakh province of Kashmir, to an Islamic way of life and thus founding a single composite culture. Under this rule Muslim, Hindu, and Buddhist Kashmiris co-existed peacefully. Over time, however the *Sufiana* governance gave way to outright Muslim monarchy.

In the beginning of 14th century a ferocious *Duluchan* army from Turkistan invaded the valley. Sixty thousand soldiers entered through the *Zojila* Pass in the North. The *Dulucha* plundered every settlement along their path and slaughtered thousands of civilians. The brave Brahmans led this attack to uninhabited tracts in the mountain passes where the *Dulucha* army perished in a snow blizzard. This savage attack practically ended the Hindu royal bloodline in Kashmir. *Raja Sunder* was the ruler at that time. It was during his reign that three rulers—Shah Mir, *Rinchan* from Ladakh and *Milmai* and *Hikmat Chak* from *Dard* territory came to Kashmir and played a notable role in the subsequent political history of the valley.

Shah Mir was the second Muslim ruler (*Rinchan* was the first as he adopted Islam) of Kashmir and the founder of *Shah Miri* dynasty. *Jonaraja*, in his famous book *Dvitiya Rajatarangini* mentioned him as *Sahamera* who was from *Arjuna*. According to *Jonaraja* his ancestors were of Hindu origin and were *Kshatriyas (warrior clan).* Shah Mir was deposed by his brother *Ali Sher* who then ascended the throne under the name of *Alladin.* Following the *Shahmiri* dynasty was the *Chak* Dynasty whose reign ended in 1586 after being defeated by the *Mughals.*

Some Kashmiri rulers, such as Sultan *Zain-ul-Abidin,* who was popularly known as *Dudshah* the king (1423-1474), were tolerant of all religions and followed the examples set by munificent Hindu rulers of Kashmir. However a majority of them did not allow non-Islamic cultures to thrive. The worst of these was *Sultan Sikander Butshikan* of Kashmir (AD 1389-1413). Historians have recorded many of his atrocities. The *Tarikh-e-firishta* records that *Sikander* persecuted the Hindus and issued orders prohibiting practise of any faith other than Islam in Kashmir. He also ordered several search parties to unearth and plunder holy relics to acquire gold, silver, gems and other riches from temples and monasteries.

The *Tarikh-e-Firishta* further states that many of the Brahmans rather than abandon their religion or country poisoned themselves; some emigrated from their ancestral home while a few escaped. After the emigration of the Brahmans, *Sikander* ordered all the temples in Kashmir to be demolished. Having destroyed several generations of religious, philosophical and spiritual traditions and defacing every ornate installation of non-Islamic shrines, *Sikander* acquired the title of 'Destroyer of Idols'.

Kalhans' metrical chronicle of kings of Kashmir called *Rajataranagini* has been declared by Prof. H. H. Wilson as the only "Sanskrit" composition yet discovered to which the appellations of "history" can with any proprietary be applied. It first became known to the Muslims when on Akbar's invasion of Kashmir in 1588, a copy was presented to the emperor. A translation into Persian was made at his order. A summary of its contents, taken from this Persian translation, is given by *Abul Fazal* in the *Ain-i-Akbari*. The *Rajatarangini* was written around the middle of 12th century. His work extending over six volumes makes use of earlier writings which are now lost.

The *Rajatarangini* is the first in a series of four books that record history of Kashmir. Compiling the history of Kashmir from very early times, the *Rajatrangani* concludes with the reign of *Sangrama Deva* (1006 AD.) The second work, by *Jonaraja* continues the history from where *Kalhana* left. Beginning from the period of Muslim rule it gives an account of the reign down to *Zain-ul-Abdin* (1412).

Srivara carried forward the record to the accession of *Fah Shah* in 1486. The fourth work called *Rajavalipataka* by *Prajnia Bhatta* completes the history to the dominions of the Mughal Emperor Akbar, 1588.

SIKH RULE

In 1819, the Sikh King Maharaja Ranjeet Singh of Lahore conquered the Kashmir Valley by defeating the *Durranis* and thus ended four centuries of Muslim tyranny in Kashmir. As the Kashmiris had suffered under the *Durrani* rulers, who invaded from Afghanistan, they initially welcomed the new Sikh rulers. However, the Sikh governor, turned out to be a hard task master and the Sikh rule was generally considered oppressive. The Sikhs enacted a number of anti-Muslim laws, which included handing out death sentences for cow slaughter, closing down the *Jamia Masjid* mosque in Srinagar and banning azan—the public Muslim call to prayer. Some historian denied this.

Kashmir had also begun to attract Europe. Visitors wrote about abject poverty of the west Muslim peasantry and the exorbitant taxes under the Sikhs. High taxes, based on some contextual accounts, had depopulated large tracts of the countryside, allowing only one sixteenth of the cultivable land to be inhabited. However after the famine in 1832, the Sikhs reduced the land tax to half the produce of the land and also began to offer interest free loans to farmers. Kashmir became the second highest revenue earner for the Sikh Empire. During this time

Kashmiri shawls garnered global fame, attracting many buyers especially from the west.

The Sikhs had already conquered the kingdom of Jammu to the South of Kashmir valley. In 1780, after the death of *Ranjit Deo* (the previous sovereign ruler of Jammu) his grand nephew Gulab Singh bought service at the court of Ranjeet Singh. He distinguished himself in later campaigns, especially the annexation of Kashmir Valley and for his services, was appointed governor of Jammu in 1820. With the help of his officer Zorawar Singh, Gulab Singh soon captured (for the Sikhs) the land of Ladakh and *Baltistan* to the East and North East respectively.

In 1845, the first Anglo-Sikh War broke out. According to the Imperial Gazetteer of India, Gulab Singh contrived to hold himself aloof till the battle of Bayou (1846), when he appeared as a mediator and the trusted advisor of Sir Henry Lawrence. Two treaties were concluded. By the first one, the state of Lahore (*i.e.* West Punjab) was handed over to the British, as equivalent for rupees one crores indemnity. By the second the British handed over to Gulab Singh, for an annual sum of rupees 75 lakhs, all the hilly or mountainous country inducted to the east of Indus and the west of Ravi *i.e.* the Valley of Kashmir.

Drafted by a treaty and a bill of sale constituted between 1820 and 1858, the Princely state of Kashmir and Jammu (as it was first called) combined varied regions, religions and ethnicities. To the East Ladakh was ethnically and culturally Tibetan and its inhabitants practiced Buddhism. Jammu to the south had a mixed population of Hindus, Muslims and Sikhs. In the centrally located Kashmir valley, the population was overwhelmingly Sunni Muslim. However, there was also a small but influential Hindu minority, the Kashmiri Brahmans (pundits). The North-Western frontier (*Baltistan*) was sparsely populated by a population ethnically related to Ladakh but which practiced Shia Islam. Though the north (beyond *Poonch*) was also sparsely populated still it was an area of diverse ethnic groups (mostly Shia Muslim).

After the Indian Rebellion of 1857, in which Kashmir sided with the British, and the subsequent consumption of direct rule by Great Britain, the Princely State of Kashmir came under the Suzerainty of British Crown. In the British census of Indian 1941, the Kashmiris registered a Muslim majority population of 77%, a Hindu population of 20% and the remaining

3% comprised of both the Buddhists and Sikhs. The same year, *Prem Nath Bazaz*, a Kashmiri Pundit Journalist wrote: "The poverty of Muslim masses is appalling Most are landless labourers working for Hindu landlords. Almost the whole brunt of official corruption is borne by Muslim masses." For almost a century, Hindu elite had ruled over the impoverished Muslim peasantry. Driven into impoverishment by chronic indebtedness to landlords and money lenders, having no education, nor awareness of rights, the Muslim peasants had no political representation.

YEAR 1947 AND 1948

Hari Singh was the reigning monarch in 1947 at the conclusion of British rule and the subsequent partition of the British Indian Empire into newly independent Union of India and the dominion of Pakistan.

According to Burto Stein's *History of India*, Kashmir was neither as large nor as old-independent as Hyderabad. It had been created rather offhandedly by the British after the first defeat of Sikhs in 1846, as a reward to a former official who had spied for the British. The Himalayan kingdom was connected to India by a district of Punjab, but its population was 77% Muslim and it shared a boundary with Pakistan. Hence it was anticipated that the Maharaja would accede to Pakistan once the British devolved power, but he hesitated to do this. So Pakistan launched a guerrilla onslaught meant to frighten its ruler into submission. Instead the Maharaja appeared to Lord Mountbatten for assistance. The Governor General agreed on the condition that Kashmir would accede to India. The Indian soldiers came to the rescue of Kashmiri citizens. The infiltrators from across the border were chased out of Kashmir leaving only some remote stretches beyond the mountain passes. The United Nation was then invited to mediate the quarrel. The U.N. mission insisted on a plebiscite by citizens of the Valley. India readily agreed to this vote and requested Pakistan to withdraw all their troops from the Valley. However Pakistan was least bothered about the opinion of the locals and disapproved voting of such sorts in the portions of the valley which they occupied. Consequently India refrained from committing to a public vote.

In the last days of 1948, a ceasefire was reached under U.N. auspices. But since the demand made by the U.N. was never met, relations between India and Pakistan soured and eventually led to two more wars over Kashmir in 1965 and 1999. India has control of about half of the area of former princely state of Jammu and Kashmir, while Pakistan controls a third of the region. According to Encyclopaedia Britannica, "Although there was a clear Muslim majority in Kashmir before the 1947 partition, the political developments during and after the partition resulted in a division of the region wherein Pakistan was left with a territory that although basically Muslim in character was thinly populated, relatively inaccessible and economically underdeveloped." The largest Muslim group situated in the valley of Kashmir (constituting more than half the population) lay in the Indian administrated territory, with its former outlets via the Jhelum valley route blocked.

CURRENT STATUS

The eastern region of the former princely state of Kashmir has also been involved in a boundary dispute. In the late 19th and 20th centuries, although some boundary agreements were signed between Great Britain and Afghanistan over the northern borders of Kashmir, China never accepted these agreements and the official Chinese position did not change with the communist revolution in 1949. By the mid 1950s the Chinese Army had entered the north-east portion of Ladakh.

By 1956-57 they had completed a military road through the Aksai Chin area to provide better communication between Xingjian and western Tibet. India's late discovery of this construction led to a serious strategic disadvantage. The ensuing border clashes between the two countries culminated in the Sino Indian War of October 1962.

The region is divided amongst the three countries in a territorial dispute. Pakistan controls the northwest portion (desolated Northern areas and Azad Kashmir and Ladakh). China controls the north-eastern portion of Ladakh as well as the northern portion (Aksai Chin and trans-Karakoram Tract). India controls the majority of Siachen Glacier area including the Saltoro Ridge Passes, whereas Pakistan controls lower territory just southwest of the Saltoro Ridge. Cumulative figures suggest India's governance over 101,338 km². (39,127 sq. m.) of the disputed territory while Pakistan controls 65,846 km² (33,145 sq. m) and China the remaining 37,555 km² (14,500, sq mi).

Jammu and Pakistan administrated Kashmir lie outside Pir Panjal Range and are under India and Pakistan control respectively. These are populous regions. The main cities are *Mirpur, Dadayal, Kotli, Bhimber, Jammu, Muzaffarabad* and *Rawalkot.*

The *Gilgit-Baltistan,* formerly referred to as the Northern Areas, are a group of territories in the extreme north bordered by the Karakoram range, the western Himalayas, the Pamir and the *Hindu Kush* ranges. With its administrative Centre at the town of Gilgit, the Northern Area, covers an area of 72,971 km (28,174 mi^2) and has an estimated population approaching 1,000,000. The other main city is *Skardu.*

Ladakh is a region in the east, between the Kunlun Mountain range in the North and the main Great Himalayas to the South. Main cities are Leh and Kargil. It is under Indian administration and part of the state of Jammu and Kashmir. It is one of the most sparsely populated regions in the area and is mainly inhabited by people of Indo-Aryan and Tibetan descent.

Aksai Chin is a vast high-altitude descent of Saltro that reaches as high as 5,000 metres (16000 ft). Geographically part of the Tibetan Plateau, Aksai Chin is referred to as the Soda Plain of the region. It is almost uninhabited and has no permanent settlements.

Though these regions are in practice administrated by their aggressive claimants neither India nor Pakistan formally recognized the occupation of the area claimed by the other. India claims these areas including the area ceded to China by Pakistan in the Trans-Karakoram Tract in 1963, as a part of its territory, while Pakistan claims the disputed region excluding Aksai Chin and Trans-Karakoram Tract. The two countries have fought several declared wars over the territory. The Indo-Pakistan War of 1947 established the rough boundaries of today, with Pakistan holding roughly one-third of Kashmir and India one half, which are divided by a line of control (LOC) established by the United Nations. The Indo-Pakistan War of 1965 resulted in another settlement and a UN negotiated ceasefire.

For a better understanding of the situation in Kashmir it is imperative that we take a closer look at the evolution of the present cultural heritage of the region. The contribution of Kashmiris is not only monumental to Indian heritage but it is a milestone of multidisciplinary advances spread over several generations of human evolution.

ECONOMY

Tourism is the main stay of income for vast sections of the population. Kashmiri economy is also dependent on agriculture. Traditionally the staple crop of the valley was rice, which formed the chief food of the people. In addition, Indian corn, wheat, barley and oats were also grown. Given its temperate climate, crops like asparagus, artichoke, seakale, broad beans, scarlet runners, beetroot cauliflower and cabbage are cultivated. Fruit trees are common in the valley and the cultivated orchards yield peas, apples, peaches and cherries. The chief trees are deodar, tir, pines, chenar, plane, maple, birch, walnut, apple and cherry.

Historically Kashmir became world renowned when *Pashmina wool* was exported to other regions. Since then the exports have ceased due to the threat of extinction to the *Chasmere* Goat and increased competition from (China). Kashmiris are well adept at knitting and making *Pashmina* Shawls, silk carpets, rugs, *kurtis* and pottery. Saffron crop is grown in Kashmir. The naturally grown fruits and vegetables are exported as organic foods mainly to the Middle East. Srinagar is known for its silverwork, papier-mâché, wood-carving and weaving of silk.

The economy was badly damaged by the 2005 Kashmir Earth Quake which resulted in more than 70,000 deaths in the Pakistan controlled part of Kashmir and around 1500 deaths in Indian administered Kashmir.

The Indian administered part of Kashmir is believed to have hydro reserves with great potential for future development.

HISTORY OF TOURISM

Jammu and Kashmir is the Northern most state of the Indian Union, famous for its extra vibrant natural beauty. This region has a widely varying geography. In the south Jammu serves as a gateway to the Himalayas. It is the land of snowy mountains that share a common boundary with Afghanistan, China and Pakistan. Nature has preserved a piece of heaven amidst the harsh abode of snow.

Much before the modern system of airways and diesel propelled cargo ships reduced the world to a global village, Kashmir served as a vital link between the East and the West with its vast network of interconnected rivers. Trade relations through these routes between China and Central Asia made it a land inhabited by various religious and cultural groups. It was during the reign of *Kashyapa* that the otherwise vagabond caravans lead a settled life. Buddhism influenced Kashmir during the rule of Asoka and the present town of Srinagar was founded by him. This place was earlier called *Srinagari* or *Puran Dhisthan*. The Brahmans who inhabited these areas were very accommodating and gave ample social space for Buddhism to bloom. From Kashmir Buddhism spread to Ladakh, Tibet, Central Asia and China. Various traditions co-existed till the invasion of the Islam.

LANGUAGE

The inhabitants of Kashmir have a distinct language called *Kashmir* or *Kashmiri*. Although there are two different views about its origin, yet a dispassionate and scientific analysis will show that it has developed from the language of the Vedas. Therefore the syntax, vocabulary and idiom of Sanskrit apply to it. During the *Pathan* and *Mughal* rule, where Persian became the court language, it adopted a number of Persian words. During the rule of the Sikhs the language of Punjab also influenced Kashmiri and later with the adoption of Urdu as the official language by Dogra rulers, during the British reign in India, it assimilated both Urdu as well as English. There are references in various chronicles that during the Buddhist period some religious books were written in *Prakirt*. But these books are now nowhere to be found, although their translations are available. The initial glimpse of this amalgamated language had verses written about the love life of the queen of *Rajajayapeed* during 8th century and in the Sanskrit work '*Setuband*' of king *Praversen*, who incidentally established Srinagar as the capital of the valley for the first time. This language was then referred to as *Isarva Gochar Bhaksha* or the language of the masses.

The Sanskrit writers used to write in this new language side by side with Sanskrit. But a systematic literature in Kashmiri started from *Mahanay Prakash* written in thirteen century by *Shitikanth*. It displayed the same *Vakh* form which was later officially accepted.

Scholars from Kashmir developed a script of their own called *Sharda* script, which largely follows the pattern of the *Devnagri* script. The alphabets and combination of vowel sounds with consonants appear to have been developed from the old *Brahmi* script. Unfortunately after the forceful religious conversion of the masses in the valley this script didn't get official recognition because of its Vedic origins and is not in use anymore. Many learned Muslim scholars like *Ghulam Mohammad Mehjoor*, the eminent poet, were also in favour of retaining the *Sharda* script but the ruling dynasties dictated that the official script must be based on Persian with some minor allowances for local dialect. It is relevant to mention that even without official recognition *Sharda* script is currently used by all the publications and journals issued from Jammu and Delhi due to its literary richness.

LITERATURE

It is the rule of nature that a change in the thinking results in a change in action which is turn changes the environment. All these changes are reflected in the literature produced from time to time. Literature is the mirror of social consciousness in a civilized society.

Kashmir was a seat of learning because of which it was called *Sharda Peeth* or "the seat of Goddess of Learning". Just as the name *Ryeshi Vaer* denoted the culture of this land, the name *Sharda Peeth* indicates the greatness and vastness of the literature produced by *Kashmiris*. Kashmir's contribution to Sanskrit literature before the establishment of the first Muslim dynasty was monumental.

SANSKRIT LITERATURE

The Sanskrit literature can be divided into two groups. The first relates to the Kashmir *Sharda Darshan*. The prominent writers of this discipline include *Uttar Deva, Soma Nanda, Vasu Gupta, Abhinav Gupta* and *Khem Raj.* Their scholarly works include *Spands Karika, Shiva Drishti, Shivastotrali, Parmartha, Sara Pratya-Bhajana Darshan, tantra Sara, Malini, Vijaya, Kudrayamal.* Of all these literary masterpieces *Acharya Abhinav Gupta*'s *Tantralok* stands alone in its subtle elucidation of the theory and practice of spirituality. A number of treaties and commentaries have been written on these works in order to bring to light the true purpose of this unique philosophy. It is a matter of concern that there is no effort on the part of the State Government to preserve or develop this important world acclaimed school of philosophy. It has been largely preserved by individual efforts and private funds received from *Sadhaka* or the disciples of *Swami Lakshman Joo.* However, there is an Abhinav Gupta Centre at Lucknow established by Dr. Pandey where this philosophy is studied by young scholars. Dr.Baljin Nath Pundita, Dr.Neelkanth Gurtoo and (late) Dr. Dwivedi of Rajasthan University have edited and translated some of the selected works of *Shaiva Acharyas.*

The second group comprises of books or subjects other than philosophy. The most distinguished name in the group is that of *Kalhana Pundit*, the author of the famous *Rajatarangini,* the only book of chronicles written in Sanskrit. This book gives an account of the rulers and events from the 8th century to the 12th century. It was later extended and supplemented by *Jonaraja, Shirvara* and *Prajna Bhatta* and brought up to date till the reign of Zainul-Ab-Din.

There are a number of books in Sanskrit written by *Kashmiris* on a variety of subjects, like linguistics, aesthetics, poetics, sexology, and fiction. *Mammtacharya* was the reigning authority in Sanskrit grammatology after unanimous acceptance of his revered work—*Kavya Prakash.* It is believed that the commonest of the common scholars would commence work in Sanskrit only after the seal of approval from Kashmir. Such was the sanctity of authority bestowed upon the Kashmiri Sanskrit Universities.

Dhvanyalok of *Anandavardhan* added a new dimension to linguistics and poetics. Earlier the definition of a *Kavya* (poetry) was "*Vakyam Rasatmakam Kavyam*" meaning "Any composition which gives tasteful pleasure is poetry". Scholars were forced to change their opinion and define poetry as "*Vakyam Dhvanyathmakan Kavyam*"—a piece of writing that gives a message by influence and suggestion is poetry.

Ksemendra, the author of *Kalavilasa* was another great writer who dazzled scholars with his witty and satirical writings. Other prominent scholars of the period included *Bilhana, Kaivyata, Udbhatta, Hayata, Koka Pundit, and Jagaddhara,* whose authoritative works in the field of literature, philosophy, spiritualism, mysticism and politics have made them immortal in the Sanskrit world. *Bilhana* wrote *Vikramanka Deva Charitan* in praise of the Karnataka king who honoured him. *Mahakha* wrote *Shri-Kantha Charitan* in 12th century. *Bharata's Natya Shastra* is an authoritative treaty on dramaturgy. During the reign of *Badshah, Bhatta Avtara* wrote *Xaina Katha* and *Zaina Villas* while *Yodha Bhatta* wrote *Zaina Prakash*. Another big name in Sanskrit Literature from Kashmir is *Gunadya*, who wrote in *Brihat-Katha Manjari*. It is felt that many of the stories from this book have been included in the great multi volume Indian story book *Katha Sarit Sagar*.

A Russian Scholar of Sanskrit revealed during the World Sanskrit Conference at Varanasi in 1981 that the story of their famous ballet Swan Lake has also been taken from this collection. There are modern scholars like *Pundit Lakshmidhar Kalla*, who have opined on the basis of the internal evidence that even *Kalidasa* hailed from Kashmir.

Thus we see that Kashmir served as a fountainhead of wisdom, formal education and a centre for systematization of various scholarly disciplines in the first millennium.

CONTRIBUTION OF KASHMIR TO OTHER LANGUAGES

When Persian replaced Sanskrit as the court language, the local Kashmiri faced a serious problem of learning the language in the shortest of time. It is said that bilingual and trilingual verses were composed, committed to memory and thus an effort was made to learn the new language. The following samples will show the ingenuity of the people:—

1. *Roni Lagan Zongla Bastan Natsun Hao Raqsidan Ast, Banda Paether Murdam, Ragas Sonth Amad Bahar.*
   —Tying the jingles are called *zongla bustan,* dancing is called *Raqsidan* male folk dance is *Murdami Raqas* and the advent of spring is called *Bahar Amad.*

2. The second is in the form of a "question and answer".
   "Kuja Budi Kahan tha, Kati Oshkh? Dere tha Khana boodan, gari oins, chi Khurds, Kyatse Khoho, Kya Khaya?
   Du name do not, rotiyan, tsechi Jorah."
   —The questions are in three languages about *"Where the person was and what did he eat"* and the answer is also in three languages that *"He was at, got home and had eaten two taxes".*

In the absence of any authentic state records we are unable to give an account of the prominent Persian scholars of Kashmir who wrote during the early periods of Islamic rule. The tribes that invaded Kashmir did not value the local art, literature, music and traditions. Their strategy had all along been to exploit the land for riches. Moreover these illiterate tribesmen from Central Asia had never received the fruits of formal education and hence a system of appreciation, preservation or propagation was not in place for any of the intellectual pursuits of human society.

However much later, after the Mughals captured Kashmir, we do have written records mentioning two very important names. Firstly a great poet named *Ghani.* He lived during *Aurangzeb's* reign. He is reported to have declined the invitation of the King to visit his court. He had a peculiar habit of closing all the doors and windows when he was in and keeping them open when he was out. His explanation was that the most precious item in his house was he himself. The inscription on his tombs reads—*Chu Shama Manzile Ma ba Payi Ma.* It means that "like a burning candle, my destination is under my very tact."

Pundit Bhawani Das Taweei was a renowned poet who showed an extraordinary control on Persian vocabulary while reciting devotional lyrics. His wife *Arnimal* too was a great poetess of Kashmiri language. There are many devotional poems written in Persian with an admixture of Sanskrit. A great saint *Krishna Kar* has written in praise of Goddess *Sharika* in these words—

Aval Tui Aakhritui, Batin Tui Zahir Tui., Hazir Tui Nazir Tui, Shrisharika Devi Naman Man Az Tu Nadi Chakri Man, Pranaz Tu Pranyayami Man, dhyan Az Tu Japa Malayi Man Shri shakira Devi Naman.

MODERN LITERATURE

Kashmiris outside Kashmir have written in Urdu as well. The well known names include *Pundit Ratan Natu Sanskar, Pundit Daya Shankar Naseem, Pundit Dattatreya Kaigi, Pundit Anand Narayan Mula* etc. More recently we have had poets and writers like *Prem Nath Dar, Prem Nath Pardesi, Gulan Rasul Nazki, Ali Mohd. Lohe, shorida Kashmir, Dina Nath Mast,* and *Pushkar Nath* who have made a rich contribution to literature both in prose and poetry. Writers have not lagged behind in Hindi either *Dr. Toshkhani, Ratan Lal Shant, Mohan Lal Nirash, Madhup, Dr. Agnishekhar, khema, kaul, Dr. Krishna Razdan, Haleem, Maharaj Krishna Bharat* have contributed both in prose and poetry. Their language is Hindi but the aspirations and feelings projected are those of Kashmiris. *T. N. Dhar Kundan* has written two books—*Main Samudra Hoon* and *Main Pyasa Hoon*—both collections of Hindi Poems that reflect the rich Kashmiri culture and are a great contribution to education and literature. From here onwards three distinct streams of poetry sprouted—the Sufi Mystic, the devotional and the romantic.

This also brings to light prominent forms in which poetry has been written in Sanskrit, Persian, Hindi as well as English. From Sanskrit *Vaku* has been derived. Lyrics in Hindi are known as *Geet,* while their counterparts in Urdu are subdivided into *Ghazal, Qita Nazami* and *Rubai.* Sonnet and the Tree verse have found their way into Kashmiri poetry in English. *Lal Ded* and *Nunda Risi* of the fourteenth century are two great names who have written mystic and spiritual questions. Poetry starts systematically from *Lal Ded* whose *Vaku* were first translated into Sanskrit by *Bhaskaracharya* and later into English and many other languages. These *Vakus* are dipped in *Shaiva* philosophy and enjoin upon us to go inwards in order to attain the reality.

"Gorun Dopnam Kunny, Vatsun, Nehra Dopnan Ander Atsun"—my preceptor advised me in nutshell to go from without to within.

Nunda Rishi wrote *Shruk,* which are replete with Sufi mysticism. He has praised *Lal Ded* in these words, *"Tas Padma Porechi Lale, Yem Gale Amreth Chyev, Shiv Tshorun Thali Twale, Tyuth Me Var Ditan Deevo"*—Lala of

Padmanpura (referring to Lal Ded) drank the nectar and perceived Shiva in everything. O God, purify my soul so that I may see the divine in a similar way.

These two poets are greatly revered in spiritual and mystic poetry. Where *Lal Ded* has propounded *Jnana* and *Shaiva* Philosophy in her *Vakhs*, *Nunda Rishi* has put forth the Sufi ideology in his *Shurkhs*. All the *Kashmiris* hold both in high esteem. During his travels *Nunda Rishi* reached village *Tsra*. He is reported to have spontaneously uttered these words there rhyming with the name of the place, *"Vola Zuva Yati Prar"*—"Let me wait here till the last", and there itself he left his mortal frame.

Rupa Bhawni is another name in spiritual poetry. Her *Vakh*, are full of *Shaiva* Philosophy and the language is Sanskrit. She lived a hundred years in 17th century and is regarded as an incarnation of Goddess *Sharika*. There are a number of anecdotes about her interaction with Muslim Sufi saints. In one encounter with *Sham Qalandar,* they were on the opposite banks of a river. The Sufi proposed, "*Rupa* (literally silver) come over to my side, I shall make you *Son* (Literally Gold)". She replied, "Why don't you come over so that I make you *Mokhta* (literally a pearl)."

By this time the Persian influence had grown deeply into Kashmir literature. Poets started writing 'Masnavis' or long tables in verse. The prominent poet of this period has been *Mohammad Gami*, who lived during 18th and 19th centuries. The Persian stories adopted by him included those of *Laila Majnun, Yusuf Zulaika, Shirin Khusro*, etc. *Yusuf Zulaika*, which been translated in German language, is the most famous of his compositions. He undoubtedly introduced the *Masanvi* but it reached its zenith at the hands of *Maqbool Masnavi, Gulrez,* who has become very popular with masses.

There is a big list of Sufi poets, who espoused the cause of purity and piety as well as mutual brotherhood between various religious groups. These included *Rahman Dar, Shamas Faqir Soccha Knal, Nyama Sahih* and a host of others. Their philosophy was monotheistic and that laid stress on ethical and moral values. Their poetry shows a deep influence of *Advaita* Philosophy.

"Sapan to doghyar travo, Pama Nishi Pan Parzanaro"—Trust in oneness and shun duality; try to know the real self.

"Oguny soruy dognyar Naba baba Ye Chhni bakamay"—Truth is one and there is no duality; all else is a falsehood.

In the second stream of devotional poets, the names of *Parkash Ram, Krishna Razdan* and *Parmananda* are prominent. While the first two wrote devotional songs called *Leela* in praise of *Shri Rama*, the latter was a devout of *Shri Krishna*.

"Darasa Manz Atsaevay, Vigne Zan Natsaevay"—let us join the circle of dancers and enjoy the ecstasy of *Shri Krishna*.

Parmanand who lived in the 19th century, has written a memorable long poem wherein he has compared the human actions with tilling of the land right from ploughing up to the time of reaping the harvest. *Ram* wrote the first Ramayana in Kashmiri and captioned it *Ram Avtar Tsaryat*.

While this spiritual writing continued as a sub-stream in the following centuries, Kashmir suddenly saw emergence of a new theme in poetry, romance. *Aruimal* wrote extensively on romance and love in the 19th Century. Her decision and selection of words and the musical metre used by her are exquisite. She had profound knowledge of classical music and is believed to have rearranged the *ragas* for *Sufiana Kalam*. As a result many hitherto unknown elements were introduced into Sufi music. One such example is the "internal rhyming", described at length in Sanskrit, which she introduced in her Persian lyrics. An example will illustrate her master craftsmanship:—

Matshi Thap Ditsnam Nyandri Hasti Masti Matshi Matsha, Band Sanith Gom Vanta Vyas Vony Kus Kas Patsi, Vunyub Karitha Gom—I was in deep slumber when he caught hold of my wrist. The gold wristband cut into the very skin of my wrist. O Friend! Tell me who is to be trusted in these circumstances. He has left me crust fallen.

Habbba Khatoon sung songs of love, separation and ill-treatment at the hands of in-laws and other human feelings. The Kashmiri poetry came down from the spiritual height to the mundane human level. Her lament was *"Varivyan Saet Vara Chhano Chara Kar Myon Malino No"*—I am not at peace with my in-laws, would somebody come to my rescue from my father's side?

In the romantic stream of poetry the next prominent music maker was *Rasul Meer. He* was the first poet who addressed his poems to a female beloved. The earlier poets had made a male their love perhaps because they were pointing to the divine and not the human. His famous poem starts with these words.

"Rinda Posh Mall Gindde Dravi Lolo Shubi Shabnam Chanippot Tshayi Lolo" —My beloved has come out to play in an ecstatic mood, praise be to her shadow that follows her.

"Raza Hanziyani Naaz Kyah Aenizini Gardam, Yazillahi Chashmi Bad Hishi Rachhan, Kam Kyan Gatshi Chani Bargahi lolo"—The gracious one has a neck like a swan. God! Save her from evil's eye. By that your grace will be no poorer.

CONTEMPORARY HISTORY

Twentieth Century saw all round progress of Kashmiri language. The three streams, that were flowing continued and some new trends also developed. Master *Zinda Kaul* is a great name among the mystic poets of this period. His book '*Surman*' won him the Sahitya Academy Award. A short poem of his:—

"Tyamber Pyayam **are** *Kharmanas alava hyoton Kanzael Vanas, taer tirna laez Phaelna dil dodum Jigar tatyom, Krakla Vaetesh Zi naar he"* —A spark fell on the haystack. The entire jungle caught fire. It didn't take long to spread. My heart burnt and the liver heated up. A shout came from the sides, Fire, fire!

He has described God in these words:—

"kaem tam Kar Tawat bonag pot today doorey dejutle must sayer Kaman tee burnt saems diles tee bynthmut" —Someday somewhere somebody has seen his shadow from a distance. We have heard it with our ears and our heart is convinced of his Existence.

Ahad Zargar is another important poet of this stream who has written notable poems on mysticism and spirituality. The immortal poet *Mehroor*, who is called Wordsworth of Kashmiri language, has elevated the romantic poetry to new heights. He was applauded by Rabindranath Tagore. In this message for his fellow countrymen:—

"*Hyund Chhu Shakar Dodh Chhuu Muslim anlii Deen, dodh ta shaker Milaneviv Pana Vaen*"
—Hindus are like sugar and Muslim like milk. Let us mix the two and create a harmonious society.

Another great name of this period is that of *Ahad Azad*. He didn't live long, but left an indelible mark on Indian literature. He was virtually the harbinger of the progressive poetry in Kashmir. His long poem *Darac* or the river is a master piece. He has ridiculed romance in the face of poverty, want and hunger:—

"*Madanvari Lagay Paeree, BA O Zara Ashga Bemart. TSE SAET Gaetsh Fursatha AAsen, Dilas Gaetsh Farhatma Arsen, Me Gaemets Nael Naadari, BA Nozara Ashqa Bemari.*"
—My love romance is not my cup of tea. It needs leisure and peace of mind. I have none and I am crestfallen due to my poverty so no romance for me please.

Post independence period is a period of renaissance for development of literature in Kashmir. Kashmiri poets were influenced by the philosophy of Karl Marx and the progressive literature of other languages. While *Aiiama Iqbal* was the ideal for many, *Faiz Jafri* served as an inspiration for the rest. In the past most of the mystic poetry was full of obscure and suggestive idioms whereas the poetry of this new breed of poets was frank and forthright, sometimes reminding one of slogans. In response to the Pakistani tribal raid the writers formed Kashmir Cultural Front for defending inter-ethnic harmony. They warned the masses and tried to educate the religious leaders about the consequences of baseless religious fanaticism. The literature created could not remain unaffected by the political and social rearing. Earlier in 1945 *Mirza Arif* had started a cultural organization by the name of *Bazame Adab*. Many enthusiastic writers got involved with this organization. *Mirza Arif* is famous for his *Kashmiri Rubaiyas*, which are crisp and meaningful. The prominent poets of this new movement are *Dina Nath Nadim Rehman Rahi* and *Amin Kamil*. *Nadim* revolutionized the entire face of poetry. He used pure Kashmiri diction for lending expression to the desire and aspiration of the common man. He wrote opera, and sonnet for the first time in Kashmiri and his poems have been translated into many languages. One of his immortal poem is against wars and strife:—

"*Mya Chham Aash Pasa Haech Pagag Sholi Duniyan*"
—I have full faith in tomorrow for tomorrow will bring new light to the entire world.

He was the torch bearer of humanistic poetry in Kashmir. His operas *Bonber* and *Ta Yambarzal Neki Ta Baedi* are milestones of not only Kashmiri but also Indian literature. *Rahi* is another recipient of the Sahitya Academy Award. His *Nav Rozi Saba* shows the influence of *Iqbal* very clearly. He has also made a rich contribution to Kashmiri poetry.

"*Tse sang Yaer Mutsraew Taer Baryan, Maer Maehd Phyur Mas Malryan, Vaer Zahir Vaets Amman TA lolo.*"
—The big benefactor has thrown the doors open and filled wine into big pitchers. It appears that the common man will get his share now.

Kamil has written short stories and poetry both. His diction is rustic and meter musical.

"*Khot sorma Ranjan Tala Raan Bhav Bahar aav*"
—The price of make-up items for ladies and the ornaments have shot up; it appears the spring has arrived.

This period produced a multitude of poets who contributed to the enrichment of Indian literature. *Noor Mohd. Roshan Aryan Dev Majboor, Ghulam Rasool Santosh, Moti Lal Saqi, Chaman Lal, Prem Nath Premi, Makan Lal Bekas, Ghulam Nabi Firaq, Vasu Dev Reh, Ghulam Nabi Khayal* were active within the valley. In the same period *B. N. Kaul, Shambhu Nath Bhatt* and *Haleem* were writing from the point of view of a Kashmiri out of Kashmir.

Prose writing also grew in leaps and bounds during this period. The names of prominent short story writers are *Akhtar Mohiudeen, Somnath Zutshi, Ali Mohammad Love, Umesh Bansi Nordosh, Hriday Kaul Bharti, Deepak Kaul, Hari Krishna Kaul, Santosh* and *Kamil*. They gave expression to the emotions and feelings of the common man visualising the life of the inhabitants of the valley. *Akhtar, Love, Kamil* and *Hari Krishna* have written novels.

Radio Kashmir and Door-Darshan Kendra at Srinagar provided multiple new media avenues and thereby played an important role in encouraging these writers. The Academy of Arts and culture has also been publishing the works of these artists and anthologies, which inspire other young writers. *Moti Lal Kyomu* has been a pioneer in the field of drama and publisher *Bhan* in Satirical Radio plays. *Hari Krishna Kaul* is also a successful drama writer.

There are a host of other writers who have not been mentioned for fear of digressing from the central point of the book. Apologies to them since all of their contribution to the Kashmiri literature are precious. This is to conclude that Kashmiri language is not only rich in literature, but it also reflects the evolution of Kashmir down the ages from time of the Vedic hymns to the progressive multicultural twentieth century.

TRANSLATIONS

There have been some translations into other languages but it is not enough. Some of the writers who have done pioneering work in popularizing Kashmiri literature are Professor *Jai Lal Kaul, Nand Lal Talib. T. N. Raina, P.K. Pushp, K.M. Dhar, B. N. Parimoo, Moti Lal Saqi* and *R.K. Rehbar*. There is a pressing need for translating the selected works from Kashmiri into other Indian and foreign languages, so that the readers in the entire country will be acquainted with its depth and vastness. Kashmir is the beloved mother tongue of all the Kashmiris irrespective of their religion. It is however a pity that the language has not been receiving official patronage that it deserves.

ART AND ARCHITECTURE

Kashmir also has a rich tradition of fine arts. The old Sanskrit and *Shonda* manuscripts are full of beautiful paintings and pictures of gods and goddesses. Life like flowers and petals are drawn along the margins of the pages. The text is written in an ancient calligraphic font. The colours used in drawing them have been made indigenously from natural dyes extracted from leaves, herbs and flowers. They are so prepared and mixed that the passage of time has only made this art more prolific and profound indicating the existence of a well researched system of chemical chromatics. Even today one can see samples of these paintings on the top of the horoscopes and along the margins of manuscripts written on handmade paper. The portraits are exquisite and a methodical research will throw light on its origin and gradual development. No wonder that the artisans of Kashmir have made a name for themselves in embroidery, papier-mâché and walnut carving. In modern times, Kashmir has produced a good number of artists who have experimented with traditional as well as modern techniques and in the process developed their own distinct styles. *Sarva Shri K.N. Dhar, Dina Nath, Gulam Rasool Santosh, P.N. Kachrou, Manhar Kaul, Bausi Parimoo* and many others fall in this category.

MUSIC

Music is another facet of Kashmiri culture, which has not received due acknowledgement. Today there are almost identical marriage songs for Hindu and Muslim marriages. The difference is only that the Hindus sing in *Vilambit* or elongated effect of *Sama Vedic* recitation while the Muslims sing them in '*Drut*' or fast tune. Kashmir has a very rich tradition of folk songs which depict the emotions, feelings, and sensibilities of the common man. Floods and famines have been vividly described in these songs. A well organised school of classical music called *Sufiana Kalam* (or the saying of the Sufi Saints) has its roots in Kashmir. It has different *Ragas* and usually the sayings of *Lal Ded*, the great poetess of Kashmir, are mentioned at the beginning of each Raga.

In recent times we have had many great exponents of *Sufiana Kalam,* two most prominent names are *Mohd. Abdullag Tibbet baquae* and *Ghulam Mohd. Qalinbat.* All these ragas, which are in vogue these days, have been formalized by *Arni Mal*, another great poetess of Kashmir. The multi stringed *Santoor* is the soul of the *Sufiana Kalam. Pundit Shiv Kumar Sharma* has successfully introduced *Santoor* in the Bollywood film industry. Other musical instruments are also popular in Kashmir and a well known name in Sitar recital is that of *Pundit Shambhu Nath Sopori.*

FESTIVAL AND RITUALS

In spite of being home to a variety of festivals based on major religions of the valley, there are a lot of similarities in the diverse rituals. Distribution of *Tahar* (cooked yellow rice) on festive occasions is common between Hindus and Muslims. Night long singing of hymns in praise of the divine is another common feature. The annual *Urs* or commemorative days of various saints are also celebrated jointly by all the ethnic groups with due reverence. The Hindus of the Valley are called Kashmiri Pundits or *Bhat*. An important festival that has become their identity is the celebrations of *Shiva Ratri* in the month of February. Here the festivities stretch over a fortnight and this festival has the same importance in Kashmir as the *Ganesh Puja* has for Marathas and the *Durga Puja* for the Bengalis.

Not much is known about the tradition of dramatics and dance in Kashmir. Sanskrit plays have always been written for the purpose of entertainment and celebration on various festive occasions like the advent of spring season. It is said that king *Zainul-Ab-Din* had patronized drama writing and theatre. During his time, *Yodha Bhat* and *Som Pundit* had written some plays with serious themes.

The popular folk dance is called *Banda Paether*. *Ruf* is a melodious group dance with strong satirical accent. On the occasion of marriage, *Veegya Natsun* expresses the emotions that dawn before the couple starts a new phase of life. This indicates that dance must have been a passionate pursuit of the nobility in the valley.

A unique style of celebration wherein synchronized steps are accompanied by lively music is prevalent in *Ladakh*, pointing to the existence of a similar Buddhist dance system in the valley. There is definitely a need for future researches to remove the veil of time from this facet of Kashmiri culture.

CULTURE AND FOOD CUISINE

Kashmiri Cuisine includes *dum aloo* (boiled potatoes with heavy amounts of spice), *tzawam* (a solid cottage cheese), *Rogan Josh* (Lamb cooked in heavy spices), *Yakhingyu* (lamb cooked in curd with mild spices), *lakh* (a spinach-like leaf), *rista-gushtaba* (minced meat belly in tomato and curd curry), *dnival Krme* and of course the signature rice which is particular to Asian cultures. The traditional *Wazwan* feast involves cooking meat and vegetables, usually mutton in several different ways.

Alcohol is strictly prohibited in most places. There are two styles of making tea in the region: Noon Chi Salt Tea which is pink in colour (known as *Chinen Posh Rans*) or Peach flower colour and popular with locals; and *Kahwa* a tea for festive occasions, made with Saffron and spices (cardamom, cinnamon, sugar, nouches leaves) and black tea.

Composite Culture

The past millennium has been a period of turmoil which brought shame to the composite culture of the valley. The Hindus had to migrate to Jammu, Delhi and other parts of the country to escape the wrath of the Pakistan sponsored militancy. During the last decade of the 20th century, Kashmiri writers have authored a lot of literature. In this literature they lament the loss of their family and hearth. The yearning to go back to their roots is not suppressed even by the pain and anguish that is triggered by the fundamentalist geo-political approach that cuts the very root of their rich culture and in the process shatters their proud tradition. The worst casualty has been the mutual trust relationship and harmony between the people of different faiths. *T. N. Dhar Kundan* concluded by reciting these verses—

"Beys Vaeth Deenaek Ta Dharmaek Fitmai, Beys Gav Byon Alfas Nish Bey.
Gotchs Nayi Rauun Hasil Koryus, Dashi Thaev Thaev Astanan Manz."

"Again we are witnessing conflict and confrontation in the name of religion. Again one is getting separated from the other. I am afraid we may lose all that we had achieved after offering prayers repeatedly at the shrines and holy places."

Srinagar

The city of Srinagar was founded by King *Pravarsen*-II over 2000 years ago. This city is situated on the hills of Mount *Shrigiri* named after Lord Shiva and lies on the banks of river Jhelum. The city is located at an altitude of 1730 metres and overlooks the snowy ridge of Peer Panjal Range. It experiences summer temperature ranging from 29.5°C to 10.6°C and winter temperatures from 7.3°C to-1.9°C. The Chinese traveller *Huen Tsang* visited this town in 631 A.D. during the reign of the last Hindu ruler of the valley King *Lalitaditya Muktapeeth,* who built a temple on the top of a plateau near the town of *Anantnag*. He dedicated this temple to the Sun God, the originator of his dynasty. This temple has eighty four columns and is an exquisite example of the marvellous architectural skill of those times. It overlooks the Kashmir Valley and offers some of the most breathtaking views of the Himalayas. The temple stands on a square shaped hard lime stone rock surrounded by snow capped mountains.

The city of Srinagar is a city of lakes and gardens. Whereas the lakes are the work of Nature, the gardens were laid out at the behest of two Mughal Emperors—Akbar and Jahangir. Out of some seven hundred Mughal Gardens once present in the Valley, only a few survive. Three of them lie on the eastern bank of Dal Lake. These gardens bear the names *Chashma-e-Shahi, Nishad Bagh* and *Shalimar Bagh.* The stately Chinar Tree (*Platanus orientalis*) was introduced in the Kashmir Valley by the Mughal Emperors when they got the gardens laid out in the valley. The lakes of Srinagar with their boat dwellings and *Shikara* (wooden boat) rides are a prominent tourist attraction. Living in the huge houseboats anchored in the lakes is a once in a life time experience. Moreover the small and swift *Shikaras* provide the tourists with considerable fun and enjoyment of the scenic beauty. Extremely bewitching handicrafts with finest wood carvings, embroidery, papier-mâché, carpets and shawls delight the tourists and contribute to the local economy. In response to the rising demands magnificent hotels are also coming up on dry land to accommodate the new inflow of foreign tourists.

The River Jhelum has eight bridges that connect various parts of the city on its either banks. These bridges have been named differently such as *Amira Kadal* and *Zena Kadal* etc. however under the British the bridges were allotted numbers as Zero Bridge, One bridge and so on.

Srinagar has a number of shrines and mosques. They are typically crafted out of wood in geometric patterns and surmounted by pagoda like steeples instead of domes. The mosque of *Shah Hamdan* in the old city, the shrine of *Shah Mukhdoom Saheb* on the slopes of *Hari Parvat*, the *Pathar* mosque, mosque of *Akhund Mullah Shah* and the *Hazratbal* mosque are the chief Holy places of local Muslims. It is believed that the *Hazratbal* Mosque contains the most sacred relic—hair from *Hazrat Mohammad Sahib's* beard. A Mughal prince built Pari Mahal, a religious college dedicated to his teacher in the 17ᵗʰ century which lies in ruins presently. Additionally the ruins of once magnificent Hindu temples at *Avantipura and Martand* Temple near *Anantnag* are really worth-seeing. One can only imagine their splendour before the Muslim occupation.

Gulmarg

Gulmarg, about 58 kilometres west of Srinagar, is known as the "meadow of flowers". It is located at an altitude of 2730 metres and was developed by the British for their leisure time pursuits. It has a golf course surrounded by fairytale cottages among pine forests. As we move higher, we reach *Khilanmarg* which is a ski resort with all world class facilities.

Pehalgam

Pehalgam lies to the west of Srinagar at a distance of 96 kilometres in the Valley of river *Lidder* along the southern slope of the Greater Himalayas. It forms the base for several treks to *Kishtwar* and *Suru* Valley and further to the holy cave shrine of Lord *Amarnath,* which is visited by millions of devotees every year. This area is dotted with mustard meadows, trout fisheries and saffron fields at every step. These crops bring considerable revenue for the state of Jammu and Kashmir and provide it with sound economic stimulus. *Pulwama* and *Pampore* produce the majority of Kashmiri saffron which is renowned world over.

Amarnath Cave Shrine

Amarnath cave is a Hindu shrine located in Jammu and Kashmir, India. It is dedicated to Lord Shiva. The cave is situated at an altitude of 3,888 m (12,756 ft), about 141 km (88 mi) from Srinagar, the capital of Jammu and Kashmir and can be reached through *Pahalgam* town. The shrine forms an important part of Hinduism, and is considered to be one of the four holiest shrines in Hinduism. The cave is surrounded by snowy mountains. The cave itself is covered with snow most of the year except for a short period of time in summer when it is open for pilgrims. Thousands of Hindu devotees make an annual pilgrimage to the Amarnath cave on challenging mountainous terrain to see an ice stalagmite formed inside the cave.

Inside the 40 m (130 ft) high Amarnath cave, the stalagmite is formed due to freezing of water droplets that fall from the roof of the cave on to the floor and grow up vertically on the cave floor. It is considered to be a Shiva Lingam by Hindus. The Cave waxes from May to August. As snow melts in the Himalayas above the cave and the resultant water seeps into the rocks that form the cave and gradually wanes thereafter. As per the religious beliefs, it has been claimed that the lingam grows and shrinks with the phases of the moon reaching its height during the summer festival.

According to a Hindu legend, this is the cave where Shiva explained the secret of life and eternity to his divine consort, *Parvati*. Two other ice formations represent *Parvati* and Shiva's son, *Ganesha*. The main purpose of the annual pilgrimage to the cave is worship of the ice stalagmite Lingam.

History

The Amarnath cave has been a place of worship since times immemorial. There are references to the legendary King *Aryaraja* (ascribed dates 300 BCE) who used to worship a lingam formed of ice in Kashmir. The book *Rajatarangini* (Book VII v.183) refers to *Amareshwara* or Amarnath. It is believed that Queen *Suryamathi* in the 11th century AD gifted tridents, banalingas and other sacred emblems to this temple. *Rajavalipataka* written by *Prjayabhatta* has detailed references of the pilgrimage to Amarnath Cave. Other than this, there are further references to this pilgrimage in many other ancient texts.

Discovery of Holy Cave

It is believed that after the middle ages this cave was forgotten by people. A shepherd discovered it once again in the 15th century. Another story relates to *Bhrigu Muni*. Long time ago it is believed that The Valley of Kashmir was submerged under water and *Kashyapa Muni* drained it through a series of rivers and rivulets. Therefore when the waters drained, *Bhrigu Muni* was the first man to pay obeisances to Lord Amarnath. Thereafter, when people heard of the Lingam, it became an abode of Lord Shiva for all believers and a pilgrimage which is done by lakhs of people each year.

Yatra

The temple is a popular pilgrimage destination for only Hindus. In 2011 it received about 634,000 persons, the highest recorded number for the site. The number was 622,000 in 2012 and 350,000 in 2013. Pilgrims visit the holy site during the 45 day season around the festival of *Shravani Mela* in July or August, coinciding with the Hindu holy month of *Shraavana*. The beginning of the annual pilgrimage, called Amarnath Yatra is marked by '*pratham pujan*' to invoke the blessings of Shri Amarnathji.

Route

Devotees travel on foot, either from Srinagar or from *Pahalgam*. The latter journey takes approximately 5 days. The State Road Transport Corporation and Private Transport Operators provide the regular services from Jammu to *Pahalgam* and *Baltal*. Also privately hired taxis are available from Jammu and Kashmir. The shorter northern route is just about 16 km long, but has a very steep gradient and is quite difficult to climb. It starts from *Baltal* and passes through *Domial, Barari*, and *Sangam* to reach the cave. The northern route is along the Amaranth valley and all along the route one can see the river Amaravathy (It is a tributary of Chenab) which originates from Amaranth Glacier.

It is believed that Lord Shiva left Nandi, the Bull, at *Pahalgam* (*Pahal* meaning bull, *Gam* meaning village). At *Chandanwari* (*Chandan* means Moon, *wari* means abode) he released the Moon from his hair (*Jataon*). On the banks of Lake *Sheshnag* (*Shesh* meaning King and *Nag* meaning Snakes), he released his snakes. At *Mahagunas Parvat* (Maha Ganesh Mountain), he left his son Lord *Ganesha*. At *Panjtarni* (*Panj* meaning five), Lord Shiva left behind the five elements—Earth, Water, Air, Fire and Sky. As a symbol of sacrificing the earthly world, Lord Shiva performed the *Tandava* Dance. Then, finally, Lord Shiva entered the Holy Amaranth Cave along with *Parvati*.

Facilities

En route the cave, various non-profit organizations set up food supply and resting tents called *Pandals* which are available for free to the pilgrims. Near the shrine, hundreds of tents which are erected by locals can be hired for a night's stay. Helicopter services from base camp to *Panjtarni* (6 km from the cave) are also available from various private operators.

Security

Every year, thousands of central police and state police personnel are deployed to provide security to pilgrims from potential terror threats. The forces are stationed at various halts and also form a perimeter around the shrine.

Deaths

Out of the 622,000 yatra pilgrims in 2012, 130 died during the yatra. The major cause was attributed to persons who were not physically fit for the arduous climb, high elevations, and adverse weather. Some also died in road accidents before reaching the base camp from where the yatra starts. Of the 130 deaths, 88 were due to purported health reasons and 42 in road accidents. The 2012 pilgrimage ended on *Shravana Purnima (Raksha Bandan)* Day, 2 August 2012

Organisers

Officially, the Yatra is organised by the State Government in collaboration with the Shree Amaranth Yatra trust. The Government agencies provide necessary facilities all along the route during the Yatra period, which includes provision of ponies, supply of power, telecommunication facilities, firewood and setting up of fair price shops.

1990s problems

The pilgrimage was banned from 1991 to 1995 due to threats from militants. In 1996, the militants had assured that they would not interfere. Thus the yatra resumed with far greater numbers than in previous years. However, unseasonal blizzards in late August of that year led to a tragedy that claimed the lives of 242 yatris, killed by exhaustion and exposure.

The Massacre

Four years later, the pilgrimage suffered another setback with the massacre in Pahalgam of 30 people by Kashmiri separatist militants. Most were yatris on their way to Amaranth or porters and horsemen who would have ferried the pilgrims to the site. The then Indian Prime Minister Atal Bihari Vajpayee blamed *Lashkar-e-Taiba* for the killings.

Controversies

On 26 May 2008, the Government of India and the state government of Jammu and Kashmir reached an agreement to transfer 100 acres (0.40 km²) of forest land to the Shri Amarnathji Shrine Board (SASB) to set up temporary shelters and facilities for Hindu pilgrims. Kashmiri separatists opposed the move citing reasons that it will jeopardize the article 370 that gives separate identity to the people of Jammu and Kashmir and prevents any Indian citizen to settle in Kashmir. People in Kashmir staged widespread protests against this decision of the government. Due to the protests, the Jammu and Kashmir state government relented and reversed the decision to transfer land. As a result, Hindus in the Jammu region launched counter agitations against this roll back.

Environmental destruction

Environmentalists have expressed concern that the number of people participating in the Amaranth Yatra is having a negative impact on the area's ecology and some have expressed support for government regulated limits on the number of pilgrims permitted to make the trek.

Hari Parbat

Hari Parbat also known as *Koh-e-Maraan* is a hill overlooking Srinagar, the largest city and summer capital of Jammu and Kashmir. It is the site of a *Durrani* fort, built in 1808. It has the famous *Shakti* Temple on the western slope and Muslim shrines of *Khwaja Makhdoom Sahib* and *Akhund Mullah Shah* on the southern slope. On the southern side of the outer wall there is a Gurudwara, which commemorates the visit of *Guru Hargobind Singh Ji*.

The first fortifications on the site were constructed by the Mughal Emperor Akbar in 1590. He built an outer wall for the fort and planned a new capital called *Nager Nagor* to be built within the wall. That project was never completed. The present fort was built in 1808 under the reign of *Shuja Shah Durrani*.

Temple.

The hill is considered sacred by the Kashmiri Pundits due to the presence of a temple of *Sharika Devi*. Temple is of goddess *Jagadamba Sharika Bhagwati*. She has 18 arms and is regarded as the presiding deity of Srinagar city. The goddess is represented by a *Swyambhu Shrichakra (Mahamaha Shrichakra)*, also called *Mahashri Yantra*, which consists of circular mystic impressions and triangular patterns with a dot at the centre. *Sharika Devi* is believed to be a form of *Durga* Mata or *Shakti*.

Makhdoom Sahib

Nestled below the imposing Mughal Fort is the shrine of Sheikh *Hamza Makhdum*, also known as—*Makhdoom Sahib, Mehboob-ul-Alam* and *Sultan-Ul-Arifeen*. Shrine is located on the southern slope of Hari Parbat Hill. It is one of the most sacred shrines in Kashmir. This double storied, multi-pillared structure displays a remarkable architectural style. This shrine is visited not only by Muslims but by people of all faiths, throughout the year. *Makhdoom Sahib*, also called *Hazrat Sultan*, was a Sufi saint.

Many mosques were built by Muslims in the Hari Parbat area since the time of Afghan *Ghaznavis* and *Ghurids*. The present fort, called Hari Parbat fort, was erected by *Durrani* Afghan rulers of Kashmir in 1808.

Gurdwara Chatti Patshahi

Gurdwara Chatti Patshahi, Kathi Darwaja, Rainwari, Srinagar is one of the most important Sikh *Gurudwaras* in Kashmir. It is believed that the sixth guru of Sikhism travelled through Kashmir, stopping to preach occasionally and stayed for a few days. An old Blind lady called *"Bag Bhari"* was a great disciple of *Shri Guru Hargobind Sahib*. She had prepared a *Khadar Chola* (tunic) for Guru Sahib and was waiting for Guru Sahib (as she being blind couldn't travel). So to fulfil her wish the Guru travelled to Srinagar and met her. She offered the tunic to the Guru and expressed her desire to see the Guru once. The Guru struck the ground with his sword and a spring of water started coming out of the ground. The Guru then asked the lady to wash her eyes with that water. When *Bhag Bhari* did that her eyesight was restored. Seeing the Guru with her own eyes, she fell on his feet. And further she requested that now having seen the Guru, she did not want to see anything else in this world. She requested the Guru to release her from this birth. Her request was accepted and she left for the heavenly abode. The guru himself cremated her body on a spot marked by the *Gurudwara*.

Legendary Origin

According to legend, the Hari Parbat hill was once a huge lake inhabited by the demon *Jalobhava*. The inhabitants called on the goddess *Parvati* for help. She took the form of a bird (*hari*/ Mynah) and dropped a pebble on the demon's head, which grew larger and larger until it crushed the demon. Hari Parbat is revered as that pebble, hence was named Hari (myna) Parbat. It is said to have become the home for all the gods of the Hindu pantheon. *Parvati* is worshipped as *Sharika* in *Shri Tsakra* (an emblem of cosmic energy pervading the universe) occupying the middle part of the western slope of the hill. The hill is also called *Predemna Peet*. On the birthday of *Sharika Bhagwati*, the devotees make a sacrificial offering of `*Taher-charvan*' (*Taher*— rice boiled with turmeric powder and mixed with oil and salt, *charvan*— cooked liver of goat) to the goddess. This day is celebrated locally as *Har Navum*.

KASHMIRIYAT

India is a young nation inhabited by people of ancient origin. Around 1500 B.C. Aryans arrived from Central Asia and settled in the Great Himalayas and along the Gangatic Plains of North India. Kashmir Valley housed the initial settlements of the migrating Aryan race. Although the Hindu caste system in Kashmir was influenced by the influx of Buddhism during the reign of Mauryan Emperor Asoka (around 3rd century B.C) the Brahmans lived on alms, practiced meditation and shared common spiritual pursuits with the Buddhist monks. As a consequence, Kashmiri Pundits are the purest of the Aryan race. Another important and vital feature of early Kashmir society was the relative high regard in which women were held when compared to their global counterparts during the same period.

The inhabitants of Kashmir valley were predominantly faithful to the *Trika* school of *Shaivism*. Popularly known as Kashmir *Shaivism,* it is a Hindu Vedic philosophy with the goal to merge in *Shiva* or realize one's already existing identity with *Shiva*, by means of wisdom, yoga and God's grace. It is categorized by various scholars as monistic idealism, transcendental materialism and some even go to the extent of calling it the "Realistic idealism". It gives primacy to universal consciousness and all things as manifestations of this consciousness.

Culture

Early accounts and Archaeological evidences such as terracotta sculptures do not record the present day dress, which comprises of items such as the *Turban, Taranga* and *Pheran*. Instead records indicate leather doublet woollen cloaks and clothes made from hemp, cotton linen and different types of silk. Many items of clothing reflected the cold winter climate of area.

Kshemendra's detailed records from the eleventh century describe many items of which the precise nature is unknown. It is clear that tunics known as *Kanchuka* were worn long-sleeved by men and in both long-and half-sleeved version by women. They used to wear a special type of turban referred to as a *Shirahshata*. The foot wear consisted of leather shoes and boots worn with socks. Some holy sites of Kashmiri Pundits include the *Skhir Bhawani, Martand Sun Temple* at *Mattan, Mahakali* Shrine in Srinagar on the banks of *Vitasta* and above all the *Amarnath* Cave Shrine, the Pilgrimage to which is conducted during *Sharavan Purunima*. The religious festivals of Hindus of Kashmir have Vedic and Proto-Indo-Iranian roots. The Kashmiri Pundits share many of their festivals with other Hindu Communities and some with Zoroastrians. The pre-Islamic elements of Persian and Central Asian cultures derived from the Proto-Indo-Iranian religion also contribute to the heritage of Kashmiri Pundits. *Shivratri* or *Herath* as it is known in Kashmir is one of the major festivals of Kashmiri Pundits. *Navreh* or the Kashmiri lunar New Year is also an important Pundit festival.

The *Chitrapur Saraswat* Brahmans are a small *Koukani* speaking community of Kashmiri Brahmans who migrated to Karnataka in 19th century, at the flame of Muslim invasion. They call themselves *Bhanars* in the *Koukani* language. Mostly educators and administrators this community adheres the *Adavita Vedanta* Philosophy of *Adi Shankar*. There are various etymologies of the word *Saraswat*. A prominent one refers to the offspring of *Saraswati* (the Goddess of learning) and is utilized to specifically address learned and scholarly people. It may also denote the residents of the *Sarawati* River Basin. The Brahmans of this region who are referred as *Saraswats* in the Mahabharata and *Puranas* were well versed in Vedic knowledge.

The Valley of Kashmir was under the governance of mighty Hindu rulers since the prehistoric times which include 2000 years of recorded history as well. The population of the valley was overwhelmingly Hindu and Buddhist by faith and the rulers belonged to the Solar Dynasty of the *Rajputs*. Other people from *Rajputana* (the land of the brave *Rajputs)* migrated to this valley and took to two possible occupations. A majority of them turned sheep herders, while others took to farming of rice, maize, herbs, saffron, vegetables, fruit and flowers like roses and tulips.

Northern India was subject to foreign invasions from 8th century onwards with the rise of Islam. Kashmir was not keenly contested due to the tough terrain encircling the valley. However in the 14th century Muslim Rule was established. This was a consequence of the disintegration of the royal court of the Hindu *Lohara* dynasty. The *Damaras* of few chiefs grew so powerful that they defied royal authority by constant revolts. Life and property were not safe anymore. Agriculture declined and trade came down to a standstill. Hence the Muslim invaders conquered a disheartened starved quarrelling group of Kashmiris.

A Mongol from Turkistan *Zulju*, wreaked devastation in 1320, when he invaded Kashmir and conquered many regions of the valley. The actions of Sultan *Shihsa Butshikan* (1389-1413) the second Muslim ruler of Kashmir were also significant to the area. The Sultan has been referred to as a "Breaker of Images" because of his destruction of many non-Muslim religious symbols. The brutal manners in which he forced the population to convert to Islam bear an uncanny resemblance to Aurangzeb's Mughal rule in the rest of India. Many followers of the traditional religions who did not want to convert to Islam fled to other parts of India. Pundits were at that time offered tracts of land by rulers elsewhere in India who wanted to utilize the high literacy and general education of the community as well as the legitimacy conferred upon them by the threat of forced religious conversion. The outcome of this shift was apparent in the demographics and the Kashmir Valley became a predominantly Muslim region.

Next came the reign of Mughal ruler Akbar. The Hindus enjoyed security of person and property. They were allotted high government Post because of better education than their Muslim counterparts. It was Akbar who was so pleased with their intelligence that he gave them the surname "Pundit". The Mughal rule was followed by that of Afghans. The 500 years of Muslim rule in Kashmir coupled with the missionary work of Sufis led to conversion of the majority of population to Islam leaving only a handful of Kashmiri Pundits.

Thus towards the end of the thirteen century and the beginning of the fourteen century Islam came to Kashmir. On one hand it brought the invaders whose sole intention was to exploit the land while on the other hand this place attracted the Muslim Sufis. These Sufis believed in *Khulwa* or spiritual retreat and propagated going from the outer exotic to the inner esoteric. This coincided with the prevailing tradition of seeking means to refine deeper realization of the divine with one's consciousness rather than engaging in critical theological discussions; realizing the possibilities of the soul in solitude and silence; and to transform the flashing and fading moments of vision into a leading light which could illumine the long years of life. Thus came into existence a composite cultural framework.

The Kashmiri Pundits used to swear by *Dastgir Sahib* (revered Muslim Sufi Saint) and any Muslim Passing by a Hindu Shrine would hold his hands in obeisance. There are innumerable holy places and shrines where both Hindus and Muslims would go to offer prayers. Hindus and Muslims equally revered *Lal Ded* and *Peer Pandit Padhshan, Nunda Rishi, Bata Mol Sahib* to name a few.

"*Afu Khodaya Fazal Kar, Badas Ta Janas Hyamdis Ta Musalmanas*" (Kashmiri)
—God shower your grace on good and bad people alike, both in Hindus and Muslims.

"*Sarve Bhavanhtu Sukhenam Sarve Santu Niramayam Sarve Bhadravi Pashyantu Ma Kaschit Duk Bhag Bhavet*" (Sanskrit)
—Let all be happy, free of worries. Let all be met with beneficial and pleasant things and let no body meet with grief and unhappiness.

To sum up we can say that the origin of the cultural stream of Kashmir is Vedic. It was, for a brief period of history, influenced by Buddhism. Majorly the peaceful periods of coexistence were shaped by *Tirka* Philosophy of Kashmir Shaivism and the Muslim Sufism. Both of which were in turn influenced by each other. The enormous literature that has been produced by the hermits and scholars of this land portray a picture of *Jnana* or Knowledge dressed in *Bhakti* or Devotion. This is *Kashmiriyat*.

KASHMIRI PUNDITS

Mere words cannot match the depth of the sorrow experienced by Pundits nor can they heal their wounded heart. These tragedies must end in the largest democracy of the world. And to end them, we must change the thinking of Muslim Kashmiri's. The international civil society and India in particular is untouched by the grief of the Hindus of Kashmir. Pundits are an important community of Kashmir. They want justice. There is not a single word of concern in this matter from India's President, Prime Minister, the cabinet or even the Chief Minister of Jammu and Kashmir. The matter is being dragged for the last 23 long years on one pretext or the other. Kashmiri Hindus are still suffering in the camps of Jammu. Media is silent on the matter. There are no pictures of homeless Pundits in magazines, no speeches from any political party addressing the topic, no interviews of grieving people of Kashmir, no analysis of what happened and why. The whole world is unaware of the emotional trauma that is associated with being an innocent civilized cultured Hindu in India, leave alone Kashmir. It is shocking to see this sad chapter of Indian history where a community which has been living in Jammu and Kashmir for the past five thousand years was forced to leave their homes in 1990 and live in exile due to Islamic religious fundamentalists. Seven hundred thousand (700000) Hindu Kashmiri Pundits were forced to flee due to a war waged by Islamic terrorists. They have been labelled as migrants in their own country by the State Administration and are on the verge of extinction as a race. Right from the dawn of freedom, Hindus in Kashmir faced and fought communalism and fundamentalism within their homeland.

Pundits are a part of the Vedic heartland of India and have lived in Kashmir from times immemorial. In fact, they are the original inhabitants of the valley of Kashmir, now reduced to a minority. The Hindu religious concept has borne the message of universal peace, brotherhood and co-existence of all creeds and faiths. The Hindus of Kashmir are the progenitors of *Shakti* and *Shaivite* monism as well as the *Hinayan* and *Sarvastavdi* Buddhism. They propounded the great Shaivite dectrive of Trika and theory of self recognition. *Kalgana, Jonanraja, Prajbhat, Shuka* and *Shrivara,* the great masters of history, compiled the historical chronicle of *Rajatarangini.* The Hindu kingdom of Kashmir reached its Zenith with ascendance of *Karkotas* when Kashmir commanded respect and tribute from its neighbourhood kingdoms till the fall of *Ultras.*

The Kashmiri Pundit, have played a major role in liberation struggle against British and their colonial imperatives in the state. The secularization of various communal movements, which rocked the state after the growth of Muslim-separation in India, was achieved mainly due to Kashmiri Pundits. They authored and sponsored the famous declaration of National Self Government, which also received its ideological content from the Kashmiri Pundits. The history is replete with contributions of Kashmiri Hindus to the nation. They served as the real founders of secularism and democracy in Kashmir. In the modernization of the state of Jammu and Kashmir, the Hindus have imparted to the Kashmiri society its scientific, progressive and human outlook. Throughout their history more specifically in the modern times, they have tried their utmost to live at peace with the Muslim companions. The secular façade which Kashmir has exhibited all through for the last 65 years has been provided mainly by Kashmiri Hindus. They did not follow a policy of "An eye for an eye." But instead, they confronted the rigorous Muslim dominance in the state with a fervent hope that universal education, free flow of democratic thought, recognition of human rights, and a genuine urge for heightened religious tolerance would bring equality and Justice in Kashmir.

Atrocities

The ascendancy of Muslim Sultans in the thirteenth century witnessed fierce religious persecution. Attempts at conversion of Kashmiri Pundits were faced with faith, dignity and determination, preferring death to surrender. Since then not much has changed. After the independence of India and accession of Kashmir to the Indian Union, the Kashmiri Hindus have continued to fight the religious precedence as well as the separatism. They were reduced to a life of slavery, misery and servitude but they did not react violently against Muslim communalism. In spite of the forces arraigned against them viz. The Muslim fundamentalists, the communalized state apparatus and the secessionist group, the Hindus suffered at the stake to save the secular and democratic image of Kashmir and India. While resisting the orchestrated moves fostered by Muslim communalism inside the state, the Hindus became the victims of communal hatred, forced hostility, ridicule and privation. The Kashmiri Hindu was the main obstacle in the attainment of the goal of fundamentalists. *Sheikh Mohammad Abdullah* credited them as the fifth pillar of Indian unity. They thus became the victims of dangerous irony, where on one hand they were persecuted because of their adherence to the values of secularism and democracy enshrined in the Indian constitution and on the other hand the rulers of India jettisoned them. The Hindus of Kashmir with almost negligible representation in the state legislature and bureaucracy became helpless onlookers as separatist leaders manoeuvred and distorted the stabilized democratic, constitutional and legal institution of state which gave rise to Muslim preponderance. Under this new system Kashmiri Hindus faced a deliberate, steady and relentless squeeze of constitutional, political and legal rights until they were forced into exile. This devilish plan started right from 1947 and the year 1990 was particularly unfortunate for Kashmiri Hindus and Pundits. Till date more than Seven hundred thousand (700,000) Kashmiri Pundits have left their ancestral home due to the various atrocities committed by Muslim majority in the state.

The terrorist violence has taken a heavy toll on marred, peace loving and tolerant Hindus of Kashmir Valley. Hundreds of Hindus—men women and children—were brutally murdered after subjecting them to inhuman torture, the worse of the lot suffered a community death. The properties left behind by them have been looted and their houses burnt or destroyed by dynamite. Presently a scorched earth policy is being followed by terrorists wherein they systematically burn the Hindu localities, Hindu Houses and Hindu Shrines and temples. The Indian Partitions of 1947 was not an accident of history. It was conceived by the British to contain the Freedom Movement. It unexpectedly culminated in a separate Muslim majority State (where the pre eminence of Muslim man was supposed to be recognized). During the last 64 years, Pakistani Hindus who constituted 30% population at the outset have been reduced to only 1%. The operative design of Muslim communalism in Kashmir is similar. The Hindus of Kashmir who formed about 9% of the population of Kashmir in 1947 have been almost wiped out. As part of the grand strategy for the attainment of an Islamic Kashmir, the exodus was inevitable.

Pakistan

Today Kashmir is on the brink of being separated from India. It is the beginning of a comprehensive plan to bring upon social unrest in India and thereby disintegrate this amalgamation of cultures. The militancy in India is being sponsored by the Pakistan Army and the Government of Pakistan in a bid to grab a vital portion of the Valley. The violence that has ravaged the state of Jammu and Kashmir for the last 65 years is the culmination of the long list of movements carried on by the fundamentalist forces overtly supporting Islam and terror. Terrorism in Kashmir is a Muslim crusade, aimed at the secession of the state from the Republic of India and its subsequent annexation by Pakistan.

It is founded on an ideological struggle which states that:—

- That Kashmir valley which has a majority Muslim population should be annexed by Pakistan on the basis of religion.
- That all the instructions of secularism and democracy are to be destroyed. And the people who believe in these are to be eliminated.
- The rich and eternal cultural traditions of Kashmir civility, which evolved from Hindu Shaivism and Muslim Sufism, be demolished and replaced by Islamic fundamentalism.

Pakistan is unconditionally involved in its attempts to sabotage the constitutional and administrative machinery of the state of Jammu and Kashmir. This it accomplishes by giving affiliation to the terrorist violence and lending moral, political as well as military support. The terrorists operating in Jammu and Kashmir are being trained in the neighbouring states of Pakistan. They are sent into India to cause large scale anarchy, destruction, arson, murder, molestation and rape. The Kashmiri Hindus have become the first victims of terrorism, but looking at intentions of Islamic fundamentalism they will definitely not be the last.

Separatist

Ali Shah Gilani and *Mir Waiz Umar Farooq* cry foul for Kashmiri Muslims, who are actually videotaped pelting stones on security forces, killing Shias, Buddhist and Hindus Pundits. These Hurriyat leaders play dirty politics to enforce a merger with Pakistan and sponsor forceful conversions to Islam. They do not consider themselves a part of India. They have no respect for India and Indian constitution. They indulged in destruction of Hindu temples and shrines, large scale killing of Hindus, smouldered Hindu homes and properties, disgraced Hindu women and children. Although a sizeable number of security personnel have been deployed along the Line of Control and within the city parameters, but still they leave no stone unturned in their attempts to target the Kashmiri Hindus. Kashmiri Hindus are a highly cultured, dignified and socially affable community. They cannot be expected to further adjust with such anti national communities.

Government

Our parliament and constitution has given equal rights and privileges to minorities. Why is there a double standard for minorities in Kashmir?

Pundits have become refugees in their own country due to the total failure of the Indian state to provide security and safety to Hindu minorities. What was the government doing when Hindus were being ruthlessly persecuted, threatened, tortured and murdered by Islamic terrorist forces in Kashmir?

All the political parties should unite and raise the matter in public and parliament. The Indian leaders served their petty personal interests, leaving the field open for fundamentalists to carry out their elaborate designs of vandalism.

Media

The national media in India repeatedly comes forward to support trade relations with Pakistan. The television rights to broadcast Indo-Pak cricket matches are much sought after. News channels rerun the video tapes of terrorist attacks. Many forums invite Pakistani delegates, including Ex-Army officers who are proud of their plunder, to participate in dialogues. The entire civil society protests against death penalty and criticizes the government for delivering swift justice. So we present the following section of the book as a testimony to the Media. To bring them face to face with the reality of being a Hindu in Kashmir. To acquaint the civil society the world over what human right "Violation" actually is.

It is indeed deplorable that some human rights organizations reporting on Kashmir situation have conveniently ignored the gross human rights violations against Hindus. Their silence on the genocide of the community and the terrible plight facing the community after the exodus is exasperating and questions the credibility of these organisations. The one-sided partisan and extremely prejudicial views of certain agencies that have chosen to blackout the bursitis and murderous killings of

Kashmiri Pundit minority in their report, implores us to conclude that such organizations have fallen victims to the dangerous ploy of terrorism.

It is a sad commentary on the perceptions and sensitivities of the civilized world. A community which has been the original inhabitants of the valley of Kashmir with a proud history of more than five thousand years, a rich cultural heritage and distinct ethnic religious entity, the proponent of and an heir to a unique concept of Hindu thought—the philosophy of Kashmir Shaivism—With its message of Universal peace, non-violence, amity and brotherhood is being deliberately and systematically destroyed.

Human Rights

This is a brief outline of the barbarities that the community faced at the hands of despotic Muslim rulers, since the 13th century. It traces the present escalation of human right violations mounting the genocide of Kashmiri Pundits to a cruel and criminal conspiracy by the fanatical and fundamentalist forces, which gained ascendency and got fresh impetus during the last four decades. It also provides a bird's eye view of the mushrooming of dormant fundamentalist forces during these years in the Islamic schools of thoughts. This indoctrination prompted and incited the youth of Kashmir to cross over to Pakistan, where they received arms training to carry out the diabolical plan for the Muslimization of Kashmir.

This appeal brings out vividly the persecution of minority communities through threats, abductions, extortions, tortures and killings in cold blood. This extremist campaign was initiated much before the exodus through radicalization of the Muslim citizens and was implemented with fanatical zeal after the exodus in order to secure total ruination of the minority community. The present plight of the community which was once synonymous with academic, philosophical and spiritual pursuits now rots without identity and the truth will be further disclosed in the book. Over one thousand Kashmiri Pundits have been killed by the terrorists and thousands more are dying in the miserable refugee camps for the want of basic amenities, shelter, Medicare and family support. Unfortunately thousands of its youth are getting scattered in search of livelihood. It is feared that at the present rate of dispersal the community will disintegrate beyond redemption and face extinction.

This appeal invokes the conscience of the civilized world so that people may gain knowledge about the grim prospects that are being faced by the Kashmiri Pundit community. Free men all over the world must stand up and speak against the violence. We must help the community regain its lost status. The people must be rehabilitated with honour and dignity in their own homeland.

EXODUS

The armed subversion by Muslim fundamentalist youth is to destroy the pluralistic, secular, socio-political character of Kashmir Valley. In its 23rd year of operation, the grand design of this separatist insurgency is aimed at snapping all historical, economic, cultural and political links of Kashmir Valley with India so that Pakistan can smoothly annex it.

The Kashmiri Pundits (Hindus) in the Valley of Kashmir irrespective of their age, sex, position, status or situation became threatened, individually as well as collectively through word of mouth, through thought insinuation and innuendo, through posters and press all over the valley. Fear loomed large and the terror shadow stalked educational institutions and other public places wherever the Kashmiri Pundits had representation. The community members were indentified and denounced, hit lists were pasted on electric poles, office doors and entry to various institutions and the public places. They were exhorted at large and hounded until it became impossible for them to continue the routine life. They were followed and kidnapped from their homes and places of work. They were interrogated and tortured. A spree of killings of the intellectuals of the community started. This was followed by indiscriminate gunning down, hanging, dismembering, tying with grenades and blasting into pieces, skinning, burning and sawing of human beings in full public eye. Many of the victims, after being butchered, were thrown into the streets as exhibits for everybody to get terrorized. The bereaved were not permitted to move the dead, pay respect or perform the last rites. Those who dared to attend the funeral were earmarked for reprisals. Molestation and rape was the order of day. These Muslim Kashmiris worked under the veil of "Foreign terrorism" and continued their depredations.

Kashmiri Pundits (Hindus) started leaving the valley temporarily to seek shelter in the Jammu Province of the State of Jammu and Kashmir, Delhi and in other towns of India during the months of January-March 1990. A large number preferred to stay behind, partly hopeful of a letup in the persecution and partly on account of the reassurance by their friends, neighbours and colleagues of the Muslim majority community. However, indiscriminate murders gained momentum along with the rigid accusations, denigrations and warnings.

Not content with the tempo of the exodus, the Muslim religious zealots pressed into service the local newspapers and started periodic write-ups full of vituperative and malicious propaganda targeting Kashmiri Hindus. All these repeated warnings culminated in a final ultimatum through the pages of Daily *Alsafa* on 14th April, 1990 giving the community "Two days" to leave the valley or face retribution and death. The good Samaritans of the Muslim majority community who had offered help, solace and protection to the Kashmiri Pundits were also threatened, coerced and subdued to fall in Line with the fundamentalist designs. Therefore, even they advised the Kashmiri Pundits to leave the Valley. Both gentle and well meaning persuasion was adopted side by side with covert and overt threats to intimidate Hindus forcing them into exile. Meanwhile unbridled violence and brutal murder went on. More than one thousand Hindus have been killed, hundreds are missing (possibly dead or kept hostages), and women have been held captive in remote hideouts of the terrorists to satisfy their lust. An unspecified number of those Hindus who are still living in the valley, because they have no place to go, amidst the unrelenting terror are victims of extortion, religious persecution or kidnappings. The communal carnage and forced exodus was followed up with a virulent campaign of vilification and disinformation against the Kashmiri Hindu Community with the objective of covering up the true communal and fundamentalist character of the so-called "Freedom struggle" of Kashmiri Muslims. This propaganda offensive was backed up by a canard floated across the country that:

(i) The Kashmiri Pundits migrated out of valley because they were touted by Mr. Jagmohan, the then Governor of Jammu and Kashmir, who promised to provide them relief, ration and land.

(ii) Those who were gunned down, hanged or tortured were informer enemies of the freedom struggle.

This canard took such deep root, inside and outside of the valley, that the poorly informed Indian public (even of cosmopolitan cities like Delhi and Bombay) who go by the corollary that majority in Kashmir valley were Hindus, failed to understand why Kashmiri Pundits (Hindu) had to flee their homes and hearths. Only the committed demographers in the country realized that Kashmiri Pundits (Hindu) are a minority in the Muslim majority Kashmir valley of Hindu majority India.

(iii) The Kashmiri Pundits are over represented in centre and State Government services and private Jobs.

This was a major source of irritation and encouraged Muslims to take up arms as a means to fight for their rights. This canard has been supplemented and reinforced by distorted statistic and the thread has been skilfully taken over by some self proclaimed humanists and overzealous politicians of the country who want to prove more secular than their credentials allow. In fact, they found it to be a useful tool to convince themselves and the world that the exodus in Kashmir was not an armed submission aimed at annexing the state from the union of India. But an act of frustration of a handful of disgruntled and misguided youth. This ill conceived notion, though countered by the exiled Kashmiri Pundits, fell on the ill-informed ears, and scored points for the terrorists and their cause, though it didn't take long for the communal, fundamentalist and subversive character of terrorism to emerge in its true colour.

(iv) The Kashmir Hindus because of their money, cunning and influence would become usurpers and takeover educational institutions, professional colleges, trade, industry, Government jobs etc.

In Jammu, Delhi and other places where they have taken refuge this disinformation caused tremendous confusion, panic, overreaction and even hostility. Especially in the small towns which were ill-equipped to accommodate such a sizeable influx of refugees.

KASHMIRI PUNDITS PLIGHT

In Jammu, where seventeen camps were set up in suburban dingy areas, students faced stiff resistance while applying for admission in various educational institutions; jobs were denied to the youth and all doors were closed for the rehabilitation of professional and non-professional personnel of the Kashmiri Hindu community. A community which took pride in its academic excellence and unmatched professionalism had been left idling and rotting for the past 23 years, while torture, persecution and killings were rampant. Side by side influence of the canards surfaced in the form of loots, raids and arson of properties. Their houses were destroyed; stores were confiscated and encroached upon until all their lands were annexed. Till date more than a lakh Hindu colonies have been blasted or razed to the ground. The remaining have been looted, vandalized or occupied.

Within months of the exodus of the Kashmir Pundits, the government (out of misplaced optimism to placate and appease the terrorists or with deliberate intent) started recruiting and promoting Muslims to the post and positions vacated by Kashmiri Pundits. This further banished any hope of the Minority Kashmiri Pundits of returning to the valley, for it had neither the jobs nor the houses for shelter which would have played a vital role in social resurrection.

So a tragedy which began with religious persecution and genocide climaxing with the exodus of the community has now attained colossal dimensions. This agro-religious minority is presently fighting for survival and faces a bleak and uncertain future. Having been forced to live under torn and tattered tents, in ramshackle camps or in one room tenements and stables vacated by cows and buffaloes and rented at exorbitant prices, they are subject to the vagaries of a harsh climate, a hostile population and an indifferent and callous administration. They have to go through a tortuous procedure to establish their credentials as exiles in order to be eligible for a meagre relief (mainly rations), for which they have to queue up for long hours and face untold miseries and humiliation. They have become the victims of bureaucratic bungling and corruption. They are pawns in the hands of political parties and power brokers. They are being pushed around and kicked out for demanding justice. Many of them have been arrested for raising their voice against the deaf administration. Thus they have been reduced to abject poverty and a life of utter helplessness and apathy. Their greatest tragedy is that they have become exiles in their own land, aliens in their own country which they inhabited for thousands of years.

This community is now caught up in a piquant and unsavoury situation. The state and central Government are treating them as expendable. The authorities are busy covering up the genocide, the exodus, the present plight, and the total abdication of their responsibility towards this minority community. Unfortunately the international community is also unaware of the refugee status of this community as countries around the world recognize refugees only when they are forced to flee into another country.

The last 23 years have witnessed a perpetuation of human rights violation against this community. Most of the nearly 700,000 (seven lakh) refugees are not even left with the bare minimum necessities of life. Families got split and scattered in the scramble for shelter and livelihood. Parents got separated from children, spouses from their partners, brother from sisters. They are still on the move from one place to another like wandering nomads looking for help and succour. As a result of this dispersal the social fabric of the community as born as under the economic structure has collapsed, material possessions have vanished and the political base has been overturned. All this heartache brought a premature end to the old and infirm of the community, while the youth at large experienced a mental breakdown. Depression, panic attacks, phobias nightmares and insomnia have seized all age groups. Unnatural deaths in the form of sunstroke, snake, and scorpion bites, hydrophobia and accidents have taken a big toll. The terror, a feeling of siege, a sense of footlessness and loss of identity, the trauma of forced migration, exposure to an alien and hostile environment, problem of acclimatization, poor housing, insanitary conditions and the lack of basic amenities like drinking water, scarce

Medicare, malnutrition and idleness compounded by hurt and humiliation have orchestrated to result in physical, mental and psychological trauma of unimaginable magnitude. The community has reached the end of its tether and its reserves of patience and hope have dried up. The spectre of disease, death and extinction are haunting the community. It seems unlikely that the community will ever be able to reorganize itself into a cohesive social and political entity, which is vital for its survival and resurgence. Far from regaining its pristine glory, it is hard pressed to even keep one's body, mind and soul together.

History is replete with records of religious persecutions and barbarities perpetrated against this community since the advent of Islam in the thirteenth century in Kashmir. While the community accommodated, mingled and absorbed the culture and traditions of all outsiders who came to Kashmir, it was repeatedly rewarded with the most inhuman and brutal treatment. From time to time various cruel Muslim rulers driven by the religious zeal diminished Hindu institutions and shrines, burnt religious scriptures and libraries of Hindus and unleashed a reign of terror leading to imposition of heavy taxes, forceful conversions and general massacre of those refusing to embrace Islam. They inflicted bestialities like the chopping off the noses and tongues, beheading, drowning in water after tying people back-to-back etc. on the community. These who escaped the forceful conversion, mutilation and death were forced into exile reducing this community to a minority in its own land.

Even after the attainment of independence and accession of Jammu and Kashmir to India the fundamentalist forces in the Kashmir Valley refused to accept the principles of secularism and democratic pluralism and in fact intensified those nefarious designs against the minority community of Kashmiri Hindus. Under a *Mecantra* programme *Maktabi* (Religious Schools) were established in every nook and corner of the Kashmir Valley with the putative aim of teaching religious scriptures to youth, but with the real motive of indoctrinating and envenoming the young impressionable minds with anti Hindu and anti India notions. Funds were lavished on these schools openly and clandestinely by local patrons as well as Muslim countries espousing Islamic fundamentalism, led by Pakistan. The schools became nurseries for the growth of radicalism and Islamic terrorism. A ban imposed by the Government of *Sheikh Mohammad Abdullah* on these schools in 1977 was lifted soon after its imposition under relentless pressure by *Jamat-i-Islam* and other fundamentalist organizations. These pressure groups gradually extended their tentacles in every sphere of administration, bureaucracy and judiciary in the state and moulded these agents in a cruel conspiracy against Kashmiri Pundits resulting in discrimination, alienation, denial and deprivation of this community over the years.

Radicalization of Islam

The process of *Islamisation* and fundamentalism which started in 1947 took firm roots by 1986. The fundamentalists rehearsed the present terrorism on a small scale by plundering Hindu temples in the *Anantnag* district of the Kashmir Valley. No serious effort was made by the administration to bring the guilty to book. This encouraged them to cross the border to attend arms training camps in Pakistan. Over the next three years, they brought with them large quantities of sophisticated arms and ammunition to carry on a full scale subversion and terrorism. The cataclysmic event, leading to genocide and mass exodus of Kashmiri Pundit community from 1990 onwards is the culmination of this long process of regimentation, indoctrination, religious frenzy and terrorism.

AFTERMATH

The hope is now shattered. Neither the Muslim brethren nor the Indian Government (which swears by secularism) came to the rescue of Kashmiri Hindus. When they were being uprooted and thrown into wilderness. Constitutional guarantees for the protection of their life, property and dignity have been trampled. The Hindus of Kashmir wherever they are, therefore unequivocally declare that:

"With their deep and firm commitment to social unity, religious co-existence, democracy and secularism they will not accept a society which is communalistic, intolerant and obstinate. They will not submit to any authority in the state that does not recognize this right to life, equality, faith and protection against discrimination. They will not be a party to the present struggle launched against secular and democratic India."

With their history of having lived and died for freedom and their open espousal of the cause of tolerance, peace, unity and brotherhood between the various ethnic, social and religious groups they cannot accept the pre-eminence and predominance of any single religious community at their cost.

CONCLUSION

Being the original inhabitants of Kashmir from ancient times and being the inheritors of a glorious cultural tradition of more than five thousand years, Kashmiri Pundits have as much right to life in Kashmir as any other religious group. Preservation of this community in its natural habitat is a political and natural necessity.

The present crusade by the terrorists against Kashmiri Pundits to drive away the last remnant, of this proud Community from its rightful place is a shame to the secular India in particular and world community in general. Any measure taken to rehabilitate this community outside Kashmir will only result in the dispersal of this distinct race and an outstanding culture will be on the verge of extinction.

Because of their equal right to the land of their birth they state their claims to be an equal pastry to any future deliberations in the process of normalisation and ultimate solutions on Kashmir Problem.

The Kashmiri Hindus represented by *Panun Kashmir* therefore passed a resolution on 28/12/91 at *Jammu Tavi* as follows:—

1. The establishment of a separate homeland for Kashmiri Hindus in the Kashmiri Valley to the East and North of the river Jhelum.
2. The constitution of India be enforced in letter and spirit in this homeland to ensure the right to life, liberty and Law.
3. The homeland be placed under central administration with Union Territory Status until it evolves its own economic and political infrastructure.
4. All the Kashmir Hindus, which includes those who have been driven out of Kashmir in the pre independence era along with those who were forced to leave on account of the terrorist violence in Kashmir, be settled in the homeland on equitable basis with dignity and honour.

The book is an effort to save Kashmiri Pundits, to save Kashmir, to save India, to save the World.

Notable Kashmiri Citizens

- ❖ Amitabh Matto (1962-Present) Vice Chancellor of Jammu University and a Padma Shri awardee.
- ❖ Birbal Dhar (early 19th century) invited Maharaja Ranjit Singh to Kashmir.
- ❖ Braj Kumar Nehru (1909-2001) ambassador of India to the United States (1961-1968) and Governor of Assam (1968-1973).
- ❖ Durga Prasad Dhar (1918-1975) ambassador of India to the Soviet Union.
- ❖ Farah Pundit (1969-Present) U.S. State Department Special Representative.
- ❖ Mehraj Mattoo (1961-Present) Global Head of Commerzbank AG.
- ❖ Mirza Pandit Dhar was a prominent Kashmiri during the rule of Azim Khan.
- ❖ Mohan Lal (1812-1877) diplomat in the First Anglo-Afghan War and a writer.
- ❖ Munir Butt (1940-Present) former British diplomat
- ❖ M. L. Madan is a veterinarian, scientist, and administrator. He was previously the Vice Chancellor at Akola and Mathura Universities; Deputy Director General (DDG)—Animal Sciences, Indian Council for Agricultural Research (ICAR); Joint Director, National Dairy Research Institute (NDRI). He is also the Creator of World's First IVF Buffalo Calf.
- ❖ Neel Kashkari (1973-Present) Interim Assistant Secretary of the Treasury for Financial Stability in the United States Department of the Treasury.
- ❖ P. K. Kaul, ambassador of India to the United States (1986-1989).
- ❖ Purushottam Narayan Haksar (1913-1998), political strategist.
- ❖ Rameshwar Nath Kao (1918-2002) was the first chief of the Research and Analysis Wing, India's intelligence agency (from 1969-1977)
- ❖ Tej Bahadur Sapru (1875-1949) lawyer, political and social leader during the British Raj.
- ❖ Triloki Nath Khoshoo (1927-2002) was the secretary of the Department of Environment in the Indira Gandhi Government.

- ❖ T.N. Kaul (1913-2000) was the ambassador of India to USA, Soviet Union and Iran. Foreign Secretary, Indian Ministry of External Affairs.
- ❖ Vijaya Lakshmi Pandit (1900-1990) was the ambassador of India to the United States (1949-1952) and the first woman President of the United Nations General Assembly (1953).

Armed Forces

- ❖ Aziz Khan (1947-Present) General in the Pakistan Army, former Chairman of the Joint Chiefs of Staff.
- ❖ Brij Mohan Kaul commanded the Indian forces in the Sino-Indian War 1962.
- ❖ Mohammed Amin Naik was a Major General in the Indian Army.
- ❖ Mushaf Ali Mir (1947-2003) was the Chief of Air Staff of the Pakistan Air Force (2000-2003).
- ❖ Rashid Minhas, Pilot Officer (1951-1971) is the only PAF officer to receive the highest valour award, the Nishan-e-Haider.
- ❖ Raja Habib ur Rahman Khan (1913-1978) was a freedom fighter and an officer in the Indian National Army. He is known as *Fateh-e-Bhimber* (Liberator of Bhimber).
- ❖ Sardar Muhammad Anwar Khan (1945-Present) retired as the Major General of the Pakistan Army.
- ❖ S. K. Kaul (1934-Present) retired as the Air Chief Marshal of the Indian Air Force (1993-1995).
- ❖ Tapishwar Narain Raina (1921-1980) was the Chief of Army Staff of the Indian Army (1975-1978).
- ❖ Tahir Rafique Butt is the Chief of Staff of the Pakistan Air Force since 2012.

Literary Marvels

- ❖ Amin Kamil, Kashmiri poet and short story writer.
- ❖ Basharat Peer (1977-Present), author
- ❖ Chandrakanta (1938-Present), novelist and short story writer
- ❖ Dina Nath Walli alias *Al-mast Kashmiri* (1908-2006), poet as well as renowned water colour artist.
- ❖ Habba Khatun 16th century poetess, known as Zoon (the Moon) because of her immense beauty.

- ❖ Hari Kunzru (1969-Present), British novelist of Kashmiri descent.
- ❖ Jaspreet Singh, novelist and playwright.
- ❖ Khalid Hasan (1935-2009) writer, senior Pakistani journalist and diplomat.
- ❖ Krishan Chander (1914-1977) Urdu and Hindi Afsaana Nigaar, or short story writer.
- ❖ Krishna Hutheesing (1907-1967), author, and sister of Jawaharlal Nehru.
- ❖ Manju Kak, short story writer.
- ❖ Maqbool Shah Kralawari (1820-1876), lyricist
- ❖ Meeraji (1912-1949) an eminent Urdu poet who lived the life of a bohemian and worked only intermittently.
- ❖ Mahmud Gami (1765-1855), composed a version of the story of *Yusuf and Zulaikha.*
- ❖ Ghulam Ahmad (1885-1952), poet, better known by the pen name *Mahjoor.*
- ❖ Momin Khan Momin (1800-1851) Indian poet known for his Urdu ghazals.
- ❖ Moti Lal Kemmu (1933-Present) playwright.
- ❖ Moti Lal Saqi (1936-1999) was a poet, writer, folklorist and researcher.
- ❖ Muhammad Iqbal (1877-1938) was a famous Muslim poet and philosopher. Commonly referred to as Allama Iqbal.
- ❖ Mohammad Ishaq Khan (1946-Present) is the foremost historian of Kashmir. Well known for his scholarly works on Islam in Kashmir with special reference to Sufism, society and culture.
- ❖ Nayantara Sahgal (1927-Present) Anglo-Indian writer, novelist
- ❖ Prem Nath Dar (1914-1976) Urdu language short story writer from the Kashmir Valley, member Progressive Writers' Movement.
- ❖ Rehman Rahi, Kashmiri poet
- ❖ Saadat Hasan Manto (1912-1955), famous short story writer and member Progressive Writers' Movement.
- ❖ Salman Rushdie (1947-Present) novelist and essayist.
- ❖ Santha Rama Rau (1923-Present) travel writer.
- ❖ Pundit Shiva Kumar Sharma (1938-Present) Indian Santoor player.
- ❖ S.L. Sadhu (1917-Present) Scholar, Professor, poet, writer, folklorist and Historian.
- ❖ Pamposh Bhat, (1958-Present) author and environmentalist.

- ❖ Qudrat Ullah Shahab (1917-1986) was an eminent Urdu writer and civil servant from Pakistan, best known for his autobiography 'Shahab Nama'.
- ❖ Zinda Kaul (1884-1965) famous poet, also known as *Masterji.*
- ❖ Hakeem Manzoor (1937-2006) was a prominent Urdu writer, poet & administrator. He has written more than 15 books some of his famous books in Urdu are Na Tamaam, Barf Ruton Ki Aag and Lahu Lamas Chinar.

Royality

- ❖ Khwaja Abdul Ghani and his Dhaka Nawab Family reigned in Dhaka from mid 19th century to mid 20th century.
- ❖ Lalitaditya Muktapida, emperor of Kashmir from the Kayastha clan (724-760).
- ❖ Raja Sukh Jivan, king of Kashmir from the Kaul clan (1754-1762).

Philosophers

- ❖ Abhinavagupta, (950-1020), one of India's greatest philosophers, mystics and aestheticians.
- ❖ Ahmad Hasan Dani (1920-2009) intellectual, archaeologist, historian, linguist.
- ❖ Anandavardhana (820-890) philosopher and author of the *Dhvanyaloka.*
- ❖ Bhaskara, notable writer on the Kashmir Shaivism.
- ❖ Bhatta Kallata, a notable Shaivite thinker.
- ❖ Gopi Krishna (1903-1980), writer and mystic.
- ❖ Jonaraja (15th century), historian and poet.
- ❖ Kalhana (12th century), historian and author of *Rajatarangini.*
- ❖ Kshemaraja (10th century), philosopher and a disciple of Abhinavagupta.
- ❖ Lalleshwari (1320-1392), saint and poet.
- ❖ Prajna Bhatta (16th century), historian.
- ❖ Somananda (875-925) a teacher of Kashmir Shaivism.
- ❖ Shrivara (15th century), historian.
- ❖ Subhash Kak (1947-Present) writer, philosopher, and computer scientist.
- ❖ Utpaladeva, a teacher of Kashmir Shaivism.
- ❖ Vasugupta (860-925), author of the *Shiva Sutras of Vasugupta.*

Politicians

- ❖ Abdul Ghani Lone (1932-2002), lawyer, politician and founder of the People's Conference.
- ❖ Abdul Qayyum Khan, former Chief minister North Western Frontier Pakistan.
- ❖ Agha Shorish Kashmiri scholar, writer, debater, and leader of the Majlis-e-Ahrar-ul-Islam, figure of the freedom movement of undivided India.
- ❖ Bakshi Ghulam Mohammad (1907-1972), Chief Minister of Jammu and Kashmir (1953-1963).
- ❖ Asiya Andrabi (1963—Present), Chief of Dukhtaran-e-Millat, prominent Kashmiri separatist leaders.
- ❖ Bilal Nazki (1947-Present) Chief Justice in India.
- ❖ Maheshdas Bhat (1528-1586), was the Grand Vizier (Wazīr-e Azam) of the Mughal court in the administration of Emperor Akbar. He is popularly known as Birbal.
- ❖ Birbal Dhar leader of the Kashmiri resistance against the Afghan rule in the early 19th century.
- ❖ Deepa Kaul (1944-Present), former minister, social worker and human rights defender.
- ❖ Farooq Abdullah (1936-Present), Chief Minister of Jammu and Kashmir (1982-1984, 1986-1990, 1996-2002), son of Sheikh Abdullah.
- ❖ Ghulam Ahmad Ashai, educator, reformer and founder of the University of Kashmir.
- ❖ Ghulam Muhammad Sadiq, Chief Minister of Jammu and Kashmir (1965-1971)
- ❖ Ghulam Mohammad Shah (1920-2009), Chief Minister of Jammu and Kashmir (1984-1986)
- ❖ Ghulam Nabi Azad (1949-Present), former Chief Minister of Jammu and Kashmir.
- ❖ G. N. Ratanpuri (1954-Present), Member of Parliament (Rajya Sabha) from Jammu and Kashmir National Conference.
- ❖ Hashim Qureshi, (1953-Present), Chairman Jammu & Kashmir Democratic Liberation Party.
- ❖ Indira Gandhi (1917-1984), Prime Minister of India, daughter of Jawaharlal Nehru.
- ❖ Ishaq Dar Ex Federal Minister Pakistan.

- ❖ Pundit Jawaharlal Nehru (1889-1964), first Prime Minister of independent India.
- ❖ Khwaja Shams-ud-Din (1922-1999), Prime Minister of Jammu and Kashmir (1963-1964).
- ❖ Khawaja Muhammad Asif MNA Sailkot PML-N.
- ❖ Kailash Nath Katju (1887-1968), freedom fighter, prominent lawyer, participated in INA trials, former governor, chief minister of several Indian states and cabinet minister under Pundit Jawaharlal Nehru.
- ❖ Maulana Mazhar Ali Azhar (1895-1974) one of founders, leader of Majlis-e-Ahrar-ul-Islam, political figure in the history of Sub-Continent.
- ❖ Mehbooba Mufti (1959-Present), female politician, member of the 14th Lok Sabha.
- ❖ Mehtab Ahmed Khan Ex Chief Minister N-W Frontier Pakistan.
- ❖ Maqbool Butt (1938-1984), co-founder of the JKLF Party.
- ❖ Mirwaiz Maulvi Farooq (d.1990), chairman of the Aawami Action Committee.
- ❖ Mohammad Shafi Qureshi, (1929-Present), former governor of Bihar and Madhya Pradesh, State Railway Minister.
- ❖ Pundit Motilal Nehru (1861-1931), Indian independence activist, president of the Indian National Congress.
- ❖ Muhammad Farooq Rehmani (1938-Present), Chairman of the Peoples Freedom League, former Convener of the Hurriyat Conference.
- ❖ Mufti Muhammad Sayeed (1936-Present), Chief Minister of Jammu and Kashmir (2002-2005).
- ❖ Muzaffar Baig (1946-Present), Deputy Chief Minister, Finance Minister, Law Minister, Tourism Minister of Jammu and Kashmir (2002-2008)
- ❖ Nazir Ahmed (1958-Present), member of the House of Lords of the United Kingdom.
- ❖ Nawaz Sharif (1949-Present), incumbent Prime Minister of Pakistan.
- ❖ Omar Abdullah (1970-Present), Current Chief Minister Jammu And Kashmir, member of the 14th Lok Sabha, son of Farooq Abdullah.
- ❖ Rajiv Gandhi (1944-1991), Prime Minister of India, son of Indira Gandhi, grandson of Jawaharlal Nehru.
- ❖ Ram Chandra Kak (1893-1983), Chief Minister of Jammu and Kashmir during 1945-47 and an eminent archaeologist.

- ❖ Grand Ayatollah Sayyed Ruhollah Mostafavi Moosavi Khomeini (1902-1989) First Supreme Leader of Iran, His Grandfather was from Kashmir.
- ❖ Raja Mummtaz Hussain Rathore (d.1999), former Prime Minister and Speaker of Azad Kashmir.
- ❖ Saif-ud-din Soz (1937-Present), long time member of Parliament, former Union Minister of Environment & Forests, former Minister of Water Resources, President JKPCC.
- ❖ Saifuddin Kitchlew (1888-1963), freedom fighter and politician.
- ❖ Sadiq Ali (1952-Present), politician, poet, writer and environmentalist.
- ❖ Sardar Muhammad Ibrahim Khan (1915-2003), founder and first President of Azad Kashmir.
- ❖ Sardar Sikandar Hayat Khan (1934-Present), politician, former prime minister and former president of Azad Jammu and Kashmir.
- ❖ Sardar Sayab Khalid (1940-Present), former Speaker of the Azad Jammu and Kashmir Legislative Assembly.
- ❖ Shehbaz Sharif, Chief Minister Punjab Pakistan.
- ❖ Shaikh Rasheed Ahmad Ex Federal Information Minister Pakistan.
- ❖ Shabir Shah (1953-Present), Founder of the Jammu & Kashmir Democratic Freedom Party. Known as Nelson Mandela of Indian Administered Kashmir.
- ❖ Syed Mir Qasim, Chief Minister of Jammu and Kashmir (1971-1975)
- ❖ Syed Ali Shah Geelani (1929-Present), prominent member of Jamait-e-Islami, Founder and Chairman of Tehreek-e-Hurriyat J&K, Chairman All Parties Hurriyat Conference.
- ❖ Sheila Kaul (1915-Present), former Indian governor and cabinet minister, social reformer, and educationist.
- ❖ Sheikh Abdullah (1905-1982), Chief Minister of Jammu and Kashmir (1948-1953, 1975-1982)
- ❖ Vijaya Lakshmi Pundit (1900-1990) Indian diplomat and politician.

SAINTS

- ❖ Bhagwan Gopinath (1898-1968), a mystic saint of early 20th century Kashmir in India.
- ❖ Hamza Makhdum (d.1563), poet, Sufi saint and social reformer.
- ❖ Lalleshwari (1320-1392), a mystic of the Kashmiri Shaivism sect and at the same time a Sufi saint.

❖ Mian Muhammad Bakhsh (1830-1907), Sufi saint and poet.

❖ Mir Sayyid Ali Hamadani, a Persian Sufi of the Kubrāwī order who had a major influence in shaping the culture of the Kashmir valley.

❖ Rupa Bhawani, a mystic poet saint of Kashmir from the Saahib clan of Kashmiri Pundits. The famous Chashme Shahi was built in her memory and consequently named after her.

❖ Swami Lakshman Joo Raina (1907-1991), scholar of Kashmir Shaivism.

❖ Sheikh Noor-ud-din Wali (1377-1440) Famous Kalahari saint who belonged to the Rishi order.

Scholars and Educationists

❖ Sa'id al-Afghani (1911-1997), half-Kashmiri half-Syrian professor of Arabic language.

❖ Ahmad Hasan Dani (1920-2009), Pakistani intellectual, archaeologist, historian, and prolific linguist.

❖ Patañjali, compiler of the Yoga Sūtras, an important collection of aphorisms on Yoga practice.

❖ Kailas Nath Kaul (1905-1983), Indian botanist, agricultural scientist, agronomist, and educationist.

❖ Braj Kachru (1932-Present), researcher in English linguistics.

❖ Gautam Kaul, Educationist, Professor and Principal Scientist in Biochemistry.

❖ Omkar N. Koul (1941-Present), researcher in linguistics, language education, communication, and comparative literature.

❖ Ravinder Kumar (1933-2001), historian.

❖ Jaishree Odin, post-modern literary theorist, professor of Interdisciplinary Studies at the University of Hawaii.

❖ Giridhari Lal Pandit, historian of science and professor of philosophy.

❖ Lalita Pandit, poet, professor of English at the University of Wisconsin—La Crosse.

❖ Balajinnatha Pandita (1916-2007), Sanskrit scholar, expert on Kashmir Shaivism.

❖ Hakeem Ali Mohammad (1906-1987), Unani Medicine scholar, physician expert on Unani Medicine.

SPORTS

- ❖ Suresh Raina (1986-Present), member of the Indian national cricket team.
- ❖ Vivek Razdan (1967-Present), member of the Indian Cricket Team.
- ❖ Mehrajuddin Wadoo (1984-Present), member of the Indian national football team and East Bengal FC.
- ❖ Munir Dar, Member of Pakistan National hockey Team.
- ❖ Aleem Dar, International cricket umpire.
- ❖ Haroon Rasheed Dar (1953-Present) is a former Pakistani cricketer who later went on to manage the Pakistan Cricket team. He is also credited with the discovery of Waqar Younis and Shahid Afridi.
- ❖ Sana Mir (1986-Present) is the captain of Pakistan women's cricket team.
- ❖ Abid Nabi (1985—Present) was regarded as fastest bowler in India.
- ❖ Parvez Rasool (1989—Present) is first Kashmir cricketer to play for India A and for Sahara Pune Pune Warriors in the Indian Premier League.

Visual Artist

- ❖ Abid Kashmiri, actor
- ❖ Abhay Sopori, Indian Santoor player, composer & musician.
- ❖ Anupam Kher (1955—Present), actor.
- ❖ Anwar Shemza (1928-1985) artist and writer of Pakistani origin who later migrated to Kashmir; Published Urdu novels and books of poetry, wrote plays performed on Radio Pakistan.
- ❖ Asif Raza Mir Pakistani actor, drama producer and director.
- ❖ Asim Butt (artist) (1978-2010) Pakistani painter and sculptor, member of the Stuckism International Art Movement.
- ❖ Bansi Kaul (1949-Present), theatre director
- ❖ Bhajan Sopori, Indian Santoor player, awarded the Sangeet Natak Akademi Award in 1993 and the Padma Shri in 2004.
- ❖ Farhan Saeed (1984-Present) former lead vocalist of the Pakistani music band Jal
- ❖ Ghulam Hassan Sofi (1932-2009) singer and harmonium player of traditional music of Kashmir.
- ❖ Ghulam Mohammad Saznawaz, proponent of Kashmiri Sufi Music.
- ❖ Ghulam Nabi Sheikh, singer and composer.

- ❖ Ghulam Rasool Santosh (1929-1997), painter.
- ❖ Hina Khan (1986-Present), actress.
- ❖ Omkar Nath Dhar (Jeevan), actor.
- ❖ Katrina Kaif (1984-Present) model, actress.
- ❖ Khawaja Khurshid Anwar (1912-1984) filmmaker, writer, director and music composer who gained extreme popularity both in India and Pakistan.
- ❖ Kiran Kumar, actor.
- ❖ Kunal Khemu, actor.
- ❖ Maanvi Gagroo (1985-Present), actor.
- ❖ Mani Kaul (1950-2011), Indian Film Maker, winner of Filmfare critic's award for best movie.
- ❖ Manohar Kaul (1925-Present), painter.
- ❖ Muzammil Ibrahim (1984-Present), model, actor.
- ❖ Mushtaq Kak (1961-Present), theatre director.
- ❖ Malika Pukhraj (1912-2004), highly popular Ghazal and folk singer in Pakistan.
- ❖ Mekaal Hasan (1972-Present) prominent Pakistani musician and record producer, leader and composer for Mekaal Hasan Band.
- ❖ Mohit Raina, Indian actor.
- ❖ Mohit Suri (1981-Present) Indian film director, most known for his films Kalyug (2005) and Awarapan (2007).
- ❖ Nanabhai Bhatt (1915-1999) film director and producer of Bollywood and Gujarati cinema, well known for fantasy and mythological films.
- ❖ Neerja Pandit, singer, Kashmiri Folk Music, Hindi Film and Television Music.
- ❖ Numeer nabi (1988-Present), model.
- ❖ Pran Kishore, Kashmiri drama writer.
- ❖ Pushkar Bhan, Padamashree recipient, a radio actor and drama writer.
- ❖ Raj Begum, singer who was awarded the Padma Shri in 2002.
- ❖ Raj Zutshi, Indian Bollywood & TV Actor.
- ❖ Ratan Parimoo (1936-Present), art historian and painter.
- ❖ Salima Hashmi Pakistani artist, painter, cultural writer.
- ❖ Samina Peerzada (1955-Present) well-known Pakistani actress and director director.
- ❖ Soni Razdan Indian TV actor and director.

- ❖ Qazi Touqeer (1985-Present), singer in Kashmiri and Hindi languages; Fame Gurukul Finalist.
- ❖ Vic Sarin (1945-Present) is an Indian born Canadian/American film director, producer and screenwriter.
- ❖ Sanjay Suri, actor
- ❖ D.K. Sapru (1916-1979), actor
- ❖ Priti Sapru, actor
- ❖ Gauri Pradhan, actor
- ❖ Alla Rakha, actor
- ❖ Aamir Bashir, actor

RELIGION IN THE VALLEY

India has given to the world four major religions—Hinduism, Buddhism, Jainism and Sikhism. India has the third largest number of Muslims in the world. Christianity has ancient roots here, introduced into the country by the apostle St. Thomas around 2000 years ago. The Zoroastrians, who were uprooted from Persia in the 9th century, also made India their primary home. Each faith has its own rituals, rules and taboos. Indians largely follow a "Live and let live" philosophy. It is this underlying spirit of tolerance that has enabled India to remain a unique bunch of flowers varied in culture and faith, notwithstanding periodic spells of strife.

While attitude towards religion tends to be relaxed, social hierarchies are far more rigid. Though inching towards obsoleteness, the patriarchal family structure with its deep rooted belief in arranged marriages, obedience to elders and emphasis on duty over individual liberties, continues to be the norm in much of the country. Poverty, illiteracy and caste based divisions remain evident, particularly in the countryside. Women continue to face inequality and the girl child is still regarded as an unwanted burden in many communities.

But Indians are changing quite rapidly keeping their morals intact by respecting other religions, creating a secular atmosphere and exporting the virtues of India to the whole world.

HINDUISM

Hinduism is the primordial culture of human civilization, with a recorded history that goes back 5000 years to the Indus Valley Civilization, where excavations reveal a sophisticated urban culture. This was followed by the arrival of Aryans from Central Asia who settled in the Great Plains of North India around 1500 B.C. The Indo-Aryans evolved a very distinct culture that continues to be a part of living tradition. The hymns of the Rig Veda composed by them are still recited in temples as well as households in the 21st century.

On paper 85% of India's population has faith in Hinduism. But this figure does not come even close to conveying the magnanimity of beliefs and practices that thrive under the broad cubic of Hinduism, which has evolved by inarching all other religions of India. It has to be said, at the cost of being labelled a cliché, that Hinduism is not a religion per se, but a way of life; In fact a very Indian way of life. Some people believe that Hinduism is the mother of all religions.

Hinduism has no single book or God or Prophet, and every community has its own favourite destination from an ever expanding pantheon of Gods. The events and life traditions that underline much of the Indian way of life are intrinsic to Hinduism as well. At one level, it is the religion of abstruse philosophy and metaphysical quest. It is the philosophical strain which has made India the Spiritual Land. For most Indians however, religion is more a matter of rituals and ceremonies that mark each day, season and passage of life. Gods are not clay idols stationed in a corner of the house, but they are treated as family members who occupy their hearts, homes, offices and street corner. Here worship can range from silent meditation to boisterous felinities.

Hinduism teaches "*Athiti Devo Bhav*" or "Guest is to be respected as God" and "*Vasudha Av Kutumbakam*" i.e. this whole world is one big joint family. Hinduism advocates love, peace, nonviolence, and respect for nature and aims to generate spirituality in human soul by means of a better disciplined life. In spite of the prehistoric roots of Hinduism, its literature and philosophy have influenced people throughout the world. Through the centuries, Hinduism has been the most important influence on the culture of India.

History

Writing about Hinduism as a religion is tough. Who is a Hindu? Or what is Hinduism? These kinds of queries require thorough study of ancient Indian civilisation. Hinduism was not founded on the shoulders of one man. Gradually it developed over thousands of years, and many cultures, races and religions helped shape it. Many sects arose within Hinduism and each developed its own philosophy and ways of worship. Hinduism's basic beliefs include divinities, life after death and personal conduct.

SACRED SCRIPTURES AND WRITINGS

Hinduism has no single book, unlike the new found religions, that serves as a source of its doctrines. It is the only religion in the world which accepts contributions to its fundamental beliefs. The most important of these writings includes the Vedas, the Puranas, the Ramayana, the Mahabharata, and the Bhagvad Gita.

MANU SCRIPTS

The Vedas constitute the oldest recorded system of knowledge. The teachings of Vedas existed for many millennia before they were finally written.

There are four Vedas:—

* The Rig Veda
* The Sam Veda
* The Yajur Veda
* The Atharva Veda

Each Veda has three parts—the Samhitas, the Brahmanas and the Upnishads. The Samhitas consist of prayer hymns. The Brahmanas deal with virtues and theology and include explanations for the Samhitas. The Upnishads are works of Philosophy written as dialogues.

The Puranas are long verse stories that contain many important Hindu myths about Gods, Goddesses and great Hindu heroes. They also describe the Hindu beliefs about material creation, manifestation and destruction. The Ramayana and the Mahabharata are two of the longest epics written in any language of the world. Ramayana tells the story of prince Rama and his attempt to rescue his wife Sita who was kidnapped by the demon King Ravana. The Mahabharata describes a nuclear war within the ruling dynasty of India.

The Bhagwad Gita is a philosophy and forms a part of the Mahabharata. Lord Krishna explains to the Pandava warrior, Arjuna, the meaning and nature of existence.

Manusmriti is the basic source of Hindu social laws. It also sets forth the basis of caste system.

DIVINITIES

Hinduism is often mistaken to be a polytheistic religion because of multitudes of Gods that are worshiped as representatives of nature, such as rain and the Sun. However, on deeper research one finds that though divinities appear in separate forms, these are multiple manifestations of a single universal spirit called Brahman. The most important manifestations are—Brahma the Creator, Vishnu the preserver and Shiva the destroyer.

One of the most important Hindu divinities is Shiva's wife who has several

forms. She is best known as Durga, Kali, Parvati, or Uma. For many Hindus these contrasting natures of the Goddess represent the way in which time and matter constantly move from birth to death and from creation to destruction. Many Hindus find great religious truth in symbolism and worship the Goddess as their most important divinity.

According to Hindu Doctrines animals, insects and human beings have souls. Hindus have reverence for cows, monkeys, and other animals. They have specific special reverence for cows.

SCHOOLS OF PHILOSOPHY

There are six schools of Hindu philosophy that have developed through the ages:—

1. Nyaya
2. Vaisheka
3. Yoga
4. Purva
5. Mimansa
6. Vedanta

Nyaya deals with logic. Vaisheka concerns the name of the world. Sankhya details the origin and evolution of the universe. Yoga is a set of mental and physical exercises described to free the soul from negligence of the body. The Purva, Mimansa and Vedant interpret the Vedas.

CASTE SYSTEM

Caste refers to India's strict system of occupational and social organization. The caste system may have existed in some form before the Aryans migrated from Central Asia to India around 1500 B.C. The Aryans or their descendents gradually gained control of most of India. They used the caste system at first to limit conduct between themselves and the native Indian people. Later the caste system became more elemental and one of the teachings of Hinduism. The Hindu caste, is grouped into four main categories called Varnas in order of rank, these hereditary groups are:—

1. Brahmans, the teachers, priests and scholars.
2. Kshatriyas, the administrators, rulers and warriors
3. Vasiyas, the mercantile class.
4. Shudras, the labour class and servants.

The caste system further includes thousands of sub-castes, each of which has its own rules and status.

Untouchables

For centuries, one large group existed outside the 4 Varnas and was ranked below the lowest Shudra caste. The untouchables traditionally have had rich occupations as tanning, which the Hindu Law forbids for a member of any caste in the four varnas. The Indian Constitution in 1950 outlawed Untouchability and gave the group full citizenship. But discrimination against untouchables has not been eliminated.

Through the years, the case system has somewhat devolved its grip on the modern Indian mindset. Some social distinctions have been abandoned, especially in the cities. Many educated Hindus of different castes mix freely with one another. Formerly they would have mixed only with the members of their own caste. But caste continues to be a strong influence in India.

REINCARNATION OF KARUNA

Hinduism teaches that consciousness is a symptom of the soul. This soul resides inside a material body. The soul is immortal and eternal. When a body is destroyed the soul abandons it and gains another body. This continuous process of changing bodies is called reincarnation and it is quite similar to our routine of changing clothes. The soul may be reborn in an animal or in human form.

The law of Karma is closely related to reincarnation. It states that every action of a person influences how the soul will be born in the next reincarnation. If a person lives a good life, the soul will be born into a higher state perhaps into the body of a Brahman. If a person leads an evil life, the soul will be born into a lower state perhaps into the body of a dog. This vicious cycle continues until a soul achieves spiritual perfection. The soul then enters a new level of existence, called Moksha, from which it never returns.

WORSHIP

Hinduism is the only religion where worship is a must and there are various forms of worship which are not found in other religions. Hinduism considers temples as dedicated buildings of Divinities. Hindus worship as individuals and not as a congregation. Most Hindu temples have many stories, each of which is devoted to a divinity. Each temple also has one principal shrine devoted to a single important God or Goddess.

The shrines portray the divinities in sculptured images. Hindus treat those images as living spiritual beings. Every day for example, priests bathe the images, dress them, bring them food etc. To an untrained eye this custom might appear as a form of idol worship but factually speaking the Hindus believe that the divinities are actually present in the images.

Hindu temples hold annual festivals commemorating events in the lives of divinities. Huge crowds gather for these festivals. They come to worship, to pray for existence, to enjoy the pageantry of the event. Millions of Hindus visit temples along river Ganges, the most sacred river in India.

HOME WORSHIP

Many observances of Hinduism take place in the home. Most households have a shrine devoted to a particular divinity. The homes of several wealthy Hindus have a room used exclusively for worship. In most homes, the husband or wife conducts are performed at home, including the one in which a new born boy officially becomes a member of the community. Other religious ceremonies include marriage and rituals connected with pregnancy and child birth.

WORSHIP OF SAINTS

Hindus worship both living and dead men as saints. Some saints may be Yogis (men who practice yoga) others may be gurus (spiritual teachers). Hinduism has many local and regional saints rather than official saints for all its followers. Many Hindu monks and Nuns have joined together in a religious order under the leadership of some saint.

FUTURE

Indians are telling the philosophy of Hinduism and Hindu culture. Hinduism teaches peace, non-violence, spirituality and simplicity as a way to attain prosperity and a better character i.e. why people believe that Hinduism is not a religion but way of life and if the whole world adopts this way of life there will be peace and the entire world would become a paradise.

SHAIVISM

"Kashmir Shaivism has penetrated to that depth of living, through where diverse currents of human wisdom unite in a luminous synthesis."
—Dr Rabindranath Tagore (winner of 1913 Nobel Prize in Literature) famously commented on Kashmir Shaivism.

Kashmir Shaivism is a Hindu Vedic Philosophy, a manifestation of universal consciousness. The goal is to merge in Shiva or realize one's already existing identity with Shiva, by means of wisdom, yoga and Divine grace.

This school of self realization was born during the Eighth or Ninth century CE in Kashmir and made significant strides both philosophical and theological until the end of the twelfth century C.E. Among the many Hindu philosophies, Kashmir Shaivism is a school of thought consisting of Trika and its philosophical articulation / *Prayabhijna*. It is categorized by various scholars as realistic idealism or "transcendental physicalism".

Shaivism Vs Vedanta

It is philosophically important to distinguish Kashmir Shaivism from the *Advaitya* Vedanta of Shankara as both are non-dual philosophies which give primacy to Universal consciousness. In Kashmir Shaivism, all things are a manifestation of this consciousness. The phenomenal World (*Shakti*) is real, and it exists to its being in consciousness (chit). In comparison, Advaita Vedanta believes that Brahman is inactive (*niskriya*) and the phenomenal World is an illusion (*maya*). Thus, the philosophy of Kashmir Shaivism, also called the Trika, can be seen in contrast to Shankara's Advaitya.

Secondly Kashmir Shaivism is based on a strong monistic interpretation of the Bhairava Tantras (and its sub-category the Kaula Tantras), which were tantras written by the Kapalikas. Contrastingly, the Advaitya Vedanta is based on Upanishads, Brahmsutras and Bhagwad Gita.

There are additional revelations of the Shiva Sutras compiled by Vasugupta. Kashmir Shaivism claimed to supersede Shaiva Siddhanta, a dualistic tradition which scholars consider normative tantric Shaivism. The Shaiva Siddhanta's goal of becoming an ontologically distinct Shiva (through Shiva's grace) was replaced by recognizing oneself as Shiva who, in Kashmir Shaivism's monism, is the entirety of the Universe. Somananda, the first theologian of monistic Shaivism, was the teacher of Abhinava Gupta who in turn was the teacher of Ksemaraja.

CONCEPTS:

Philosophical overview

The point of view of Kashmir Shaivism can be summarised in the following four concepts of *Chiti, Mala, Upaya and Moksha*.

1. Chiti: Universal consciousness (*chiti*) is the fundamental constituent of the universe. This consciousness is one and includes the whole. It could also be called God or Shiva.

2. Mala: Consciousness contrasts itself. The one becomes many. Shiva becomes the individual (*Jiva*). This expansion is called, *Mala* (impurity). There are three *Malas* or expansions, the Mala of individualization (*Anava mala*), the Mala of the limited mind (*Mayiya Mala*) and the Mala of the body (*Karma Mala*).

3. Upaya: An individual caught in the suffering of embodied existence afflicted by the three *Malas*, eventually yearns to return to his or her primordial state of universal consciousness. To attain this, he or she undertakes *Sadhana* or spiritual practice. Kashmir Shaivism describes four methods or Upayas—*Anavopaya*, the method of body. *Saktopaya*, the method of the mind, *Sambhvopaya*, the method of consciousness, and *Anupaya* the "Method-less" method.

4. Moksha: The fruit of the individual's *Sadhana* is the attainment of self-realisation or *Moksha*. In Kashmir Shaivism, the state of liberation (*mukti*) is called *Sahaja Samadhi* and is characterized by the attainment of universally blissful consciousness while living one's ordinary life.

ANUTTARA, THE SUPREME

Anuttara is the highest principle in Kashmir Shaivism and as such, it is the fundamental reeling underneath the whole universe. According to the multiple interpretations, *Anuttara* are above all and form the supreme unsurpassed reality. In the Sanskrit alphabets *Anuttara* is associated with the first letter "A". As the ultimate principle *Anuttara* is indentified with Shiva / Shakti (as Shakti is identical to Shiva).

The supreme consciousness (*Chita*) sheds light (*Prakasha*) upon the supreme subject (*Aham*) and a temporal vibration (*Spanda*). The practitioner who realizes direct transmission by the grace of Shiva / Shakti is liberated and perceives absolutely no difference between the self and the body of the universe. Being and beings become one. In the absence of erotic friction the subject perceives the object non-differently from itself and that act of perception is filled with non-dual beings / consciousness / bliss. *Anuttara* is different from the notion of transcendence because even though it is above all, it does not imply a separation of the being from the universe.

AHAM, THE HEART OF SHIVA

Aham is the concept of supreme reality as heart. It is considered to be a non-dual interior space of Shiva which supports the entire manifestation, as the supreme member and is identical to Shakti.

PRATYABHIJANA

Pratyabhijana is the philosophical articulation of Kashmir Shaivism. It literally means "spontaneous recognition", because it does not have any *Upayas* or means to practice. The only thing to do is recognize who you are. This means that it can actually be called *"Anupaya"*—the Sanskrit word for "without means". *Kremaraja*, the student of *Abhinava Gupta* used a mirror analogy to explain *Pratyabhijana*.

KAULA

Although domesticated into a householder tradition, Kashmir Shaivism recommends a secret performance of *Kaula* practices. This was to be done in seclusion, thereby allowing one to maintain the appearance of a typical house holder.

SWATANTARYA, SELF-CREATED WILL

The concept of the will plays a central role in Kashmir Shaivism. Known under the technical name of *Svatantarya,* it is the cause of the creation of the universe. According to this concept a primordial force stirs up the absolute and manifests the world inside the supreme consciousness of Shiva. *Svatantarya* is the sole property of God, all the remaining conscious subjects being co-participant, in various capacities, of this divine sovereignty. Humans have a limited degree of freewill based on their level of consciousness. All subjects have freewill but they can be ignorant of this power. Ignorance too is a force, projected by *Svatantarya* itself upon the creation and can only be removed by *Svatantarya,* by the divine grace of *Saktipath*. In this philosophical system spiritual liberation is not accessible by mere effort, but depends only on the will of God. Thus the disciple can only surrender himself and wait for the divine grace to come down and eliminate the limitations that imprison his consciousness. Causality in Kashmir Shaivism is considered to be created by *Swantantarya* along with the Universe. Thus there can be no contradiction, limitation or rule to force Shiva to act one way or the other. *Swantantarya* always exists beyond the limiting shield of cosmic illusion, *Maya*. Ultimately, Kashmir Shaivism, as monistic idealist philosophical system, views all subjects to be identical. All are one and that one is Shiva, the supreme consciousness.

THE SHIVA SUTRAS

The first great initiate recorded in the history of this spiritual path was *Vasugupta* (C. 875-925) *Vasugupta* compiled, for the first time in writing, the principles and main doctrines of this system. A fundamental work of Shaivism, traditionally attributed to *Vasugupta* is the Shiva Sutras. These Sutras are considered to have been revealed to *Vasugupta* by Shiva. According to myth *Vasugupta* had dreams in which Shiva told him to go to the Mahadeva Mountain in Kashmir. On this mountain he is said to have found verses inscribed on a rock. Shiva Sutras outline the teachings of Shaivism. The work is a collection of aphorizes. The sutras expound a purely non-dual (*Advaita*) metaphysics. These sutras are classified as a type of Hindu Scripture known as *Shivarahasyagama Samgraha*.

CLASSIFICATION OF WRITTEN TRADITION

The first Kashmiri Shaiva text was written in the early ninth century CE. *Trika* Shaivism also draws teachings from *Shrutis* such as the monistic Bhairava Tantras and the Shiva Sutras of *Vasugupta*. A unique version of the *Bhagvad Gita*, known as the *Gitartha Samgraha*, as a commentary by *Abhinava Gupta,* also finds its way into the written tradition. *Tantraloka* of *Abhinava Gupta* is also a prominent work of philosophy. Scriptures belonging to Shaivism can be divided into three fundamental categories, *Agama Sastra, Spanda Sastra* and *Pratyabhijana Sastra*.

1. *Agama Sastras* are those writings that are considered as direct revelations from Shiva. The writings were first communicated orally, from the master to a worthy disciple. They include essential works, Shiva Sutra having most of them.
2. *Spanda Sastra* are commentaries. *Spanda Karika* by *Vasugupta* is the most prominent work of literature in this category. The *Spanda Sandoha* talks only about the first verses of *Spanda Karika* and *Spanda Nirnaya* is a commentary of the complete text.

3. *Pratyabhijna Sastras* are those writings which mainly have a metaphysical content. Due to their extremely high spiritual and intellectual level, this part of the written tradition of Shaivism is the least accessible for the uninitiated. Nevertheless, the corpus of writings refer to the simplest and most direct modality of spiritual realization and refers to the spontaneous recognition of divine nature hidden in each human being (*atma*). The most important works in this category are: *Israra Pratyabhijna* by *Utpaladeva*. *Prayatbhijana Vimarsami*, a commentary to *Ishvara Prayatbhijana* means in fact the "Direct recognition of Lord as identical to one's heart". Before *Utpaldeva*, his master *Somananda* wrote *Shiva Drasti* (The Vision of Shiva), a devotional poem written on multiple levels of meaning.

PROMINENT SAGES OF KASHMIR SHAIVISM

ABHINAVGUPTA

All the four branches of Kashmir Shaivism were put together by the great philosopher Abhinav Gupta (950-1020 AD). His most important work is the *Tantraloka* (the Divine Light of *Tantra*), a work in verses which is a majestic synthesis of the whole tradition of monistic Shaivism. Abhinava Gupta succeeded in smoothing out all the apparent differences and disparities that existed among the different branches and schools of Kashmir Shaivism before him. Thus he offered a unitary, coherent and complete vision of this system. Due to the exceptional length of verses in *Tantraloka*, Abhinava Gupta himself provided a shorter version in prose, called *Tantrasara* (The Essence of *Tantra*).

JAYARATHA

Another important Kashmir Shaivite, Jayaratha (1150-1200 AD), added his commentary to *Tantraloka*—a task of great difficulty which was his lifelong pursuit. He provided more contextual examples, numerous quotes and clarifications without which some passages from *Tantraloka* would be impossible to elucidate today.

RELATED TEACHINGS

KARMA

"Teran Karma" means "Progressive gradation". Spiritual progression or gradual refinement of the mental processes occurs at the ultimate level, in the supreme consciousness (*chita*). Even as the Karma School is an integral part of Kashmir Shaivism, it is also an independent system both philosophically and historically. Karma is significant as a synthesis of *Tantra* and *Sakta* traditions based on the monistic Shaivism. Karma is similar in some regards to *Spanda* as both centre around the activity of *Shakti* and also similar with *Kula* in their Tantric approach. Inside the family of Kashmir Shaivism, the *Pratyabhijana* School is the most different from Karma. The most distinctive feature of Karma is its monistic dualistic *Bhedabhedopaya* discipline in the stages precursory to spiritual realization.

Even if Kashmir Shaivism is an idealistic monism, there is still a place for dualistic aspects in introductory stages on the spiritual path. So it is said that in practice Karma employs the dualistic-cum-non-dualistic methods, yet in the underlying philosophy it remains non-dualistic. Karma has a positive epistemic bias aimed at forming a synthesis of enjoyment (*bhoga*) and illumination (*moksa*).

SPANDA

The Spanda system, introduced by Vasugupta (800 AD), is usually described as a "liberation movement of consciousness". Abhinava Gupta uses the expression "Some sort of Movement" to imply the distinction from physical movement. It is rather a vibration or sound inside the Divine, a throb. The essence of this vibration is the ecstatic self recurrent consciousness. The central tenet in this system states that "Everything is Spanda, both the objective exterior reality and the subjective world." Nothing exists without movement. Yet the ultimate movement takes place not in space or time, but inside the supreme consciousness. It is a cycle of internalization and externalization of consciousness (*Chita*) relating to the most elevated plane in creation (Shiva-Sakti Taitva). In order to describe the connotations of the Spanda Concert, a series of equivalent concerts, are enumerated, such as self recurrent consciousness—*Vimarisa*, unimpeded will of Supreme consciousness—*Swatantarya*, supreme creative energy—*Visarga*, heart of divine—*Herdanga* and the ocean of light consciousness—*Chidananda*. The most important texts of the system are *Shiva Sutras, Spanda, karika* and *Vijnana Bhairava Tantra*.

THE REVIVAL OF KASHMIR SHAIVISM IN 20TH CENTURY

Kashmir Shaivism went underground for a number of centuries after the Muslim invasion. While there might have been yogis and practitioners secretively following the teachings, there were no major writers or publications after perhaps the 14th century.

In the 20th century Swami Lakshman Joo laid the cornerstone of modern Kashmir Shaivism. His contribution is enormous. He inspired a generation of scholars, who made Kashmir Shaivism a legitimate field of enquiry within the academy. The contribution of Swami Muktananda cannot be overlooked, although he did not belong to the direct lineage of Kashmir Shaivism. Muktananda felt a great affinity for the teachings which were validated by his own direct experience. He encouraged and endorsed Motilal Banarsidass to publish Jaideva Singh's translation of *Shiva Sutras, Pratyabhijnahrdayam, Spanda Karikas* and *Vijnana Bhairya*. He also introduced Kashmir Shaivism to a wide audience of western meditational practitioners through his writings and lectures on the subject.

CONTEMPORARY KASHMIRI SHAIVITES FROM KASHMIR

Laleshwari (1320—1392)
Bhagwan Gopinath (1898—1968)
Swami Lakshman Joo (1907—1991)

Swami Lakshaman Joo Raina (9th May 1907—27th September 1991) was a mystic and scholar of Kashmir Trika Shaivism. He was known as Lal Sahib (Friend of God) by followers, who considered him a fully realized saint. He attracted the attention of western writers such as Mignel Serrano, the *Chilam* mystical writer and Paul Reps, whose rendering of the *Vigyan Bhairav Tantra* was later used by Osho, brought Lakshman Joo and the meditation methods of his school to International prominence.

Swami Lakshman Joo was also the founder of Srinagar based Ishwar Ashram Trust which continues his teachings on Kashmir Shaivism and Tirka

Philosophy. Lakshaman Joo was involved in teaching Kashmiri Shaivite text throughout his adult life. He translated the texts, which he considered the most important inheritance of his people, into both Hindi and English.

His works include:—

1933—Sanskrit *Gitartha Samgraha*, Abhinavgupta's commentary on the *Bhagvad Gita*.

1943—Hindi Translation of *Sambpanchasika*.

1958—*Sri Kramanayadipika* (Hindi) on the 12 forms of Goddess Kali.

1964—Hindi translation of Uppaladeva's *Shivastotravali*.

1982—Lectures on practice and discipline in Kashmir Shaivism.

1985—*Kashmir Shaivism: The Secret Supreme* edited by John Hughes (the essence of the first fifteen chapters of Abhinavagupta's *Tantraloka*).

1986—Hindi Commentary by Swami Lakshmajoo on Abhinavgupta's *Bhagvad Gitartha Samgraha*.

1987—Hindi translation of *Panchastavi*.

1994—Self Realisation in Kashmir Shaivism, Oral Teachings of Swami Lakshmanjoo, edited by John Hughes.

2002—English translation of Shiva Sutras of Vasgupta edited by John Hughes.

2002—Shiva Sutras of Vasgupta along with original audio recordings.

2005—Revelations, Grace and Spiritual Practice, original audio and DVD recordings.

2006—*Trika Rahasya Prakirya* by Swami Lakshman joo (Sanskrit verses with Hindi commentary)

2007—*Vijinana Bhairava,* original audio and transcript introduction by John Hughes.

2009—*Bhagvad Gitartha Samhraha* of Abhinavgupta (Revisited Chapters 1-6 translated by Swami Lakshman joo DVD.)

Over a period of nineteen years John Hughes recorded Lakshman Joo's translation of the following library.

Bhagawad Gitartha Samgraha of Abhinavgupta: translation and commentary by Swami Lakshman Joo, original audio recordings (Kashmir, 28 November 1978 to 3 June 80).

Bhodhapancadashika of Abhinavgupta: Translation and commentary by Swami Lakshman joo, original audio recordings (Kashmir, 18 to 22 October 1980).

Dehastadevatacakra of Abhinavgupta: Translation and commentary by Swami Lakshman Joo, original audio recordings (July 1974).

Janma Marana Vicara: Translation and commentary by Swami Lakshman Joo, original audio recordings (Kashmir, May, 1975).

Kashmir Shaivism: The Secret Supreme (Special Lectures in English), Swami Lakshman Joo, original audio recordings (Kashmir, 1972).

Kashmir Lectures on Practice and Discipline, Swami Lakshman Joo original audio recordings (Kashmir, 1980).

Paramarthasar (Abhinavgupta's commentary): Swami Lakshman Joo's comments on John Hughes reading original audio recordings (Kashmir, 26 April to 6 September 1972).

Parapraveshika of Kshemaraja: Translation and commentary by Swami Lakshman Joo, original audio recordings (Kashmir, 26 April, 1972).

Paratrishika Laghuvriti of Abhinavgupta: Translation and commentary by Swami Lakshman Joo, original audio recordings (Kashmir, 25 May 1974 to 6 July 1974).

Paratrishika Vivarana of Abhinavagupta: Translation and commentary by Swami Lakshman Joo, original audio recordings (Kashmir, 26 May 1982 to 24 August 1985).

Revelations on grace and Practice: A collection of Swami Lakshman Joo's original audio recordings and transcripts, edited by John Hughes (USA, May 9, 2005).

Shivastrotravali of Utpaladeva: Translation by Swami Lakshman Joo, original audio recordings Kashmir, June 1976 to September 1978.

Shiva Sutra Vimarishini of Vasugupta: Translation and commentary by Swami Lakshman Joo, original audio recordings (Kashmir, 7 June 1975)

Spanda Karika of Vasugupta: Translation and commentary by Swami Lakshman Joo original audio recordings (Kashmir, 5 August to 26 August 1981).

Spanda Samdoha of Kashemaraja: Translation and commentary by Swami Lakshman Joo, original audio recordings Kashmir, 29 August to 9 October 1981.

Special Verses on Practice Swami Lakshman Joo Original audio recordings Nepal, 1988.

Stavacintamani of Bhatta Narayana: Translation and commentary by Swami Laksham Joo, original audio recordings Kashmir, 26 November 1980 to 17 July 1981.

Tantraloka of Abhinavgupta (Chapters 1-18): Translation and commentary by Swami Lakshman Joo, original audio recordings (Kashmir, 1976 to 1981).

Vatulanath Sutras of Kshermaraja Swami Lakshman Joo, original audio recordings (Kashmir, 1975).

Vijinana Bhairava Question Swami Lakshman Joo, original audio recordings (Kashmir, July 1985).

AUDIO (KASHMIRI LANGUAGE)

- *Kalika Sotra* of Shivanandanatha: Recitation by Swami Lakshman Joo and devotees, Kashmir, 1977.
- *Maharthamanjari* of Maheshvarananda: Translated by Swami Lakshaman Joo, (Kashmir, 1977).
- *Prartrishika Vivarana*: Translated by Swami Lakshman Joo, (Kashmir, 1982-83).
- *Shiva Sutras Vimarshini* of Vasugupta: translated by Swami Lakshman Joo (Kashmir, 1978).

- *Shiva Strotravali* of Utpaladeva with Kashemaraja's commentary translated by Swami Lakshman Joo, 9Kashmir, 1975-85).
- *Stuti Kushmanjail*: Translated by Swami Lakshman Joo, (Kashmir, 1977).
- *Tantraloka* of Abhinavagupta: (Selected chapters) Translated by Swami Lakshman Joo, (Kashmir, 1975-85).

DVD LIBRARY ENGLISH

- *Bhagvadgitarthasamgraha* of Abhinavgupta: Translation and commentary by Swami Lakshman Joo original video recordings (Nepal, 1990).
- *Parmarthasara* of Abhinavgupta: Translation and commentary by Swami Lakshman Joo, original video recording (Nepal, 1990).
- Revelations on Grace and Spiritual Practice: Selections from translation and commentaries on *Bhagwadgitarthasamgrah* (video), *Paramrthasara* (video) and *Tantraloka* (audio) (Los Angeles, 2006).
- Special Verses on Practice Swami Lakshman Joo, original video recordings (Nepal, 1988).

BUDDHISM

In 8th century B.C., North India saw the rise of several urban centres fuelled by widespread trade. This urbanisation led to changes in social stratification and encouraged the emergence of new religious sects, which challenged the Brahman dominance. Chief among these were Buddhism and Jainism, founded respectively by Siddhartha (566—486 B.C.) who became the Buddha and Vardhman Mahavira (540—467 B.C.). These two religions gained much public favour as they neither had caste nor creed. They were open to everyone irrespective of their gender. These religions gave simple teachings that had a mass appeal.

The King Amongst Saints

In 566 B.C. Prince Siddhartha Gautama was born in the kingdom of Kapilavastu. Though born in Lumbini, Nepal, all the places associated with his life as an ascetic and the subsequent teachings are in Bihar and Uttar Pradesh (India). These are now pilgrimage sites—starting from Bodh Gaya (where Siddhartha attained enlightenment) to Sarnath where he preached his first sermon through other places he visited regularly and finally to

Kushinagar (where he left his body) in 486 B.C.—for the people who have adopted Buddhism.

Siddhartha renounced his princely life style and left his family at the age of 30 to seek the meaning of human existence. Impoverished by fasts and penances, while he spent 6 years living with ascetics and wandering as a beggar, he found that such self-notification gave him no answer. Enlightenment came at Bodh Gaya after 49 days of Meditation under the Bodhi Tree. Siddhartha discovered that the cause of sufferings is desire and desire could be conquered by following an Eight Fold path of righteousness.

In 528 B.C., Siddhartha delivered his first sermon at Deer Park in Sarnath near Varanasi. He explained the *Dharamchakra* or "the Wheel of Law". In those days Sarnath was one of ancient India's greatest centres of learning. Sarnath was often visited by foreign scholars, including the Chinese travellers Fa Hien and Hiuen Tsang who wrote of its flourishing monasteries. The central monument at the existing complex in Sarnath is the 5th century A.D. Dhameksh Stupa, which is built at the site where it is believed that Buddha delivered his sermon to five disciples.

Buddha preached life as a continuing cycle of death and domination. Each person's position and well being in life was determined by his or her behaviour in previous lives. For example, good deeds may lead to birth as a wise and wealthy person or as a being in heaven. Whereas a person's evil deeds may lead to rebirth as a poor and sickly person or even in hell.

Buddha also taught that as long as individuals remain within the cycle of death and rebirth, they can never be completely free from pain and sufferings. Buddha said people could break out of this cycle by eliminating any attachment to worldly things. By ridding themselves of such attachment, people would gain perfect peace and happiness. Buddha called this state of peace and happiness "Nirvana". According to Siddhartha, those who are willing to follow the Middle Way and are able to commit their life to the noble eight fold path conquer their attachment to worldly things and thus achieve nirvana.

The "Middle Way" is a way of life that avoids both the corporal satisfaction of human desires and extreme forms of self-denial and self torture.

EIGHT FOLD PATH:—

1. Knowledge of Truth.
2. Intention to resist evil.
3. Saying nothing to hurt other.
4. Respecting life, morality and property.
5. Holdings and job that does not injure others.
6. Striving to free one's mind of evil.
7. Controlling one's feeling.
8. Practicing proper forms of concentration.

In 86 B.C. Buddha fell ill after eating wild mushrooms prepared by one of his followers and died in a groove of Sal Trees at Kushinagar, where a Stupa still marks the site. After the death of Lord Buddha, his disciples and followers summarized the traditions that had developed around the dharma. The oldest of the many Buddhist schools compiled a scripture called the *Tripitika*, This worldly discipline deals with the rules for regulating the order of Buddhist Monks. The second part, the Basket of Discourses, consists largely of original sermons recited by the Buddha. The third part is the Basket of Dharma, which contains more systematic discussions of the doctrine. Later schools have added their own scriptures.

Sects of Buddhism

Mahayana

The Mahayana can be described as a loosely bound collection of many teachings with large and expansive doctrines that are able to coexist simultaneously. Buddhism practiced in China, Indonesia, Vietnam, Korea, Tibet, and Japan is Mahayana Buddhism. Much of the early extant evidence for the origins of Mahayana comes from early Chinese translations of Mahayana texts. These Mahayana teachings were first propagated into China by *Lokakṣema*, the first translator of Mahayana Sutras into Chinese during the 2nd century CE.

Ideology

Mahayana constitutes an inclusive tradition characterized by plurality and the adoption of new Mahayana Sutras in addition to the earlier

Āgama texts. Mahayana sees itself as penetrating further and more profoundly into the Buddha's Dharma. An Indian commentary on the *Mahāyānasaṃgraha*, entitled *Vivṛtaguhyārthapiṇḍavyākhyā*, gives a classification of teachings according to the capabilities of the audience. According to disciples' grades the Dharma is classified as inferior or superior. For example, the inferior was taught to the merchants *Trapuṣa* and *Ballika* because they were ordinary men; the middle was taught to the group of five because they were at the stage of saints; the eight fold *Prajñāpāramitās* were taught to bodhisattvas, because the *Prajñāpāramitās* are superior in eliminating conceptually imagined forms.

There is also a tendency in Mahayana Sutras to regard adherence to these Sutras as generating spiritual benefits greater than those that arise from being a follower of the non-Mahayana approaches to Dharma. Thus the *Śrīmālādevī Sūtra* claims that the Buddha said that devotion to Mahayana is inherently superior in its virtues to the following the *śrāvaka* or *Pratyekabuddha* paths.

The fundamental principles of Mahayana doctrine were based on the possibility of universal liberation from suffering for all beings and the existence of Buddhas and bodhisattvas embodying Buddha Nature. The Pure Land school of Mahayana simplifies the expression of faith by allowing salvation to be alternatively obtained through the grace of the *Amitābha Buddha*, by having faith and devoting oneself to mindfulness of the Buddha. This devotional lifestyle of Buddhism has greatly contributed to the success of Mahayana in East Asia, where spiritual elements traditionally relied upon mindfulness of the Buddha, mantras and *dhāraṇīs*, and reading of Mahayana Sutras. In Chinese Buddhism, most monks, as well as the lay people, practice Pure Land, some combining it with Chán (Zen).

Most Mahayana schools believe in supernatural bodhisattvas who devote themselves to the perfections (*pāramitā*), ultimate knowledge (*sarvajñāna*), and the liberation of all sentient beings. In Mahayana, the Buddha is seen as the ultimate, highest being, present in all times, in all beings, and in all places, and the bodhisattvas come to represent the universal ideal of altruistic excellence.

ORIGIN

The origins of Mahayana are still not completely understood. The earliest Western views of Mahayana assumed that it existed as a separate school in competition with the so-called "Hīnayāna" schools. Due to the veneration of Buddhas and bodhisattvas, Mahayana was often interpreted as a more devotional, lay-inspired form of Buddhism, with supposed origins in stūpa veneration, or by making parallels with the history of the European Protestant reformation. These views have been largely dismissed in modern times in light of a much broader range of early texts that are now available. These earliest Mahayana texts often depict strict adherence to the path of a bodhisattva, and engagement in the ascetic ideal of a monastic life in the wilderness, akin to the ideas expressed in the *Rhinoceros Sutra*. The old views of Mahayana as a separate lay-inspired and devotional sect are now largely dismissed as misguided and wrong on all counts.

The earliest textual evidence of Mahayana comes from Sutras originating around the beginning of the Common Era. Jan Nattier has noted the use of the term "Mahayana" in some of the earliest Mahayana texts such as the *Ugrapariprccha Sutra*, yet there is no doctrinal difference between Mahayana in this context and the early schools, and that "Mahayana" referred rather to the rigorous emulation of Gautama Buddha along the path of a bodhisattva seeking to become a fully enlightened Buddha.

There is also no evidence that Mahayana ever referred to a separate formal school or sect of Buddhism, but rather that it existed as a certain set of ideals, and later doctrines, for bodhisattvas. Paul Williams has also noted that the Mahayana never had nor ever attempted to have a separate *Vinaya* or ordination lineage from the early schools of Buddhism, and therefore each *bhikṣu* or *bhikṣuṇī* adhering to the Mahayana formally belonged to an early school. Membership in these *nikāyas*, or monastic sects, continues today with the *Dharmaguptaka nikāya* in East Asia, and the *Mūlasarvāstivāda nikāya* in Tibetan Buddhism. Therefore Mahayana was never a separate rival sect of the early schools. Paul Harrison clarifies that while monastic Mahayanists belonged to a nikāya, not all members of a nikāya were Mahayanists. From Chinese monks visiting India, we now know that both Mahayana and non-Mahayana monks in India often lived in the same monasteries side by side.

HINAYANA

According to Jan Nattier, it is most likely that the term *Hīnayāna* post dates the term *Mahayana*, and was only added due to antagonism and conflict between bodhisattvas and śrāvakas. The sequence of terms then began with *Bodhisattvayāna*, which was given the epithet *Mahayana* ("Great Vehicle"). It was only later, after attitudes toward the bodhisattvas and their teachings had become more critical, that the term *Hīnayāna* ("Inferior Vehicle") was created as a back formation, contrasting with the already established term *Mahayana*. The earliest Mahayana texts often use the term *Mahayana* as an epithet and synonym for *Bodhisattvayāna*, but the term *Hīnayāna* is comparatively rare in early texts, and is usually not found at all in the earliest translations. Therefore, the often perceived symmetry between *Mahayana* and *Hīnayāna* can be deceptive, as the terms were not actually coined in relation to one another in the same era. While evidence of a conflict is present in some cases, there is also substantial evidence demonstrating peaceful coexistence between the two traditions. The Chinese monk Yijing who visited India in the 7th century CE, distinguishes Mahayana from Hīnayāna as follows:

Both adopt one and the same Vinaya, and they have in common the prohibitions of the five offences, and also the practice of the Four Noble Truths. Those who venerate the bodhisattvas and read the Mahayana Sutras are called the Mahayanists, while those who do not perform these are called the Hīnayānists.

Spread of Buddhism

The great Chinese scholar-monk Hiuen Tsang travelled across forbidding deserts and mountains to come to Nalanda University in the early 7th century A.D. He spent 12 years studying and teaching there. During his stay he was dazzled by Nalanda's soaring domes and Pinnacles, peer-red pillars, ornamented and adorned balustrade. Upon his return to China he settled down at the Big Goose Pagoda in Xian, where he translated the Buddhist Scriptures he had brought back with him from Nalanda into Chinese.

Mauryan emperor Asoka, the grandson of Chandragupta, (269-232 B.C.) became one of the greatest rulers of India. His Empire extended from Afghanistan to Karnataka. But after the bloody conquest of Kalinga, Asoka gave up violence and became a great patron of Buddha. He gave literally his entire empire to charity. Animal killing was forbidden in his kingdom and people were encouraged to respect all religions. He got Buddhist ethics engraved on rocks and pillars all over his vast empire. These edicts were written in the Brahmi Script, from which most Indian scripts have evolved—Asoka also built many Stupas to safeguard Buddhist relics including the one of at Sanchi.

After Asoka, the Mauryan Empire soon declined. Local kingdoms arose across North India. Invaders from Central Asia attacked and established a brief rule of Indo-Greeks from 200 B.C. to 300 C.E., which included the Bactria, the Scythians, the Parthians and the Kushanas. The territory of Kanishka, the greatest Kushana King, covered Northwest Kashmir and most of the Gangatic Valley. He too was a pattern of Buddhism. Mahayana Buddhism, which developed during his reign, was reflected in two great schools of art, the Greco-Roman Gandharva style in the northwest and in a more indigenous style at Mathura.

The monks in Ladakh are a very peaceful and God fearing community. They are spreading the light of Buddhism to the whole world while struggling to survive in the cold desert of the North Eastern region of the Indian state of Jammu and Kashmir. From Kashmir (Ladakh) Buddhism has spread to Tibet, China, Japan, Indonesia, Korea, Vietnam, Thailand, Myanmar, Nepal, Taiwan, Honk Kong, Singapore, Afghanistan, Tajikistan, Java, Sumatra, Bali Malaysia, Bhutan, Magnolia, Sri Lanka, and Philippines.

Buddhist Architecture

Earliest Buddhist monuments consist of Stupas, hemispherical funerary mounds, rock shrines (Chaityas) and monasteries (Viharas). While chaityas were places of worship, the Viharas were dwelling places for Buddhist monks. They consisted of small cells arranged around four sides of an open court. The Stupas were monumental reliquaries in which the ashes of Buddhist Teachers, including the Buddha were interred. Chaityas served as halls (grihas) for congregational worship and enshrined a model Stupa at one end. Chaityas have distinctive barrel shaped ceilings, expressed on the exterior as a horseshoe shaped arch.

Buddha Jayanti and Mahavir Jayanti

The Buddha was born, attained enlightenment and died on the full moon of the forth lunar month. Buddhists gather in Viharas for prayer. It is a national Holiday in India.

SANGHA

The word Sangha sometimes refer to the ideal Buddhist Community, which consists of those who have reached the higher ranges of spirituality. In addition to the order of Buddhist monks and Nuns it may also refer to the laity. The order of the monks has always had a special role in preserving and spreading Buddhism. In many Buddhist groups, the dissipative monastery life is considered essential for those who seek nirvana. In most Buddhist countries monks, are expected to live a life of poverty, meditation and study. Monks are also expected to avoid sexual activity. Sangha Members are expected to honour Buddha, to follow basic sword rules and to support the monks. They are also expected to pay special honour to images of Buddha and objects that are associated with him.

Many of the laities have influenced the history of Buddhism. Asoka, the Indian emperor, made Buddhism a kind of State religion. B. R. Ambedkar, one of the principle framers of Indian constitution, led a mass convention in India that brought more than one million Hindu farmers into the Sangha.

THE MANTRAYANA

The word "Mantrayana" means sacred recitation vehicle. A bodhisattva is a person who vows to become a Buddha by leading a life of virtue and wisdom. At the highest level, a bodhisattva is the one who postpones venturing into nirvana in order to relieve the sufferings of others on the same path through love and compassion.

The schools of Mantrayana are in Himalayan regions like Ladakh, Mongolia and Japan. The Japanese call it Shinson. Mantrayana Buddhism accepts some Mahayanist doctrines. But it also emphasized a close relationship between a spiritual leader, sometimes called a guru, and his small group of disciples. The disciples spend much of their time reciting spells called mantras, performing sacred dances and gestures, and meditating. Some branches of the school in Tibet stress sexual symbiosis and believe that sex should be used for holy purposes. Many followers of Mantrayana Buddhism traditionally keep many of their beliefs and practices secret from outsiders.

Contemporary Significance

In the whole world, Buddhism is considered as a symbol of simplicity, peace and unity. It is respected by all religions for its selfless service to mankind. At various times, Buddhism has been a dominant religion, culture and social practice in most of Asia. In each era Buddhism has mingled with elements of other religions specific of the region. Though it was widely adopted because it did not discriminate on the basis of classes, caste or creed, its teachings are however still valid in the world where terrorism is at its peak. People are fed up with the monster called Jihad. Today Buddhism is one of the major religions of the world.

ISLAM

More than 90% population in the Kashmir valley follows Islam. We must explore the origin of this modern religion and follow the journey of its global proliferation to understand the repercussions of its establishment in the valley of Kashmir.

Islam is the name given to the religion preached by Prophet Muhammad. The Prophet was an Arab, who was born in Mecca around 570 A.D. He believed that he had been sent to guide his people and to call them to worship God (Allah). The prophet announced that there is only "One God" and Muhammad himself was the only messenger of that God. Those who believe in this God and accept Muhammad as his messenger are called "Muslims".

Both 'Islam' and 'Muslim' are Arabic words and when translated to English mean "Submission and peace" and "Submitting oneself To Allah" respectively. West often calls "Islam" Muhammadanism and its followers Muhammadans. Muslims feel that these terms give an incorrect impression that Muslims worship Muhammad.

Islam is the second most widespread religion in the world with majority of the followers residing in the Middle East, North Africa, Indonesia,

Bangladesh, Pakistan, India and the Soviet Union. Islam is also the principal religion in European Turkey and Albania. However the Great Muslim Empire no longer exists. But Muslims are still united by the faith of Islam, which forms a common bond of culture among them.

GROWTH OF ISLAM

The Prophet around the year 610 A.D. began preaching in Mecca. Most of the powerful and rich citizens of Mecca discarded his teachings. Some were so angered and frightened that they plotted to kill him. In 622 the Prophet was forced to flee to the city of Medina (then called Yathrib) and seek shelter from a group of nine people. This immigration of Muslims is called the *Hegira*. Muslims date their calendar from this year.

In 630A.D. Muhammad and his followers, returned to Mecca and occupied the city. They destroyed all the idols in the temples and the holy shrines inside the *Kabba*. This was followed by a theological restructure that converted the same holy place into a mosque (Muslim house of worship). The residents of Mecca had no other alternative but to accept Islam and acknowledge Muhammad as the only Prophet. After the fall of Mecca, other tribes hastened to submit to the Muslims. Those who did not submit were harried until they submitted. Mecca and Medina became sacred cities of Islam.

SPREAD

In the name of God, several army expeditions were launched from Mecca and Medina to spread Islam throughout the Middle East and North Africa. After Muhammad died in AD 632, Abu Bakar was elected the Caliph or the Muslim ruler. He and his successors encouraged Jihad or the Muslim Crusade. Within a century of its inception, the Muslims built an empire that stretched from Northern Spain to India. The rapid spread of Islam engulfed the Persian Sassanid Empire and much of the Christian Byzantine Empire. The Muslim did threaten Western Europe once, but Charles Martel marred their evil plot by defeating them and annihilating all their supporters at the Battle of Poitou, also called the battle of Tours in 732A.D.

Islam united millions of different people into one large society. Muslims established a vivid civilization in Iraq, Persia (Iran), Palestine, North Africa,

Spain and Syria. They transmitted much of the classical knowledge of the ancient world, and built such magnificent structures as the Alhambra in Spain and the Taj Mahal in India.

TEACHINGS

Teachings of Islam were compiled in the Holy Book called "Quran", the Arabic word meaning "Recitation". The Caliph *Uthaman Miya* ruled from 644 to 656 and ordered the first official edition of "Quran". He sent one copy to the chief mosque in each of the capital cities of the Muslim provinces. Muslims consider the Quran to be the words of God himself as spoken to Muhammad by an angel.

Parts of the Quran have been adapted from the Bible, the Apocrypha and Talmud. The Quran contains many stories about the prophets that appear in the Old Testament. The Quran also has stories from the New Testament about Jesus, which is again referred to as the word of God.

HUMANITY

Quran teaches the absolute unity and power of God, the creator of the whole universe. It also teaches that God is just and merciful and wishes people to repent and purify themselves so that they can attain paradise after death. The Muslims believe Muhammad was the last of the prophets, his predecessors being Jesus, Noah and Moses who have been mentioned in the Old Testament. The Quran forbids the representation of human and animal figures so orthodox Islamic art rarely pictures living beings. The Quran also denounces singing, games of chance (gamble), eating pork and consuming wine (alcoholic drinks).

ETHICS

The Quran, like the Bible forbids:—

1. Worship of multiple deities.
2. Lying
3. Stealing
4. Adultery
5. Murder

Punishment for some offences, such as theft or adultery can be severe, but the Quran soften the ancient law of "An eye for an eye, a tooth for a tooth" by permitting the payment of blood money and by pleading for forgiveness. The Quran permits slavery under certain conditions but urges that slaves be freed. It permits a man as many as four wives under certain conditions. The Quran teaches honour for parents, kindness to slaves, protection for orphans and widows, and charity to the poor. It teaches the virtues of faith in God, benevolence, honesty, industry, honour, courage and generosity. Head of the family should treat household members kindly and fairly. It empowers a wife to protest against many forms of physical, mental or sexual abuse dealt out by her husband. According to Islam God judges the dishonest petitioner and rewards the compassionate in this and the next world. Islam teaches that life on earth is a period of testing and preparation for life to come. The angel in heaven records a person's good and bad deeds. People should therefore try their best to be good and help others and then trust in God's justice and mercy for their reward. Death is the gate to eternal life. Muslims believe in a judgment day when everyone will receive the record of his or her deeds on earth. The record book is placed in the right of the good and the left hand of the wicked after they have been judged. Depending upon the placement of the book people either go to heaven or hell. The sorrows and fortunes of hell resemble those described in the Bible. The Muslim heaven is a garden with flowing streams, luscious fruits, richly covered couches and beautiful maidens.

DUTIES

A Muslims chief duty is the profession of the unity with God and the prophet hood of Muhammad, which composes of prayers, charity, fasting and pilgrimage.

Practicing Muslims pray five times daily at dawn, at noon, in the afternoon, in the evening, and at nightfall. A muezzin reminds the followers to come for prayers by announcing the azan from the mosque minaret. Muslims wash their face, hands and feet before commencing prayers. On Friday, similar to the Jewish Sabbath and Christian Sunday, Muslims are expected to attend noon prayers at a mosque. The prayer reader faces in the direction of Mecca. The men stand in rows behind him and the women stand behind men. The prayer consists of reciting passages from Quran and other phrases in praise of the God. They include such movements as bowing and kneeling with the face to ground. Friday prayer, are preceded by a sermon. A usual Muslim prayer consists of recitation of the Ninety Nine names/qualities of God.

ALMS GIVING

Islam recommends *Zakat* (Alms Giving). Muslims must give 2.5% of their wealth each year as a trust fund for the needy. Islam does not limit freewill charity, except that Muslims cannot deprive their fixed legal inheritance by giving all their wealth to charity.

FASTING

Ramadan, the ninth month of the Muslim year, is the holy month of fasting. Muslims may not eat or drink from dawn to sunset. Travellers, the sick, nursing mothers and soldiers on march are exempted, but they must make up for the days missed. Muslims joyfully celebrate the end of the long fasting period during the three day festival organized around the end of the month (Little *Bairam*).

HAJJ (PILGRIMAGE)

Hajj to Mecca is recommended in Quran. All able Muslims are required to make the pilgrimage at least once. The most important ceremony is walking seven times around the *Kabba* and kissing its sacred black stone wall. Most Muslims include a visit to the mosque of Muhammad in Medina. The pilgrimage is concluded with the festival of sacrifice—a sheep, goat or camel and the meat is usually given to the poor.

SECTS

Like all religions, Islam is divided into sects. After the death of Prophet Muhammad, the Muslim world split into two factions. The majority, Sunni population, believes that after the death of their religious guide Muhammad in 632 A.D. the Caliph who was chosen by the tribe of Muhammad should wield the seat of political power. Whereas the members of Shia sect believe that the leadership was restricted to descendants of Ali. They believe God chose Ali, who was also Muhammad's son-in-law, to be Muhammad's successor. Muhammad, before his death, designated Ali as his successor. The Shiite settlements are scattered throughout Asia and Africa and more recently, in Europe and America.

There have been a number of smaller sects as well. In the early years, a group called *Kharijites* broke away from the Muslim community and formed a puritanical and democratic sect. The *Kharijites* have disappeared as an active group. Aga Khan IV is the 49th Imam of the *Ismaili Khoja Muslims*, a sect that has been in existence almost from the beginning of Islam. Another prominent sect the *Wahhabis* of *Ikhwan*, also formed a puritanical group in late 1500. They are dominant in Saudi Arabia. The Baha'i faith grew out of Shiite groups. Members of this Islamic group live scattered throughout Asia and Africa.

Until recently, Islam had no organized missionary movement. But today Al-Ajar University of Cairo, which is the intellectual centre of Islam, trains students for missionary work. Several Islamic sects especially the *Amadiya* of Pakistan work as missionaries throughout Europe, America, Asia and Africa.

Islamic Structures and Architecture

Islamic architecture has an unmistakable technique which is distinguished by an overbearing dome, cone topped minarets, and pyramid shaped inns (*Khans*). Mosques, *Madrasas*, tombs, rest houses etc all follow a similar pattern with green being the dominant colour. The mosque or Muslim place of worship is the most important building for Muslims. The word "Mosque" is derived from the Arabic word *Masjid*. which means a place of kneeling. A typical mosque has a minaret (*niche*) that points to Mecca. It also contains a pulpit for preachers and a lector for the Quran. Most mosques have one minaret from which the muezzin announces the prayer time. A court and a water fountain are generally provided for the ceremonial washing before prayer. The mosque is often decorated with colourful arabesques and Quran verses. Many mosques have a religious elementary school where young scholars learn to read and memorize the Quran. In some mosques, especially in Muslim countries, a *Madrasa* (*Dini* School) is built within the complex where students may complete their religious education. Only Graduates, sometimes called Mullahs, are qualified to preach the Quran in a mosque. The imam or leader is the Chief Officer in the mosque. He leads the congregation of devotees in prayers and other political and *Dini* matters. Prophet Muhammad led the prayer in his mosque in Medina. In the surrounding *Kabba* in Mecca the Caliphs led the people in all religious and political matters, so they were known as the Chief Imams. Islam does not have organized Priesthood. Any virtuous and able Muslim can lead prayers in most mosques.

ISLAMIC ART

Islamic Art is the art of a civilization based on the Islamic religion. The Prophet first preached his new religion in Arabia around 600 CE. Arabian Muslims began a series of conquests in the sixth century and united all the tribes they conquered into a single civilization. The Arabs, being nomads and desert dwellers, themselves had little knowledge of fine arts but through their conquest they came into contact with highly skilled craftsmen of Persia (Iran), Syria, Egypt and Mesopotamia (now Iraq, Kuwait and parts of Western Iran). The people who accepted Islam blended these cultural influences. It was this adoption and assimilation of traditions ranging from Spain to India that developed a distinct and fairly uniform style of art known as Islamic Art.

In Spain Islamic Art is called 'Moorish" after the Muslim group Moor who were the initial Muslim settlers around 700CE. From the 900CE onwards local variations in art appeared but the general interrelation sustained. Islamic art flourished from the 8th century to 17th century A.D. Islamic Artists were most inventive in architecture, especially in mosques and such socially useful institutions as shopping areas and hospitals. They also produced beautiful textiles, hand woven carpets, metal wares, pottery, carved and moulded plasters, glassware, ivory carvings and book illuminations (decorations) and bindings. The best of these works show extraordinary mastery of technique, design and colour. They illustrate a consistent concern to ornately titivate all aspects of daily life. The prohibition of life like images channelled Islamic Art into a different direction. Artists usually avoided the realistic portrayal of human beings and animals. In paintings they designed highly stylized people, animals and birds. These works have an abstract flat character that makes them more like symbols than lifelike pictures. Even the designers who preferred floral motifs were forced to draw in an abstract style. Artists developed a special type of decoration consisting of winding stems with abstract leaves. The scroll work called arabesque became common in Islamic art in Muslim countries. Geometric patterning of remarkable sophistication developed in Iraq and Iran in 10th century and then spread elsewhere as geometry acquired an almost mystical significance.

CALLIGRAPHY

Another characteristic feature of Islamic art is the wide use of Arabic Script which extensively promoted calligraphy as a field of study. Arabic is written from right to left. It is widely used in the Middle East. Its script was adopted for Persian, Turkish, Urdu and most other languages used by Muslims. The Islamic text from their holy book (Quran) often appears on the walls of religious buildings and on art objects. These writings and various styles are beautifully executed. Sometimes they are combined with floral or geometric designs but only rarely with animal or human figures. Common styles of Arabic calligraphy include *Kufic* and *Neskhi*. *Kufic*, the formal angular style of writing received its name from the city of Kufa in Iraq, where this type of writing developed. Islamic scribes used *Kufic* for copying the Quran from the late 600CE to about 1000CE. In late 11th century a flowing script, *Neskhi*, replaced *Kufic* traditions. The new script was often complemented with a background of arabesque designs.

While *Neskhi* calligraphy was increasingly used for writing the Quran, *Kufic* was reserved for chapter headings. Other, more elaborate writing styles developed in Iran and Turkey and were also used for literature.

DECORATIVE ARTS

Traditionally, people sat or slept on the floors. Hence weaving carpets developed into a household industry where both the men and women contributed equally. Gradually this industry nurtured a rich tradition of fine hand woven carpets which garnered global acclaim. They primarily used wool and silk threads of various colours and tied them into knots forming a specific design or pattern. Some silk rugs have 10,001 knots per sq. inch and are broached with gold and silver. Scholars generally classify the rugs according to their designs, period, and their country of origin. The main areas of rug production in Muslim world were Central Asia, Turkey, Iran and Caucasus region of Russia. The weavers of Persia and India preferred floral designs, scrolls, arabesques, and medallions, occasionally combining them with animal or human figures. Many of these rugs seem to create the atmosphere of a garden. A few of them actually follow the general lay out of a formal Persian garden with trees, flowerbeds, and bodies of water stocked with ducks and fish. Most rugs that are made by the Turkish weavers display abstract geometric designs. In many cases the precise origins of the rugs are unknown or is a subject of disagreement among experts.

TEXTILES

The art of weaving on a handloom reached its apex in Islamic countries. The popular tradition became humdinger after the 700CE. Though initially

used for clothing but later it expanded to decorative elements such as wall hangings, covering, gifts and even tents. Early fabrics had designs based on those used in silk of pre-Islamic Persia. After 1250CE, craft workers used Chinese motifs. In the 15th and 16th century Persian weavers created scenes with figures inspired by contemporary miniature paintings. Other textiles used floral designs and geometric patterns.

METAL WARE

Islamic religious authorities frowned upon the use of precious metals. As a result metal workers achieved beautiful effects by chasing (tracing) bronze or brass objects. They sometimes inlaid these metals with copper, silver or gold to form inscriptions or designs. At times, metal workers decorated them with a black sulphuric alloy called nylon. Artisans working with base metals usually traced or embossed them. Mosul, in Iraq became one of the principal centres of inlaid bronze work. Cairo, Damascus and earlier Persia were also important production centres. Few objects of gold or silver by Islamic artisans have been preserved.

POTTERY AND GLASSWARE

In the period from 800CE to 1300CE pottery received much patronage and Muslim artists developed many new techniques that are used even today. For example, they engraved on earthy coatings under the glaze, or painted one and then added transparent glazes of many colours. These techniques were imitated by Byzantine and Italian ceramists. Islamic potters also painted with metallic pigments on a white or blue blaze to produce so called lustre painting. This difficult technique was practiced in the Middle East and Spain from the 8th century through the 16th century and was later adopted by the potters of renaissance period. Builders used bright tiles decorated with geometric designs on wall surfaces and fountains. Outstanding examples of this tile work decorate the mosque walls, domes and minarets in Isfahan, the ancient capital of Iran. Tile work was ancient Persian Art.

Glassware formed an integral part of Islamic decors in mosque lamps, utensils, vases and windows. Initially Islamic glassware had designs of animal and arabesques. Glass making flourished in Iraq, Persia and Egypt from the 700CE to the 1100CE. Syrian glassmakers became famous in the 12th century for glass bottles, drinking vessels and mosque lamps decorated with coloured enamel. Builders used richly coloured glass windows in many buildings, especially in mosques and private mansions. They filled wooden or stucco frames with bits of coloured glass attached with plaster. The design often consisted of abstract trees and flowers or a geometric pattern. Most of the glass making process has remained unchanged till present day.

CARVING

The intricate skill of artisans found varied expressions in day to day life with carvings on doors, boxes, ceiling, panels, prayer niche and pulpit. Wood workers often carved elaborate insertions into the plain geometrical framework of some designs. Sometimes they made use of ivory. They also carved ivory for valuable objects, especially for round boxes, chests and hunting horn in Spain, Egypt and Southern Italy. Egyptian craft workers often covered the domes and arched doors of mosques with arabesque carvings in stone. Indian art features carved marble window screens. The artisans made these by cutting geometric or realistic motifs out of slabs of marble until it was perforated by tracery.

BOOKS

Although there are examples of early wall paintings, but the better known Islamic fine Art originated as book illustration. Most of the early examples belong to the 12th century. The Persians had rich literary traditions and illustrated many poems such as the epic *Shahnama* (book of kings) by the poet *Firdausi*. They also choose the Quintet by the poet *Nizami* and the prose of *Saadi*. This included *Bostan* (Fruit garden) and the *Gulistan* (rose garden). Another popular subject was a book of fable, *Kalila* and *Dimna* which came from the Indian collection—the *Panchtantra*. Artists also painted miniatures in books representing plants, animals and constellations. Persia developed several styles of painting as the country was conquered by several warring Muslim tribes, including the Turks and Mongols. The greatest period of Persian Art extended from the early 13th century to the late 16th century. The best known Persian painter *Kamala-us-din-Bihzad* illustrated many famous manuscripts with miniatures in the late 14th century. Indian artists came to the forefront in the 15th century and produced a more realistic style of painting which was extensively used to create portraits for safekeeping in personal albums. Painters in Ottoman (Turkey) constricted their expertise in illustrating historical works in a realistic manner. Manuscript of Quran never had decorations showing human figures or animals. The Islamic painters decorated the sacred book with graceful scrolls and floral ornaments around the calligraphically written texts. Islamic books are enclosed in delicately crafted leather bindings, which nearly always have a flap on the lower cover, which can be folded over the pages. Persian craft workers made book bindings with moulded or tooled designs on the outside and cut out patterns on the inside. Some of these date back to 14th century. Many book bindings had a part of their designs imprinted in gold. Experts consider Islamic book binding to be among the most beautiful bindings ever produced.

ISLAMIC CALENDAR

The Islamic calendar or *Hijri* calendar is a lunar calendar consisting of 12 months in a year of 354 or 355 days. It is used to date events in many Muslim countries (concurrently with the Gregorian calendar) and used by Muslims everywhere to determine the proper days on which to observe the annual fast (Ramadan), to attend Hajj, and to celebrate other Islamic holidays and festivals.

The first year of the Islamic calendar began in AD 622, during which the emigration of the Islamic Prophet Muhammad from Mecca to Medina known as the Hijra, occurred. Each numbered year is designated either H for *Hijra* or AH for the Latin *Anno Hegirae* (in the year of the *Hijra*). Muslims typically call their calendar the *Hijri* calendar.

The current Islamic year is 1434 AH. In the Gregorian calendar 1434 A.H. runs from approximately 14th November 2012 (evening) to 4th November 2013 (evening).

Quran

We should make an effort to understand the holy Quran. Most of the people in this world including Muslims have minute or no knowledge of this holy book. Muslims believe it to be the word of Allah. Many a times the scriptures of Quran are misinterpreted and people fail to grasp the context in which it was written. After much study a simple fact comes to surface that Quran is not an intellectual or political document but a call to recognize the Lord and submit to him. It drives one towards purification of heart, mind, body and soul.

In the year 610 A.D. revelations occurred to Prophet Muhammad. It took 23 years to complete. The holy book is a very powerful and extraordinary text divided into chapters of variable lengths. It contains six thousand two hundred and thirty six verses (*Ayat*) divided into 114 chapters (*Surah*).

For Muslims simply believing in God is not enough. The holy book needs to be read with the guiding spirit. They should understand, act upon and also translate the meaning of the book into prayer, righteous intend and behaviour. Without this "Allah" remains just an abstract idea. Prophet Muhammad created and provided varied interpretations of the message, after which countless sages, scholars, jurists and theologians down the centuries have given their own interpretations of the holy book. Keeping in mind the exigency of the time and the words of the Prophet this difference of opinion among Islamic scholars is a blessing as it establishes that Islam requires unity to form but encourages diversity in creative and positive religious expressions.

The Quran describes itself as a book of wisdom and guidance for the pious. With its all inclusive vision, it attempts to build a global community. One cannot be a Muslim without affirming to all the prophets who came before Muhammad. According to Islamic belief and tradition 124,000 Prophets were sent on the earth by Allah. The holy book informs that there has never been a time when God did not send a messenger who spoke the language of the people—"To every people was sent an apostle". The story of *Miraj*—Ascension of Prophet Mohammad to the heavens—has motivated Muslims to follow him and make that ascension themselves. It is a tale of pluralism where prophet journeyed to the heart of the older Semitic tradition, temple on the Mount of Jerusalem. Here, Mohammad led all the previous prophets in prayer and they journeyed on *Alburaq*, the heavenly steed, to meet Allah. On different levels of heaven he encountered Abraham, Jesus, Moses and other prophets who shared their thoughts, insights and concerns for all of creations.

The wonderful story of Omar, the third Caliph, is a testament to the fact that Islam stands for tolerance, appreciations and justice. After conquering the city of Jerusalem in 638 A.D. Omar was escorted by the Greek Patriarch to the main church of the city. It was time for Muslim prayer, so the Patriarch invited Omar to pray right beside the Tomb of Christ. The Caliph declined, walked across and prayed on the Street. Omar explained that if he had prayed inside the church of the Holy Sepulchre, some misguided Muslims attempting to celebrate the first Muslim prayer in Jerusalem, might convert the Church into a Mosque and that should not happen. Later a small mosque was built in this place and it still exists across the road from the church. The Caliph signed an edict allowing Christians to keep their churches in the best part of the town. Omar then asked the way to the great mosque of Prophet Solomon, mentioned in the holy book (Quran). The Christians thought that he was going to burn it down like the Jewish temple and store its ruins as an evidence of Jewish subjugation. To Omar's horror he discovered the Byzantines using it as a garbage dump. He got Muslims to clear the rubble, sprinkle rose water and restore the place of worship. He asked Jews if they wished to return to the city. Some 70 Jew families were invited to settle in Jerusalem and live alongside Muslims. Jerusalem is the third holiest city of Muslims after Mecca and Medina. Today the modern world is torn apart by strife and conflict. Muslims need to reclaim their heritage of compassion, moderation, submission and quest for knowledge. They need to be righteous ambassadors of the message that was revealed in the Holy Quran. After the death of Prophet Muhammad in 632 A.D. a sort of war ensued amongst his successors. Four claimants stepped up: Abu, Omar, Othman and Ali. The first two almost succeeded but the political unrest brought forward shrewd diplomatic manoeuvres and two rival factions emerged. One faction supported Othman and the other favoured Ali. Ali got married to Fatima, the prophet's only daughter. He hoped that being the custodian of Prophet's only surviving bloodline would ensure his candidature as the next caliph, but destiny supported Othman. Ali joined forces with Muwaiya from Syria and the struggle picked up. Khilafat descended to Husain the younger brother of Hassan and the struggle escalated at Karbala in Iraq. Husain lost his life. This game of throne ended in much bloodshed and a distasteful showdown.

These unsavoury incidents are mourned in a collective manner by observing Muharram. Thus, Muharram evolved as an exercise in introspection by solemnity and repentance. On this day the regrettable past is recapitulated and a resolve is made that such incidents will not be allowed again. Muharram is marked by a ten day period of atonement and highlights the commencement of the Muslim calendar on a melancholic note which is in stark contrast to the joyous New Year celebrations of other communities. A huge procession of devotees demonstrates their deep sense of sorrow and atonement by carrying *Tazias* over their shoulders to symbolize the burial of all the hostility, abhorrence, carnage and vindictiveness that was unbecoming and derogatory of Islam. Muharram implies sadness and sorrow and no social functions are held on these days. Only prayers can be offered in mosques in order to signify the much needed atonement for the act of violence. It is an occasion when one can purify one's heart and mind. It is a day when we hope to refrain ourselves from being unjust and exploitative of other people's weakness and shortcomings. It is a day when we should extend our hands of friendship and cooperation. An Islamic scholar of Sufi Sect says that the Quran itself is a book of wisdom and guidance with an all inclusive vision to build a global community.

Islam in the Valley

During the pre-partition days the Muslims respected Kashmiri Pundits wholeheartedly as they had Hindu roots and even after conversion they mostly believed in a true secular state. Pakistan invaded Kashmir in 1947 and occupied a sizable portion from Muzafrabad to Siachen Glacier, which is called Pakistan Occupied Kashmir (POK). After the partition the Pakistani mullahs and rulers introduced a new religion for Kashmiri Muslims. Their propaganda was simple. Ban radio, music, satellite TV, flying kites, playing chess, dining out, drinking wine, educating women; Once a society is curtailed like this, its pent up resentment often perforates through spikes of violence. This violence was directed against the non Muslims through channels of Jihad. Hate speeches against other communities brought public attention to jihad and multiplied the number of suicide bombers willing to attack local markets, places of worship and educational institutions in the name of *Azadi* (freedom). All this was to enforce the Pan-Islamic movement upon the peace loving people of the Kashmir valley.

Wahabism

In Kashmir Valley most of the Sunni Muslims are radicals and practice *Wahabi* Sect of Islam. They believe in violence, endorse jihad and kill innocent people to bring the valley in their fold. Their aim is to destabilize the elected government of India and annex Kashmir. For this they systematically target the Indian defence forces, Hindus, Sikhs and Christians living in the valley. The misguided youth joins these extremists in their Pan Islamic movement and unknowingly buries the morals laid down by Prophet Muhammad and the Quran.

Wahabi sect is very active in the state of Jammu and Kashmir. On every Friday they address the public which assembles for afternoon prayers. They make hollow claims of "Purification" and persuade the otherwise nonviolent Muslim population to break away from local traditions and adopt some rules and regulations that were relevant 14 centuries ago in the time of Prophet Muhammad. They rant against the worship of Tombs and relics of saints describing them as leftovers of ancient Greek and Hindu Mythologies, which is not true. Every fragment of Hindu, Buddhist, Mughal, Sufi and Muslim heritage is an integral part of the composite culture that is the pride of Kashmir and India. Impertinence to this culture is unacceptable and must be avoided at all costs.

Salafism

Salafism is becoming popular in Kashmir. The Saudis provide free literature over the web, mobile phones and satellite television which is laced with the venomous *Salafi* message. In a region already wrecked by internal division and foreign pressure, *Salafism* represents yet another potentially destabilizing force. Orthodox *Salafis* are aggressive expansionist. Such a process if propelled by the *Deoband* seminary may succeed in converting Muslims to blood thirsty monsters that conformist Islam once trained and successfully deployed to forcefully spread its faith all over Central Asia.

In Kashmir the influence of radical elements is so profound that they regularly distribute calendars for Stone pelting, union strikes, civil boycott and violent demonstrations which not only disturb the public life but also send a distrustful message to the world about Islam in general and a doomed Kashmiri society in particular. Their arguments are supported by a lot of people residing in Pakistan or other wealthy Islamic countries, which fund weapon procurements, assist trafficking and sponsor the families of suicide bombers. They consist of people belonging to the educated class who have gone out of their way to claim the supremacy of Islam. An absurd idea of attaining bliss from "Allah" by indiscriminate killing of other faiths is very effectively communicated to the illiterate isolated Kashmiri population. The propagandas of the separatist leaders tread along divisional politics which emotionally blackmail the poor civilian population on the pretext of a holy war wherein they must sacrifice everything to save Islam from India and attain freedom to live a Muslim way of life. However the world has already witnessed this archetypical "Muslim way of Life" thanks to Taliban, Kuwait, Egypt, Iraq, and Pakistan etc. The politicians who control the religious institutions have very little regard for the holy texts. Their prime concern is to establish, consolidate and expand their authoritarian rule. The fact of the matter is that, in any state which sponsors a particular religion or exclusively adheres to some religious doctrine the welfare of its citizens takes a back seat. The driving force for its government becomes an impalpable righteous haven that is described in a book instead of the tangible demands of the society. And inevitably in such a society the worst afflicted are the un-wealthy, the women, the labourers, and any individuals who have the intellect to question archaic bondages. Kashmiri population doesn't realize that a secular democracy like India is the only society where people and their rights are supreme.

Sufism

An almost antithetical sect of Islam—*Sufism*—is also widespread in the valley. *Charare Sherif* or the *Dastgir Sahib Dargaha* (which was burnt down by militants not long ago) is an example of this movement in Islamic culture. Sufism is often described as a very moderate and non radical approach which focuses on spreading Allah's message rather than Islam itself. They have respect for other religions. Sufism has deep roots in Kashmir and shrines like the *Charar-e-Sharif* still attract people from all faiths.

Originally the Kashmiris were Sufi moderate Muslims but after the partition in 1947 they were misguided by Pakistan to lead a life of violence on some manipulated concept of Jihad. Sufism has the moral basis and ethical force to revive tolerance, peace and reconciliation amongst the diverse religious communities which once flourished in the valley. The relevance of promoting a tradition which has preserved the harmonious sentiments of Islam down the ages must be imbibed in institutions of Islamic learning. These institutions have decayed to the level of a fungal contamination and serve as the breeding ground of fundamentalist version of Islam. A significant dimension missing in finding the way forward on the Kashmir issue is the urgency to prescribe and promote the profound syncretism spirits of Kashmiri Sufism or *Kashmiriyat*.

Sufis neither condemn women as an object of desire nor censor modern means of entertainment. For them the distinction between virtue and vice is determined by intent, not by appearance. It is the fusion of spirituality and modernity that creates the unique aesthetic experience that is so appealing to the young and that is what makes them reject extremism.

Islamic Studies

Deoband in Uttar Pradesh is the hub of Islamic studies. Here Muslim scholars from around the world come for *Dini* (religious education). In Islamic world *Deoband* is considered the haven of Islamic learning in India. The *Deobandi Madrasas* are very popular and common in Kashmir Valley. Even non Muslims are joining *Deoband* to study Islam and return to their country as great Islamic Scholars. It was set up in the wake of India's first war of independence in 1857. *Deoband* was also a centre of resistance to British Rule. It was considered as a fortress of Islamic knowledge, a bull work against secular western ideas. Many subjects sidelining the *Deobandi* curriculum—history, geography, mathematics, science—had initially made strides under Islamic scholars. However learning in these disciplines had long since receded as they came to be associated with the West. All the more baffling was the fact that Islamic scriptures never provided any justification for sidelining of the so called secular subjects.

Afghanistan government never allowed institutes of Islamic learning to flourish within its own border. It had wholeheartedly adopted the secular system of educating champions like the West which had previously benefitted only the most progressive nations of the Muslim world— Iran, Turkey. To a great degree, this is the basis of the current schism in Kashmiri society. On one had there is a state that promotes a system of education that teaches sciences, arts, vocational courses without any discrimination of caste or creed while on the other there is a Kashmiri population that largely prefers religious studies, which are manipulated by Pakistan to misguide the unaware masses, in their search for knowledge.

The modern tripartite system of education received a lot of resistance from the *Madrasa* Community. The religious leaders who operated form the *madrasas* also influenced much of the popular vote by condemning the scientific education model with hollow justifications. Post 1947 the predominant destination for Afghan and Kashmiri students of religion switched from India to Pakistan. The focus shifted from *Deoband* to *Lahore, Karachi, Peshawar, Akora, Khatak, and Multan.* These 'politicians of religion' converted the educational institutions into breeding houses of puppet warriors. The students who attended these *madrasas* for spiritual knowledge were brainwashed and recruited in an army. Consequently rest of the world perceived Islam to be a nurturer of radicalism. In the 80s when it suited the vested interests of governments of Pakistan, USA, Afghanistan they promoted Jihadist ideologies among the Kashmiris. These houses of worship were not able to abstain from polarization and the eventual radicalization. The world is still living with the consequences of militancy and radicalism that was not only allowed but strategically fostered to serve as means to an unforeseeable end.

However the *Deobandi* scholars have an entirely different story to narrate, "The havens of Islamic Learning in India are still intact. They have not been politicized or radicalized. Some of these are admirably progressive and shunned the traditional abhorrence of secular subjects. In fact they extensively incorporated western subjects in their curriculum. If the Islamic youth receive a progressive education similar to the *Deoband* in the field of science, art, literature, etc then their energy would be directed towards constructive vocational fields instead of fulfilling someone else's depraved political agenda and in the process pursue the enlightened path as shown by the Quran.

Comparison

If we visit Pakistan we will find that the Wahabi dominated North-West was on the verge of falling into the hands of Taliban. While no such problems surfaced in Sufi dominated province of Sindh. In Southern Pakistan Sufi Islam continues to act as a powerful deterrent against fundamentalist Islam and Wahabi Mullahs. To propagate Wahabi cult Saudis have poured money directly from their oil wells in to the *madrasas* in North West Frontier Province of Punjab, thereby radically changing the religious outlook of an entire region.

So in other words here is an entirely indigenous Islamic resistance movement to counter fundamentalism. Deep rooted in South Asian culture, it is one of the few sources of hope left in the increasingly bleak political landscape of Pakistan. Sufism is integral to the revival of Islamic civilization which is facing grave threats on one hand from politically motivated mullahs and on the other from extremist Islam.

Research And Development(RAND) Corporation came out with a report in 2007 titled "Building moderate Muslim Network", which stressed Sufis to be moderate traditionalists who were open to change, and thus highlighted them as potential allies against violence. Britain is befriending the popular Sufi order and is assisting organizations like the British Muslim Forum and the Sufi Muslim Council—its main dialogue partners in the Muslim Community.

Philip Jenkins Institute for Studies of Religion at Baylor University makes a plea to Sufis—"Convince disaffected young Muslims that the quest for peace is not to be mistaken as surrender to Western oppression. Instead of perceiving peace as a betrayal of Islam they must welcome it as a return to the faith's deepest roots. Let us carry forward the message of *aman* (Peace) *Garibnawazi* (welfare of poor) and *Insaniyat Pasandagi* (love and spirituality) for greater good of human civilization as preached by great Sufi saints."

Sikhism

Sikhism originated in the Punjab province of North India around 14th Century. Adherents of Sikhism are known as Sikhs (Student or disciples) and number over 30 million across the world. It does not come as a surprise that India is the home to majority of the Sikh population. It is the 5th largest organised religion in the world.

Sikhism is a monotheistic religion founded by Guru Nanak. It evolved over a period of two hundred years under the guidance of ten successive Sikh Gurus (the last teaching being the Holy Scripture Guru Granth Sahib). This system of religious philosophy and expression has been traditionally known as the *Gurumat* (literally meaning "Wisdom of the Guru").

Sikhism expects to embody the qualities of a *Sant Sipahi, i.e.* the Saintly-Soldier. One must have control over the internal vices of the mind and be constantly immersed in virtues delineated in the Guru Granth Sahib.

Faith in Waheguru is the principal belief of Sikhism represented by the phrase "Ek Oankar" meaning "One God who prevails in everything". A Sikh is enjoined to engage in social reformation through the pursuit of Justice for all human beings. Sikhism teaches that God is *Akal Purakh* (eternal) and advocates the pursuit of salvation in a social context through the congregational practice of meditation on the name and message of God. The followers of Sikhism are ordained to follow the teachings of the ten Gurus, or enlightened leaders, as well as the Holy Scripture entitled the Guru Granth Sahib Ji. Their holy scripture includes the writings of six out of the original ten Sikh Gurus along with the work of many devotees from diverse social economic and religious backgrounds. Guru Gobind Singh Ji, the tenth guru, conferred the leadership of the Sikh community to the Guru Granth Sahib and the council body called the *Khalsa Panth* (the *Granth* and the *Panth).*

The traditions and teachings of Sikhism are associated with the history, society and culture of Punjab. Most Sikhs live in Punjab (India) although there is a significant Sikh diaspora. Before the partition of India millions of Sikhs lived in what is now called the Pakistani Punjab.

Philosophy

Maya—defined as illusion or unreality—is one of the core deviations from the pursuits of God and salvation. People are distracted from devotion by worldly attractions which give only illusory satisfaction. However Guru Nanak Ji emphasized *Maya* is not a reference to the unreality of the world, but its values. In Sikhism, the influences of ego, anger, greed, attachment and lust (known as the Five Evils) are believed to be particularly pernicious. The fate of people vulnerable to the Five Evils is separation from God, and the situation may be remedied only after intense and relentless *Nasabad or Shabad* (the divine word).

Nasabad emphasizes the totality of revelations. Guru Nanak designated the word Guru as the Voice of God and source of guidance for knowledge and salvation. Salvation can be reached only through rigorous and disciplined devotion to God. Nanak distinctly emphasized the irrelevance of outward observations such as rites, pilgrimages or asceticism. He stressed that devotion must take place through the heart with the spirit and the soul. According to *Gurubani* the supreme purpose of human life is to reconnect with the truth. However, our ego (mind and body) is the biggest disease. With Guru's grace the seeker meditates honestly on the word which leads to the end of ego. Guru is indistinguishable from God. One gets connected with a Guru only with accumulation of sheltered search of truth. Ultimately the seeker realizes that it is the reunion with the truth. Truth is a form of matter which lies within the human body but it is beyond the realm of time and death. The verbal repetition of the name of God or a sacred syllable is an established practice in most of the religious traditions of India, but Guru Nanak's ideal is the total exposure of one's being to the divine name and a total conformation to Dharma or the Divine order. Guru Nanak Ji described *Simran* (chanting) as the process of growing towards and into God gradually in steps. The last of these stages is the *Sach Khand* (The Realm of Truth)—the final Union of the Spirit with God.

Guru Nanak Dev Ji stressed that a Sikh should be *"Karta Purak"* i.e. balance work, worship and charity, and should defend the rights of all the creatures and particularly fellow human beings. They are encouraged to endorse a *"Chardi Kala"* or an optimistically resilient view of life. Sikh teachings also stress the concept of sharing—*"Vand ke Chhako"*—through distribution of food (*Langar*) at Sikh temples or Gurudwaras. Giving charity and working for the good of the community and other (*Seva*). Sikhs believe that all are equal in God's eyes irrespective of their caste, colour or gender. Men and women are equal and share the same rights and women often lead in prayers.

THE SIKH GURUS

The term guru comes from Sanskrit, meaning a teacher, guide or mentor. The traditions of Sikhism were established by ten specific Gurus from 1469 to 1708. Each Guru added to and reinforced the message taught by the previous, resulting in the creation of Sikh Religion. Guru Nanak Dev Ji was the first Guru and appointed a disciple as his successor. Guru Gobind Singh Ji was the final Guru in human form. Before his death, Guru Gobind Singh Ji decreed that the Guru Granth Sahib would be the final and perpetual Guru of the Sikhs.

Guru Angad Dev Ji succeeded Guru Nanak Dev Ji. Later an important phase in the development of Sikhism came with the third successor Guru Amar Das Ji. While Guru Nanak's teachings emphasized the pursuit of salvation, Guru Amar Das began building a cohesive community of followers with initiatives such as sanctioning distinctive ceremonies for birth, marriage and death. Guru Amar Das also established the *Manji* comparable to a system of clerical supervision. Guru Amar Das Ji's successor and son-in-law

Guru Ram Das Ji founded the city of Amritsar. Amritsar, which surrounds the Golden temple or *Hari Mandir Sahib*, is widely regarded as the holiest city of Sikhism. When Guru Ram Das's youngest son Arjun Ji succeeded him, the line of male Gurus from the Sondhi Khatri family was established. All succeeding Gurus were direct descendents of this blood line. Guru Arjun Dev Ji was captured by Mughal authorities who were suspicious of and hostile to the religious order he was developing. His permeation and death inspired his successors to promote a military and political organization of the Sikh communities to defend themselves against the attack of Mughal forces. Guru Hargobind became the sixth Guru of Sikhs. He carried two swords—one for spiritual and the other for temporal reasons (known as *Miri* and *Piri* in Sikhs). Sikhs evolved themselves as a trained fighting force to defend their independence. In 1644, Hari Rai became Guru followed by Har Kishan Ji, the boy Guru in 1661. Hymns composed by these three gurus are included in guru Granth Sahib. Tegh Bahadur Ji became the guru in 1665 and led the Sikhs until 1675. Guru Tegh Bahadur Ji was martyred by the Mughal emperor Aurangzeb. Muslims under the injunction of Aurangzeb were killing Hindus who refused to convert to Islam. Guru Tegh Bahadur Ji sheltered the Hindus and incurred the inhuman torture of Islamic fanatics. He was succeeded by his son Gobind Rai who was just nine years old at the time of his fathers' martyrdom. Gobind Rai Ji further militarised his followers and baptized the *Panj Piare (Blessed Five)*. He formed the *Khalsa Panth* on 30th March 1699 and was henceforth known as Guru Gobind Singh Ji. This was a purely defensive stance against the merciless Muslims.

Further the Sikh Gurus established a mechanism which allowed the Sikh religion to react as a community to changing circumstances. The sixth Guru Hargobind Ji was responsible for creation of the concept at *Akal Takhat* or the "Throne of the Timeless One", which serves as the supreme decision making centre of Sikhism and sits opposite the *Darbar Sahib*. The *Sarbat Khalsa*, a representative portion of the *Khalsa Panth*, historically gathers at the *Akal Takhat* on special festivals such as *Vaisakhi* or *Holla Mohalla*, when there is a need to discuss matters that affect the entire Sikh community. A *Gurumatta* (literally, Guru's intention) is an order passed by the *Sarbat Khalsa* in the presence of the Guru Granth Sahib. A *Gurumatta* may only be passed on a subject that affects the fundamental principles of Sikh religion. It is binding upon all Sikhs. The term *Hukamnama* (literally edict or royal order) is often used interchangeably with the term *Gurmatta*. However, a *Hukumnama* formally refers to a nymph from Guru Granth Sahib which gives order to Sikhs. Shortly before his death, Guru Gobind Singh Ji ordered that the Guru Granth Sahib (the Sikh Holy Scripture), would be the ultimate spiritual authority for the Sikhs and temporal authoring would be vested in the Khalsa, the Sikh nation.

HISTORY OF SIKHISM

Shri Guru Nanak Dev Ji (1469—1539) the founding father of Sikhism was born in the village Rai Bhoj Di Talwandi, now called Nanakana Sahib (in present day Pakistan). His parents were Khatri Hindu of the *Bedi* clan. As a boy, Guru Nanak Dev was fascinated by God and religion. He did not participate in religious affairs and customs, rather meditated alone. His desire to explore the complexities of life eventually led him to leave home and take missionary journeys. In the early years of his life, Guru Nanak gained the attention of Rai Bhullar Bhatti who, along with Guru Nanak's sister Bibi Nanki, was amongst the first few to witness many incidents that established the divine qualities in Guru Nanak. Both of them then encouraged and supported Guru Nanak to study and travel. At the age of thirty, Nanak Ji went missing and was presumed to have drowned after going for one of his morning baths to a local stream called the *Kali Bein*. On the day he arrived he declared, "There is no Hindu and no Muslim" (*na koi Hindu na koi Musalman*). That historic moment onwards Nanak Ji began his lifelong journey of teaching, which was later christened as Sikhism. Although the exact details of his travels are disputed, he is widely acknowledged to have made five major journeys, spanning thousands of miles. The first tour towards Bengal and Assam in the East; the second Southwards to Andhra and Tamil Nadu; the third major journey brought him to Kashmir in the North, and the fourth journey took him to as far as Mecca in the West. Finally he returned to the banks of Ravi River to end his days. In the final years of his life he lived and worked as a farmer in Kartarpur (Punjab).

GROWTH OF SIKHISM

The tenth Guru of Sikhism, Guru Gobind Singh created the *Khalsa Panth* in the year 1699, which means *Akal Purakh De,* the army of God.

The creation of Sikh Empire began when Guru Gobind Singh sent his brave Sikh General Banda Singh Bahadur along with some hundred Sikhs to punish those who had committed atrocities against Pir Buddhu Shah and avenge the murder of his youngest sons. Banda Singh with a large group of Sikhs advanced towards the main Muslim Mughal City of Sirhind and following the instructions of the Guru punished all the culprits. Soon after the invasion of Sirhind, Mughals tried to assassinate the Guru. Jamshed Khan, a Pathan assassin, stabbed the Guru in the left side below the heart while the latter was resting in his chamber after the *Rehras* Prayer. Guru Gobind Singh killed the attacker with his sword, while the assassins' companions were killed by some guards who had rushed in upon hearing the noise. A European surgeon stitched the Guru's wound. However the wound reopened as the guru tugged a strong bow after a few days and caused profuse bleeding.

The death of Guru Gobind Singh reached Banda Singh and Sikhs all over Punjab. After this the Sikh took over many Muslim and Mughal lands, establishing a Sikh Empire. Other existing Muslim Emperors, proclaimed a Jihad or a holy war against Banda Bahadur and the *Khalsa*. However, majority of the Muslim armies and their generals fled in dismay and despair after Wazir Khan's head was stuck up on a spear and lifted high up by a Sikh who took his seat at Sirhind in 1710. A chill crept up the spine of Muslim troops as they beheld the head. Many Muslims embraced Sikhism and joined Khalsa. Banda Singh at this time also married the daughter of a Muslim General. Banda Singh Bahadur's mission played an important role in development of the *Dal Khalsa* and the Sikh *Misls*, which eventually led to a new king Maharaja Ranjeet Singh, who captured Lahore in 1799 and established the Sikh Kingdom of Punjab. The New King and the *Misls* rose to power in a series of sweeping military and diplomatic victories. Increasing the number of Sikhs and spreading the Empire. His vast empire comprised almost 200,000 Square miles of what is now called Afghanistan, Pakistan and Northern India. The empire of the Sikhs was widely feared by many natives, including Afghans, Persians and other Asian neighbours. Even the Pathans who had previously lived there during the Islamic rule attempted to attack the empire with over 20,000 troops. In response Maharaja Ranjeet Singh sent his bravest Sikh Warrior named *Phoola Singh Nihang* (at the age of 65) and a few hundred Sikhs to deal with the invading Pathans and bring them under control. The Sikhs retained control of the Sikh Empire. However, another challenge was yet to come.

In the East, the British Empire took over most of the Princely states including thousands of sq. miles in many South East Asian countries. The British were considered unbeatable, but Maharaja Ranjeet Singh and the Sikhs were gutsy people who could stand toe to toe with British forces. There were huge losses on both sides during the Anglo-Sikh wars and for the first time during the British conquest of India, the British were unable to invade. This resulted in a stalemate and the English were not able to come to terms with this loss. Consequently the Anglo-Sikh wars continued. In 1839, with the death of Maharaja Ranjeet Singh, the responsibility of the enormous empire fell on the shoulders of his son, Maharaja Dalip Singh, (at the age of 11) who was unable to resist the scheming British.

Sikh Plot

From the peaceful age of Guru Nanak Dev Ji the Sikhs had significantly transformed. Even though the core spiritual philosophy was never affected, the followers now began to develop a political identity. Conflict with the Mughals escalated during the tenure of Guru Teg Bahadur and Guru Gobind Singh Ji. The latter founded the Khalsa in 1699. The Khalsa is a disciplined community that continues its spiritual purpose and goals with political and military duties.

A former ascetic was charged by Guru Gobind Singh Ji with the duty of punishing those who had persecuted the innocent people of Punjab. After the Guru, Banda Singh Bahadur became the commander-in-chief of the Khalsa and was responsible for several attacks on the Mughal Empire. He was executed by the emperor Farukh Siyar after he refused to adopt Islam and endorse its violent means.

The Sikh nation's embracement of military and political agenda made it a considerable regional force in medieval India and it continued to evolve after the demise of Gurus. After the death of Baba Banda Singh Bahadur, Sikh confederacy formed bands of Sikh warriors known as *Misls*. With the decline of the Mughal Empire, a Sikh capital was established in Lahore that yielded control all the way to the Khyber Pass, along the Chinese border. The further development of the tradition and peculiarities lasted for another century or two and finally culminated in the reign of Maharaja Ranjeet singh. A common religious and social identity was established that the term Sikhism describes.

After the death of Maharaja Ranjeet Singh, the Sikh empire fell into disorder and was eventually annexed by the United Kingdom after the hard fought Anglo-Sikh Wars. This brought Punjab under the British Raj. Sikhs formed the Shiromani Gurudwara Prabandhak Committee and the *Shiromani Akali Dal* to preserve Sikhs religious and political rights respectively. A quarter of a century later, with the partition of India in 1947, thousands of Sikhs were killed in violence and millions were forced to leave their ancestral homes in West Punjab.

Sikhs faced initial opposition from the Government in forming a linguistic state while other states in India were afforded. The Akali Dal started a non-violent movement for Sikh and Punjabi rights. Jarnail Singh Bhindrawale emerged as a leader of Damdami Taksal in 1977 and promoted a militant solution to the problem. In June 1984, Indian Prime Minister Indira Gandhi ordered the Indian army to launch operation Blue Star to remove Bhideranwale and his followers from the Darbar sahib. Bhinderanwale and his accompanying followers were killed during the army operation. In October, Indira Gandhi was assassinated by five of her Sikh body guards. This incident was followed by the 1984 anti Sikh riots and led to Hindu Sikh conflicts in Punjab as a reaction to operation Blue Star and the assassination.

In 1984 riots three thousand Sikhs were killed. Till date justice has not been delivered to the member of this proud community who have time and again sacrificed everything in the service of India. The cases are still pending in the court. In 1947 Sikhs sacrificed their Lahore seat on the altar of partition and accepted India as their country. In Jammu and Kashmir the first army contingent comprised of Sikhs who were sent to expel the Pakistan sponsored Pashtu invaders from the Kashmir valley. Through this book we appeal to the lethargic judiciary and implore the secular citizens of India to support Sikhs in their pursuit for justice.

SCRIPTURE

There is one primary source of spiritual guidance for the Sikhs: the Guru Granth Sahib. The Guru Granth Sahib may also be referred to as the Adi Granth, which is actually the version of the scripture created by Guru Arjan Dev Ji in 1604. The Guru Granth Sahib in its present form was compiled by Guru Gobind Singh Ji. There are other sources of scriptures such as the

Dasam and the so-called *Janamsakhis.* These however, have been the subject of controversial debate amongst the Sikh community.

ADI GRANTH

The Adi Granth was compiled primarily by Bhai Gurudas under the supervision of Guru Arjun Dev Ji. It is written in the Gurumukhi script. The Gurumukhi script, which is a derivative of the Landa Script used in Punjab at that time, was standardized by Guru Angad Dev—the second Guru of Sikhs—for the use of Sikh Scriptures. Some major influences have also been accredited to the Sarada and Devnagri scripts. An administrative scripture was created to protect the integrity of hymns and teachings of the Sikh Gurus and fifteen Bhagats. The 15 Bhagats are—Namdev, Ravidas, Jaidev, Tirlochan, Beni, Ramanand, Sahu, Dhanna, Sadhna, Pipa, Sur, Bhikan, Parmanand, Farid, and Kabir.

The scripture held sacred by the Sikhs was compiled by Guru Arjun Dev Ji at the end of the sixteenth century. It includes the writings of Guru Nanak and thereof the nine Gurus who succeeded him along with the saints who lived between the twelfth and the seventeenth centuries. The common thread throughout the *Adi Granth* is the importance of the Divine word or the Name of the God and the need for a perfect master to pursue the spiritual path. *Adi Granth* contains 407 hymns of Guru Amardas Ji. Guru Amardas Ji the third Sikh Guru who wholeheartedly imbibed "Guru-minded" devotion succeeded his Guru in 1552. At that time, Guru Arjun dev Ji submitted to prevent undue influence from followers of Prithi Chand, the Guru's other older brother and rival. The third version of the Guru Granth Sahib was compiled by Guru Gobind Singh in 1678. It consists of the original *Adi Granth* appended with Guru Teg Bahadur's hymns. The Guru Granth Sahib is considered the eleventh and final spiritual authority of the Sikhs. All Sikhs are commanded to take the Granth as their Guru along the spiritual path of self realization. It contains compositions by the first nine Gurus and one Salok (couplet) from Guru Gobind Singh. It also contains the traditions and teachings of Sants (Saints) such as Kabir, Namdev, Ravidas and Shekh Farid.

The bulk of the scripture is classified into "*Raggs*" with each *ragg* subdivided according to length and author. There are 31 main *raggs* within Guru Granth Sahib. In addition to the raggs there are clear references to the folk music in *Sant Bhasa*—a language related to both Punjabi and Hindi which was used extensively across medieval northern India by proponents of popular devotional religion. As per the name *Gurumukhi* it is not only a script but it is the language which comes out of guru's mouth. By using this definition, all words in Guru Granth Sahib constitute *Gurubani*, thus completing Gurumukhi language, which consists of two components—spoken Gurumukhi words in the form of *Gurbani* which originated from different languages and Gurumukhi script. The text further comprises of over 5000 *Sabads* or hymns, which are poetically constructed and set to classical form of music renditions. The Guru Granth Sahib begins with the Mulmantra, an iconic verse created by Guru Nanak Dev Ji.

"Ek Oankara Sati amu Karata Purakhu Nirabhav Niravairu Akala Murati Ajuni Saibham Gur Prasad."

Meaning: There is but one god. Truth is his name. Creative his personality and immortal his form, he is without fear, sans enmity. Unborn and self illumined. By the Guru's grace he is obtained.

"Guru hai Bani Surat"—Word is the Guru and Guru is the word.

All text within the Granth is known as *Gurbani*. The *Shabad* is the Guru, upon whom one lovingly focuses consciousness. Therefore as evident from the message of the first guru, Guru Nanak Dev Ji, *Shabad* (or word) was always the Guru (the enlightened).

However, as Sikhism evolved the dual stand of *Miri* and *Piri*, the Guru in Sikhism became a combination of a teacher and leader. Therefore the lineage from Guru Nanak to Guru Gobind Singh was of the teacher-leader amalgam. Eventually the temporal authority was passed into the *Khalsa* and spiritual authority, which always was with, passed to the *Adi Granth*. Therefore, Guru Granth Sahib is the 11th body in the Khalsa as the Guru or teacher-cum-leader of the Sikhs till eternity.

DASAM GRANTH

The *Dasam Granth* is a scripture of Sikhs which contains texts attributed to the Tenth Guru. The *Dasam Granth*, no matter how significant in the history of Sikhism, does not have the same authority as the *Adi Granth*.

Some compositions of *Dasam Granth* like *Jap Ji Sahib, Amrit Savaiye* and *Benti Chaupai* are part of the daily prayers or lessons (*Nitnem*) of Sikhs.

JANAMSAKIS

The *Janamsakis* are birth stories of Nanak. Although not scripture in the strictest sense, they provide an interesting look at Nanak's life and the early start of Sikhism. They are often contradictory and sometimes unreliable.

OBSERVANCES

Observant Sikhs adhere to longstanding practices and traditions to strengthen and express their faith. The daily recitation of specific passages from the Guru Granth Sahib, especially the *Jap Ji* hymns (*Jap Ji* means chant) are recommended immediately after rising and bathing. Family customs include both teaching passages from the scriptures and attending the communal recitals in places of worship called *Gurudwara* (meaning the doorways to God).

There are many Gurudwaras prominently constructed and maintained across India, as well as in almost every nation where Sikhs reside. Gurudwaras are open to all, regardless of religion, background, caste or race.

DISPUTES

Incredible India is the most diverse nation in the world. Kashmir exemplified this diversity and abundance. There is no denying the fact that even today this state of India (Jammu and Kashmir) is considered a reflection of Heaven on Earth. Though Ladakh in the northernmost reaches of the state is merely a cold desert with little vegetation and no rain, it still enjoyed economic prominence as a vital trade route between Central Asia and the Indian main land in the past. A cursory glance over the town of Leh and the Nubra valley in some standard text book of Geography will surely clarify any doubts regarding this fact.

The western part of the state of Jammu and Kashmir is full of glacial wealth and three great Indian rivers—the Indus, the Ganges and the Brahmaputra—originate from the glaciers of this region. If we come to the modern political importance, the *Siachen* glacier occupies the highest strategic position in the world today. With an expanse of 700 km, it is the world's second longest Himalayan Glacier. It occupies the Karakoram Range that borders Ladakh (India) Gilgit (POK) and Aksai Chin area (ceded to China by Pakistan in 1963). The temperature on this glacier dips to -50°C.

PARTITION

The Pakistan Declaration of 1933 had envisioned the princely state of Jammu and Kashmir as one of the five Northern units of India that were to form the new nation of Pakistan on the basis of its Muslim majority. Maharaja Hari Singh was the reigning monarch of the princely state of Jammu and Kashmir in 1947. With the end of foreign rule in India came the inevitable partition of the British Indian Empire into two countries the Sovereign Socialist Secular Democratic Republic of India and the Islamic dominion of Pakistan. It was anticipated that the Maharaja would accede to Pakistan as 77% of the local population was Muslim but the Maharaja hesitated. So Pakistan launched a guerrilla onslaught meant to frighten its ruler into submission. Instead the Maharaja appealed to Lord Mountbatten, the last Governor General of colonized India, who agreed to help upon the condition that Jammu and Kashmir would accede to India. The Indian soldiers came to the rescue of Kashmiri citizens. The infiltrators from across the border were chased out of Kashmir. They only occupied some remote stretches beyond the mountain passes. The United Nation was then invited to mediate the quarrel.

Following negotiations and agreements among the parties, the Security Council adopted resolution 47 (1948) on 21st April 1948 which promised a free and fair plebiscite under the supervision of the United Nations to enable the people of Jammu and Kashmir to determine whether they wish to join Pakistan or India. The Council increased the size of the commission established by United Nations Security Council Resolution 39. Now a five member committee instructed the Commission to go to the subcontinent and help the governments of India and Pakistan in restoring the peace and order in the region. They laid the foundation for a plebiscite to decide the fate of Kashmir. One of the earliest applications of Chapter VI of the United Nations Charter was on the Kashmir dispute. Resolutions passed under Chapter VI of UN charter are considered non binding and have no mandatory enforceability as opposed to the resolutions passed under chapter VII.

The resolution recommended that in order to ensure the impartiality of the plebiscite Pakistan must withdraw all tribesmen and nationals who entered the region for the purpose of fighting and that India leave only the minimum number of troops needed to keep civil order. The Commission was also to send as many observers into the region as it deemed necessary to ensure the provisions of the resolution were enacted fairly. Pakistan ignored the UN mandate and continued fighting and strengthening its hold on the illegally occupied portions of Kashmir. Subsequently India refused to implement the plebiscite claiming the withdrawal of Pakistan forces was a prerequisite as per UN resolution 47. The Kashmir issue was taken to the UN by India in January, 1948 and remained active in the UN Security Council till the late fifties.

The Indian viewpoint is succinctly summarized by Ministry of External affairs, Government of India as follows:—

- India holds that—the Instrument of Accession of the State of Jammu and Kashmir to the Union of India signed by Maharaja Hari Singh (erstwhile ruler of the State) on 25th October 1947 and executed on 27th October 1947 between the ruler of Kashmir and the Governor General of India—was a legal act, completely valid in terms of the Government of India Act (1935), Indian Independence Act (1947) and international law and was total and irrevocable. There is no evidence of any deceit practiced by India on Kashmir.
- The constituent assembly of Jammu and Kashmir had unanimously ratified the Maharaja's Instrument of Accession to India and had adopted a constitution for the state that called for a perpetual merger of Jammu and Kashmir with the Union of India. India claims that the constituent assembly was a representative one, and that its views were those of the Kashmiri people.
- India does not accept the two-nation theory that forms the basis of Pakistan's claim and considers that Kashmir, despite being a Muslim-majority state, is an integral part of secular India.
- The state of Jammu and Kashmir was provided significant autonomy in Article 370 of the Constitution of India.

Since 1947 Pakistan and India remained at loggerheads for over a decade because of the Kashmir conflict. They were looking for opportunities to oust the other not only territorially but also in global politics and trade. The first major confrontation occurred in 1965. Pakistani troops began patrolling the territory controlled by India in January 1965, which was followed by attacks by both countries on each other's posts on 8 April 1965. Initially involving the border police but soon inviting the escalated scale and attention of the armed forces. In June 1965, British Prime Minister Harold Wilson successfully persuaded both countries to end hostilities and set up a tribunal to resolve the disputed Rann of Kutchh.

After its success in the Rann of Kutch, Pakistan, under the leadership of General Ayub Khan, planned a quick military campaign in the disputed territory of Kashmir. He expected the Indian army to be an easy target after suffering heavy losses to China in the Sino-Indian war of 1962. Operation Gibraltar was the brain child of General Ayub Khan. The delusional General believed that the population of Kashmir was generally discontent with the elected Government, so he attempted to ignite an insurgent movement by means of a covert infiltration operation. On 5th August 1965 thirty thousand Pakistani soldiers crossed the Line of Control dressed as Kashmiri locals. Indian forces, tipped off by the locals, crossed the cease fire line on 15th August. A brief but furious war began. What was supposed to be a clandestine Pakistani instigation across the Kashmiri cease fire line, ended up being a parade of Pakistan's vulnerability.

Although the borders remained unchanged but according to the Library of Congress Country Studies conducted by the Federal Research Division of the United States—

"The war was militarily inconclusive. Each side held prisoners and some territory belonging to the other. Losses were relatively heavy on the Pakistani side, twenty aircraft, 200 tanks, and 3,800 troops. Pakistan's army had been able to withstand Indian pressure, but a continuation of the fighting would only have led to further losses and ultimate defeat for Pakistan."

TIME magazine reported that India held 690 mi^2 of Pakistan territory while Pakistan held 250 mi^2 of Indian Territory in Kashmir and Rajasthan. Additionally, Pakistan had lost almost half its armour temporarily. Severely mauled by the larger Indian armed forces, Pakistan could continue the fight only by teaming up with Red China and turning its back on the U.N.

Devin T. Hagerty wrote in his book *South Asia in world politics*—

"The Indian forces outfought their Pakistani counterparts and halted their attack on the outskirts of Lahore, Pakistan's second largest city. By the time United Nations intervened on September 22, Pakistan had suffered a clear defeat."

Dennis Kux's *India and the United States estranged democracies* also provides a summary of the war-

"Although both sides lost heavily in men and material, and neither gained a decisive military advantage, India had the better of the war. New Delhi achieved its basic goal of thwarting Pakistan's attempt to seize Kashmir by force. Pakistan gained nothing from a conflict which it had instigated."

The next direct military conflict between India and Pakistan occurred in 1971. International sources consider the beginning of the war to have been Operation Gengiz Khan, when Pakistan launched pre-emptive air strikes on 11 Indian airbases on December 3, 1971. The war lasted just 13 days.

Water Dispute

Another reason for the dispute over Kashmir is water. Kashmir has several glaciers which are the source of many rivers. One of the most fertile river basins of the world is the Indus River basin. The river tributaries are the Jhelum and Chenab rivers, which primarily flow into Pakistan while other branches namely the Ravi, Beas, and Sutlej irrigate northern India. Historians confirm that the earliest civilizations of Harappa and Mohenjodaro flourished along the Indus River Basin and its tributaries. The architectural remains of these cities reveal a cosmopolitan lifestyle with all the modern day amenities and utilities of a sea port, public bath, granary, town hall, sewer system etc. However we know very little about their culture because their script is yet to be deciphered.

While arbitrating the conflict in 1947, Sir Cyril Radcliffe decided to demarcate the territories instead of handing over the complete control of water resources to either India or Pakistan as it was a main economic resource for both areas. The Line of Control (LoC) was recognised as an international border establishing that India would have control over the upper riparian and Pakistan over the lower riparian of Indus and its tributaries. Pakistan alone has about 60 per cent of the catchment area while India, Afghanistan and Tibet share the rest. The Indus is a river system that sustains communities in both countries India and Pakistan. They both have extensively dammed the Indus River for irrigation of their crops and hydro-electricity systems. Thus the Kashmir conflict and the Indus River dispute are closely related and the fight over the water remains as one of the main problems when establishing good relationships between the two countries. In the early days of independence, the fact that India was able to shut off the *Central Bari Doab Canals* at the time of the sowing season, caused significant damage to Pakistan's crops. Nevertheless, military and political clashes over Kashmir in the early years of independence appear to be more about ideology and sovereignty, rather than sharing water resources. But the minister of Pakistan stated the opposite.

The Indus Waters Treaty was signed by both countries in September 1960, giving exclusive rights over the three western rivers of the Indus river system (Jhelum, Chenab and Indus) to Pakistan, and over the three eastern rivers (Sutlej, Ravi and Beas) to India. As India and Pakistan cooperated and neither one of them tried to break the regulations established, they see no more problems with this issue.

The Second War

In the 1970 Pakistani election, the East Pakistani *Awami* League won 167 of 169 seats in East Pakistan and hence secured a simple majority in the 313 seat lower house of Parliament. *Awami* League leader *Sheikh Mujibur Rahman* claimed the right to form the government. The leader of the Pakistan People's Party, *Zulfikar Ali Bhutto*, refused to yield the premiership of Pakistan to *Mujibur*. President *Yahya Khan* called the military, dominated by West Pakistanis, to suppress the public dissent. The Pakistan army conducted a widespread genocide against the Bengali population of East Pakistan, especially the minority Bengali Hindus. Approximately 10 million people fled East Pakistan and took refuge in the neighbouring Indian states. The governments of West Bengal, Bihar, Assam, Meghalaya and Tripura established refugee camps along the border. The resulting flood of impoverished East Pakistani refugees placed an intolerable strain on India's already overburdened economy.

General Tikka Khan earned the nickname of 'Butcher of Bengal' due to the widespread atrocities he committed. General Niazi commenting on his actions noted, "On the night between 25/26 March 1971, General Tikka struck. A Peaceful night was turned into a time of wailing, crying and burning. General Tikka let loose everything at his disposal, as if raiding an enemy; not dealing with his own misguided and misled people. The military action was a display of stark cruelty more merciless than the massacres at Bukhara and Baghdad by Genghis Khan and *Halaku Khan* . . . General Tikka . . . resorted to the killing of civilians. His orders to his troops were: "*I want the land not the people* . . ." Major General Farman had written in his table diary, "*Green land of East Pakistan will be painted red*". It was painted red by Bengali blood."

The Indian government repeatedly appealed to the international community but failed to elicit any response. Apparently no one in the

West cared about the blood of the "Brown" man. Prime Minister Indira Gandhi on 27 March 1971 expressed full support of her government for the independence struggle of the people of East Pakistan. It was obvious that in order to end the genocide an armed action against Pakistan was more effective than to simply give refuge to those who made it across to refugee camps. Exiled East Pakistan army officers and members of the Indian Intelligence immediately started using these camps for recruitment and training of Mukti Bahini Guerrillas.

The mood in West Pakistan had also turned increasingly jingoistic and militaristic against East Pakistan and India. Throughout September, thousands of people led by West Pakistani politicians marched in Lahore and across West Pakistan, calling for Pakistan to "Crush India". India responded by starting a massive build up of Indian forces on the border with East Pakistan. By November, war seemed inevitable. The Indian military waited until December, when the drier ground would make for easier operations and Himalayan passes would be closed by snow, preventing any Chinese intervention. On 23 November, Yahya Khan declared a state of emergency in all of Pakistan and told his people to get ready for the inevitable. Prime Minister Indira Gandhi ordered the immediate mobilisation of troops and launched a full scale war. This involved Indian forces in a massive coordinated air, sea, and land assault. Indian Air Force started flying sorties against Pakistan from midnight. The main Indian objective on the western front was to prevent Pakistan from entering Indian soil. There was no Indian intention of conducting any major offensive into West Pakistan.

During the course of the war, Indian and Pakistani forces clashed on the eastern and western fronts. The war effectively came to an end after the Eastern Command of the Pakistani Armed Forces signed the Instrument of Surrender, on 16 December 1971 in Dhaka. Thus India laid the foundation of the new sovereign nation of Bangladesh. The Indian Army captured more than 90,000 Prisoners of War who served the Pakistan Government and were responsible for an estimated 2.5 million civilian deaths and up to four hundred thousand rapes in Bangladesh especially the minority Bengali Hindus. As a result of the conflict, a further eight to ten million people fled the country at the time to seek refuge in India.

The war stripped Pakistan of more than half of its population and nearly one-third of its army in captivity. It clearly established India's military dominance in the subcontinent. In announcing the Pakistani surrender, Prime Minister Indira Gandhi declared in the Indian Parliament—"*Dhaka is now the free capital of a free country. We hail the people of Bangladesh in their hour of triumph. All nations who value the human spirit will recognize it as a significant milestone in man's quest for liberty.*"

In 1972 the Simla agreement was signed between India and Pakistan. The treaty ensured that Pakistan recognised the independence of Bangladesh in exchange for the return of the Pakistani prisoners of war. India treated all the POWs in strict accordance with the Geneva Convention rules established in 1925. It released more than 90,000 Pakistani PoWs in five months. As a gesture of goodwill nearly 200 soldiers who were sought for war crimes by Bengalis were also pardoned by India. The accord also gave back more than 13,000 km² of land that Indian troops had seized in West Pakistan during the war, though India retained a few strategic areas. India's generosity was important to sustain the fragile democracy in Pakistan. The cease fire in Jammu and Kashmir after the war of 1971 established the de facto Line of control (LoC) between India and Pakistan. This LoC is 740 kilometres long and is imprecise beyond the northernmost point of Siachin glacier. Beyond this line, according to the Simla Agreement (1972), the boundary shall proceed further north of the glacier. According to the treaty signed, the cease fire line runs north towards the glacier while Pakistan disputes it saying that the line curves North-East towards the Karakoram pass. Obviously Siachen is of utmost strategic significance from India's point of view especially when China has built the Karokoram Highway through Aksai Chin. India has been incessantly rejecting Pakistan's claim because the occupation of this glacier is essential to thwart a two-prong threat from China and Pakistan. Pakistan revealed its evil intentions in 1984 when India successfully defended the Siachin glacier and this also reaffirmed India's concern about the strategic importance of this glacier.

In 1990 after nearly four decades, the United Nations changed its position and is no longer urging a plebiscite in Kashmir, saying the dispute should be settled through direct negotiations between India and Pakistan.

Fishing in Troubled Waters

The issue of fish worker arrests by the Maritime Security Agency (MSA) of Pakistan and Indian Coastal Guards has seen a persistent debate since the two countries achieved their independence in 1947. But only in the late 1990's the intensity or the number of people arrested became alarmingly high.

Sir Creek Dispute

Sir Creek is a 96 km (60 miles) marshy wasteland between India and Pakistan in the Rann of Kutch. Some experts believe that the region is also rich in oil and gas, which are to be found below the sea-bed. Sir Creek separates the Indian state of Gujarat from Pakistan's Sindh province. The dispute primarily involves demarcation of the India-Pakistan border along the Sir Creek and its adjoining maritime borders from the mouth of the Creek towards the Arabian Sea. Once these boundaries are defined, it would help in determination of the respective Exclusive Economic Zone (EEZ).

It is believed that Sir Creek issue began in 1908, between the ruler of Sindh and the Rao of Kutch over a pile of firewood lying on the banks of the Kori Creek, situated east of Sir Creek, which separated the two principalities. The Bombay Government, under British rule, took up the matter and brokered an agreement between the two principalities in 1913. The result was in the form of a map numbered B-44, which was subsequently implemented as map number B-74 in 1924. Both the maps are now referred to as the "1914 Resolution Maps".

The dispute resurfaced in July 1948, after partition. Pakistan raised the issue of Sindh / Kutch border. It remained dormant for a couple of years but erupted again in 1965 leading to a full-fledged war.

India states that the Sir Creek boundary lies in the middle of the channel, while Pakistan contends that it is situated on the East bank. India cites the Thalwag doctrine in its support, which states that the river boundaries between the two countries will run through mid-channel. Pakistan argues that the doctrine is not applicable in this case since it applies to bodies of water that are navigable. India counteracts by mentioning the fact that Sir Creek remains navigable in high tide and further points out that fishing

194

trawlers use it to go to sea. Pakistan challenges this claim because the creek remains dry most of the year, and hence non navigable. This litigious issue has been tangled in polemics.

After the war of 1965, the British Prime Minister Harold Wilson persuaded India and Pakistan to end hostilities and set up a tribunal to resolve the dispute. Accordingly, an arbitration panel was set up, which published its report on February 19, 1968, and redefined the boundary between Kutch and Sindh. It asked both the governments to erect pillars along the newly defined boundary, but neither of the two countries was too enthusiastic about this and, thus the demarcation remains incomplete till date.

Plight of the Fishermen

Gujarat has a huge coastline of 1600 kilometres and thousands of fishermen and their families are dependent on fishing, many of which are from Kharva and Koli traditional fishing communities. The fishermen from Saurashtra go to mid-sea to catch fish as the areas adjacent to the beach neither yield a quality catch nor a high quantity to make up for it. This raises the concerns about high levels of pollution along the coast line, not just in India but also in Pakistan. Thermal power plants or nuclear power plants on the coastline cause the worst kind of environmental pollution. They pump hot and contaminated water, and in the case of nuclear power plants, they dump toxic waste that leads to radiations in the sea. Chemical industries add to the devastation immensely. Over the years, fishermen have been forced to go far deeper into the sea, due to depletion of marine resources on the Gujarat Coast.

It is also important to note that each trawler costs between 30-35 Lakh Indian rupees. When trawlers are confiscated, it gets very difficult for the owners to repay the loans taken for the trawlers. As a norm, banks do not give loans for buying trawlers since it is officially counted in the "risky investment" category. The fishermen take loans from private money lenders at high interest rates and when the boat is confiscated or capsized many of them succumb to pressure of repayment and commit suicide.

Hence, Sir Creek is the scene of numerous arrests of Indian fishermen who have unwittingly strayed either into the disputed areas or into territorial waters of Pakistan.

Ray of Hope

Several groups of activists worked towards primarily reducing the number of fishermen in Pakistani and Indian jails. As a result, the figure in 2012 reached a historic low of less than a hundred fishermen belonging to the other side in their respective jails. Unfortunately, it has been observed that the heightened tension at the Line of Control (LoC) between the two countries (at the beginning of 2013) again led to an increase in the number of arrests of fishermen.

However the efforts made for the release of fishermen have been recognized at certain levels and Pakistan's former Interior Minister Rehman Malik issued an order early this year according to which all Indian fishermen in Pakistan jails are to be released. These kinds of achievements have come into being due to systematic efforts over the past many years. Some of the major steps taken include the creation of a mechanism for information and data sharing through local fish worker organizations. A constant effort to persuade the media and journalist fraternity to adequately cover the troubled fishing communities has reaped benefits in the form of a Government channel to communicate information and data. Several Public Interest Litigations (PILs) in supreme courts of both countries sufficiently addressed the judiciary and also led to the formation of a joint judicial mechanism at the civil society level involving former judges and legal luminaries from both countries. Visiting fish workers in prison and organizing visits by eminent personalities including former judges to the concerned coastal villages also raised the level of awareness amongst the Fish workers community.

Amicable Solution

A Maritime Economic Cooperation Agreement aimed at shared marine resources and implementation of "Release at Sea" policy, is the way ahead, as many commentators have pointed out. It also requires political will from the leadership of India and Pakistan, including permanent resolution of the Sir Creek issue.

There has been considerable progress since 2006-2007 and joint surveys have begun. The Indian Navy conducted a survey to check where the creek is present by checking the pillars. The two countries also decided to make maps separately and then exchange them. It was noticed that most part of the area has the same boundaries for both countries and the differences are on merely fifty nautical miles.

Industries are not in this area and so it could be easily declared a mutual fishing zone and no lines need to be demarcated. Cooperative solutions as practiced elsewhere can be adopted. Demands have been made that 25 nautical miles towards Pakistan and the same towards India can be declared common fishing ground or a "free fishing zone" and "No arrest zone", but this has not been considered yet. Fishermen from both the countries are demanding joint fishing licenses and identity cards for joint fishing to begin, since fish from both the countries do not adhere to manmade borders.

KARGIL CONFLICT

The Indian National Highway NH 1D connects Srinagar to Leh. It is one of the only two roadways connecting Ladakh to the rest of the country. Kargil is situated some 200 km from Srinagar along this highway. Thus any entity controlling the 160 km long stretch of ridges in Kargil is in possession of this vital military life line. As mentioned above the 1972 Simla agreement, binding on both India and Pakistan, clearly marked the new boundaries between the two countries however they were still trying to create as many outposts as possible in the upper reaches of Siachin glacier. India with its operation Meghadoot had been largely successful in gaining control of the glacier due to its far superior arsenal and tactically proficient officers. Kargil on the other hand, given the terrain surrounding it, was an easier target. So the Pakistanis devised another malevolent plan.

As a token of mutual understanding and a sign of civilized society the armed forces on either side of the border abandon their forward posts and reduce patrolling in the infiltration prone areas during the cold winter months, when the temperatures can even dip to—40°C. Also it is an unsaid truce that neither India nor Pakistan will take advantage of this fact. When weather conditions become less severe they reoccupy the outposts and resume patrolling.

The deceitful Pakistani Prime Minister Nawaz Sharif invited Indian Prime Minister A.B. Vajpayee to sign the Lahore declaration in February 1999.

This declaration was to ensure that India and Pakistan resolve the Kashmir conflict through peaceful political dialogue and was only one of the large number of attempts made by India to reconcile with their neighbours. Unexpectedly during the same month Pakistani army began to reoccupy the posts it had abandoned and also sent forces to occupy some posts on the Indian side of the LOC in the Kargil region. Troops from the elite Special Services Group as well as four to seven battalions of Northern Light Infantry covertly seized the unoccupied military positions which offered tactically vital features and well prepared defensive posts atop the peaks. Pakistan knew that once they acquire these posts, defending them from the high ground would be a cake walk. But they underestimated the resolution of the Indian armed forces which retaliated with far higher ratios of attackers to defenders and braved the high altitude and freezing temperatures. Pakistani infiltrated the heights of the Mushkoh Valley, the Marpo La ridgeline in Dras, Kaksar near Kargil, the Batalik sector east of the Indus River, the heights above of the Chorbatla sector where the LoC turns north and in the Turtok sector south of the Siachin area.

Indian army was unaware of these infiltrations but they were quick to act upon the information passed on by the local shepherds. Initially they misjudged the infiltrators as Islamic extremist but after a few encounters and based on the scale of infiltration it was clear that Pakistan had launched a full-fledged invasion yet again. The top priorities for Indian forces were the forward posts overlooking National Highway 1D which formed the arterial road for army supplies. Due to the mountainous terrain and continuous shelling by Pakistan the highway had been reduced to a narrow, steep shooting corridor. In many vital points, neither artillery nor air power could dislodge the outposts manned by the Pakistani soldiers, who were out of visible range. The Indian Army mounted some direct frontal ground assaults which were slow and took a heavy toll given the steep ascent that had to be made on peaks as high as 18,000 feet (5,500 m). Since any daylight attack would be suicidal, all the advances had to be made under the cover of darkness, escalating the risk of freezing as the temperatures were often as low as -15 °C. Two months into the conflict, Indian troops had slowly retaken most of the ridges that were encroached by the infiltrators.

As the Indian counterattacks picked up momentum, Pakistani Prime Minister Nawaz Sharif flew to meet the U.S. President Bill Clinton on July 4 to obtain support from the United States. However Clinton rebuked Sharif, and asked him to rein in the militants and withdraw Pakistani soldiers from Indian Territory. Clinton would later reveal in his autobiography that "Sharif's moves were perplexing" since the Indian Prime Minister had travelled to Lahore to promote bilateral talks aimed at resolving the Kashmir problem and "by crossing the Line of Control, Pakistan had wrecked the bilateral talks." The Indian army launched its final attacks in the last week of July. The fighting ceased on July 26. By the end of the war, India had resumed control of all territory south and east of the Line of Control, as was established in July 1972 as per the Simla Agreement.

The global community condemned Pakistan for shattering another peace accord. Of course the primary diplomatic stance of Pakistani Government denied any links with the war and even went on to blame the local Kashmiris and termed this battle as a "Kashmiri freedom fight". Veteran analysts argued that the battle was fought at heights where only seasoned troops could survive, so poorly equipped "freedom fighters" would neither have the ability nor the wherewithal to seize land and defend it. Moreover, while the army had initially denied the involvement of its troops in the intrusion, two soldiers were awarded the *Nishan-E-Haider* (Pakistan's highest military honour). Another 90 soldiers were also given gallantry awards, most of them posthumously, confirming Pakistan's role in the episode. Concurrently, Pakistan made several contradicting statements, confirming its role in Kargil, when it defended the incursions saying that the LoC itself was disputed. Pakistan also attempted to internationalize the Kashmir issue, by linking the crisis in Kargil to the larger Kashmir conflict. But such a diplomatic stance found few backers on the world stage. The Global Media was largely sympathetic to the Indian cause, with editorials in newspapers based in the West and other neutral countries observing that Pakistan was largely responsible for the conflict.

On the other hand, Indian army had again raised the bar for officer like conduct by restraining themselves from crossing the LoC and thereby preventing an all out war. This example cost India dearly as many lives could have been saved if Indian army had simply cut off the supply routes from Pakistan, thereby laying a simple mountain top siege. We Indians, try to minimize the collateral damages and prevent escalation of conflicts even at the cost of our own life. After the war, the Indian government severed ties with Pakistan and increased defence preparedness. India increased its defence budget as it sought to acquire more state of the art equipment. Soon after the war the BJP government set up an inquiry into its causes and to analyze perceived Indian intelligence failures. The high powered committee was chaired by eminent strategic affairs analyst K. Subramanian and had powers to interview anyone with current or past associations with Indian security establishment, including former Prime Ministers. The committee's final report led to a large scale restructuring of Indian Intelligence. In a departure from the norm the final report was published and made publicly available.

The legacy of Kargil war still haunts Pakistan and General Musharraf repeatedly appeared on national television to justify the causes and preludes of the Kargil war. The Pakistani masses were naive enough to expect a victory over the Indian military. They were dismayed by the turn of events and questioned the eventual retreat. The military leadership is believed to have felt let down by the prime minister's decision to withdraw the remaining fighters. With Sharif placing the onus of the Kargil attacks squarely on the army chief Pervez Musharraf, there was an atmosphere of uneasiness between the two. On October 12, 1999, General Musharraf staged a bloodless coup d'état, ousting Nawaz Sharif.

Benazir Bhutto, an opposition leader in the parliament and former prime minister, called the Kargil War "Pakistan's greatest blunder". Many ex-officials of the military and the Inter-Services Intelligence also believed that "Kargil was a waste of time and could not have resulted in any advantage on the larger issue of Kashmir." A retired Pakistan Army's Lieutenant-General Ali Kuli Khan, lambasted the war as "A disaster bigger than the East Pakistan tragedy", adding that the plan was "flawed in terms of its conception, tactical planning and execution" that ended in "sacrificing so many soldiers." The Pakistani media criticized the whole plan and the eventual climb down from the Kargil heights since there were no gains to show for the loss of lives and it only resulted in international condemnation

Through the Kargil conflict, the Kashmir dispute came into limelight again. It clearly showed the world that Pakistan was least interested in a bilateral solution since the infiltration followed a peace dialogue between the two countries. The sanctity of the LoC too received international recognition. President Clinton's move to ask Islamabad to withdraw hundreds of armed militants from Indian administered Kashmir was viewed by many in Pakistan as indicative of a clear shift in US policy against Pakistan. Finally after fifty years, four bloody wars and several hundred thousand deaths Pakistan realized that India was laid on the foundation of Unity in diversity. They had earlier failed to acknowledge the fact that while Pakistan's leadership had exhausted all their resources for that one unattainable ploy to supersede India, the latter had devoted a lion's share of all economic, social, political, infrastructural as well as human resource on creating a country that was deserving of its forthcoming global stature. India defended and evolved whereas Pakistan attacked and grew weary. Every Pakistani is fed on falsified facts and figures through a widespread network of *Madrasas* (Islamic Schools) which misguide the youth and most of the children grow up hating India as their foremost enemy. The greed envy ignorance and wrath of Pakistan imprudently led them to a grave which was supposedly for India but as history books would have it, the one who digs pits for others often falls into them. For the major part of the twenty first century, the state of Pakistan has degraded to an all out anarchy. The *Madrasas* and their parent schools of thought overpowered the military and subdued the government. Nobody knows who is in-charge anymore. Nobody is willing to take the responsibility for the actions of the country which often undermine the whole concept of civilization. All the major surveys which quantify human resource development, social safety, infrastructure, political solidarity and an overall Mean Quality of Life published by Government sponsored organizations or independent editorials, including the United Nations Organization, the Telegraph the Independent and the Economist Intelligence Unit, have listed Pakistan and its major cities amongst the ten worst places to live in the world. Thus a very prolonged ordeal has settled the question of supremacy in the Indian Sub-continent.

PROXY WAR

Pakistan had learnt it the hard way that though modern India might have petty disputes within its states but it amalgamates into an unsurpassable mountain against a foreign intruder. That is probably the only lesson India inherited from a long lineage of enslaved forefathers. So in 1965 and then again in 1972 India made a mockery of Pakistan's armed forces, the latter leading to the complete and unconditional surrender of Pakistan.

The Inter-Services Intelligence (ISI) which is Pakistan's peace time espionage agency concluded that, if the technologically and tactically superior Indian armed forces would have been preoccupied with internal security issues then Pakistan would succeed in destabilizing the country in the long term. Moreover its cost would be a fraction of the cost of an actual full-fledged invasion. Pakistan Army Generals were able to convince the elected leaders of the government that sponsoring terrorist activities in the valley would prevent India from becoming the paramount military and economic power of South Asia.

In 1979-80 the United States of America sought General Zia-ul-Haq's assistance to train the Afghan Mujahedeen groups and Arab mercenaries. This clandestine Army of Islam was to fight against the Soviet troops with arms and ammunition to be provided by the US. General Zia, who was the military dictator of Pakistan at that time, gladly accepted this responsibility in return for US military and economic assistance. So General Haq set up a committee to take control of 1000 *Madrasas* (Muslim religious schools) and also establish new ones all over Pakistan. In these schools of Islam, Major General introduced military training by serving and retired officers of the Pakistan Army. The most important and the most active of these *Madrasas* chosen by them were the *Jamiya Uloom-e-Islami* in the *Binori* mosque, Karachi, set up by *Maulana Yusuf Binori* soon after Independence in 1947, the *Darul Uloom Akora Khattak* in the North-West Frontier Province (NWFP), and the *Jamiya Ashrafiya* in Lahore. Most of the terror masterminds leading the unscrupulous Army of Islam, including Maulana Masood Azhar, Osama Bin Laden, graduated in terrorism from these three *Madrasas*. In the 1990s, many of the Taliban leaders also passed out of this *Madrasa*. The second in command to Dictator Zia-ul-Haq were General *Musharraf* and *Aziz*. They took great care to ensure that this Army of Islam included as many mutually conflicting groups as possible so that while they kept the Soviet troops bleeding, none of them would subsequently emerge as a threat to the primacy of the Pakistan Army in the local power structure. This was a proxy war waged by USA and Pakistan. Their weapons were misguided youths of Afghanistan who were fed on religious fanaticism. Jihad or crusades were waged again, but this time under the covet intention of political and economical propaganda. Neither the US intelligence agencies nor the Pakistan military had the foresightedness to understand that Jihad is a primitive concept of Islam and the consequences of such narrow minded ideology would jeopardize world peace. After the withdrawal of the Soviet troops from Afghanistan in 1988-89 Pakistan started using the proxy war techniques it learnt from the CIA against India.

In the 1987 State legislative assembly elections in Jammu and Kashmir some of the results were disputed. This resulted in the formation of militant wings after the election. The ISI played a direct role in providing monetary and tactical support to the many insurgent groups that sprouted in the State of Jammu and Kashmir. Pakistan defended its actions by labelling its militant operation as an independence movement by the people of Jammu and Kashmir. A large number of these insurgent groups received ISI assistance from the Hizbul Mujahedeen (HM) of the Jamaat-e-Islami which assured the militant groups of a better life if Jammu and Kashmir became a part of Pakistan. The militant groups however wanted to be sovereign. Consequently the period from 1988 to 1992 saw emergence of two ideologically different but equally appalling factions— the pro-independence groups and the pro-Pakistan groups. The Western countries did not interfere until 1992. They shamelessly accepted the killing of security personnel in the Kashmir valley as a freedom struggle because of their vested interests in Pakistan. However all that changed when foreign tourists in the Kashmir valley also became victims of this violence. These European and American countries, that were silent when Indians, Pakistanis and Tibetans died in the valley, took an offense as soon as the blood of the "White" Man spilled in the supposed territorial dispute of two nations. Hiding behind the veil of democratic propaganda they soon realized that they had created a monster; a monster which was thirsty for human souls, a monster that once unleashed targeted bustling markets, primary school, medical facilities and above all humanity. It became clear that Kashmir as a sovereign entity would be highly unstable and thus Pakistan got an unofficial sanction from its allies in the west to restructure the militancy in Jammu and Kashmir.

So from the year 1993 Pakistan intelligence agency restrained itself from direct involvement with militant groups and instead introduced intermediaries like Jamat-e-Islami. A huge arsenal and financial aid were given to Jamat-e-Islami. These were in turn used to run the training camps in Pakistan Occupied Kashmir and Afghanistan. The second tactical change was the withdrawal of Pakistani support for all those militant groups which wanted a free Kashmir. And the pre-condition for disbursal of any funds or arms was the recipient group's support for merger with Pakistan. Most of the assistance went to the Hizbul Mujahedeen. In absence of foreign aid most of the local insurgent groups disbanded establishing the fact that the prerequisite for a peaceful Jammu and Kashmir is a neutralized Pakistan. One such example is Yasin Malik, a leader of one faction of the Jammu Kashmir Liberation Front (JKLF). He was one of the *Kashmiris* to organize militancy in Kashmir. Malik has renounced the use of violence and calls for strictly peaceful methods to resolve the dispute as the senior members of JKLF had sided with Pakistan in lieu of tactical support.

In December 1992 the Babri Masjid was demolished and ISI saw an opportunity to tap the anger of the Indian Muslim community. Once again the Hindus and the Muslims of India stood divided thereby adding to the difficulties of the Government of India. Pakistan followed a two pronged approach by misguiding the Muslim youth in *Madrasas* (school of Islam) that operated in India and further alienating them from the peaceful Hindu community, moreover the extremist groups supported by Pakistan in Kashmir targeted the Hindus of the Jammu region in order to drive them out. As expected the Hizbul Mujahedeen and Jamat-e-Islami did not venture beyond Jammu and Kashmir because they consisted of the Kashmiris who were sick and tired of violence. Their prerogative was a Kashmir free from all political and military propaganda. Though the means they used were violent and showed utter disregard for human values but they did have some little sanity inside, which made them cling on to the idea of peace at the end of the jihad (holy war). This can also be attributed to the fact that most of the Muslims in Kashmir are actually the descendants of Hindus who were forcefully converted in 14th Century. This opportunity was grabbed by Lashkhar-e-tayeiba and Harkat-e-Mujahedeen, which won them the favour of ISI. These groups had little to do with local Kashmir issues and were actually perpetrators from Afghanistan. They had been trained at the Pakistan militant camps and were now brainwashing the Muslims of India.

It is impossible to list all the atrocities that have been hurled at the civilian population of Jammu and Kashmir, but we have tried to chronologically arrange the following incidents that bring to light the attempts of terrorists to destabilise the Indian democracy. In July and August 1989 three CRPF personnel along with politician Mohammad Yusuf Halwai of NCF were killed. In the same year the daughter of the then Home Minister of India Mufti Sayeed was kidnapped. After that the terrorists got a new modus operandi, they tried to finance their militancy by kidnappings and extortions. Similar kidnappings were reported in 1995 in Jammu and Kashmir where 6 foreign trekkers from *Anantnag* district were kidnapped by *Al Faran*. One was beheaded later, one escaped and other four remain untraced, presumably killed. On 22nd March 1997, seven Kashmiri Pundits were killed in *Sangrampora* village in the *Budgam* district.

January of the following year witnessed the massacre of twenty four Kashmiri Pundits living in the village of *Wandhama* by Pakistani militants. According to the testimony of one of the survivors, the militants dressed themselves as officers of the Indian Army, entered their houses and then started firing blindly. The incident was significant because it coincided with former US president Bill Clinton's visit to India. Inaction by the Indian authorities as well as the lack of international political consensus led to several similar genocides in 1998 where 50 Hindus were massacred by Islamic militants in *Udhampur* district of Jammu and Kashmir. Even the elderly pilgrims who were on their way to the *Amarnath* cave shrine were not spared by the Islamic militants. The attacks not only targeted Hindus but also on other non-Muslim communities in the valley. One such incident was the *Chittisinghpura* massacre where 36 Sikhs were massacred by Lashkhar-e-Taoiba militants.

After terrorising the populace, these militants engaged the state government head on by targeting the Jammu and Kashmir legislative

205

assembly. On October 1, 2001 a bombing at the Legislative Assembly in Srinagar killed 38.

The next weapon used by Islamic militants was the suicide bombers. First such attack occurred on 30 March 2002 when two suicide bombers attacked a temple. Eleven persons including three security personnel were killed and 20 were injured. The *fidayeen* (suicide bomber) squad attacked the temple again on 24 November 2002 when two suicide bombers stormed the temple and killed fourteen devotees and injured 45 others. On July 13, 2002, armed militants believed to be a part of the Lashkar-e-Toiba threw hand grenades at the Qasim Nagar market in Srinagar and then fired on civilians standing nearby killing 27 and injuring many more. The violent streak of Lashkar-e-Taiba did not end anytime soon and 24 Hindus were killed in *Nadimarg*, Kashmir on March 23, 2003. A car bomb exploded near an armoured Indian Army vehicle in the famous Church Lane area in Srinagar killing 4 Indian Army personnel, one civilian and the suicide bomber. Militant group Hizbul Mujahedeen, claimed responsibility for the attack. A militant attack on July 29, 2005 at Srinagar's city centre, Budshah Chowk, killed 2 and left more than 17 people injured. Most of those injured were media journalists.

On October 18, 2005 Kashmiri militants killed the education minister of Jammu and Kashmir Mr. Ghulam Nabi Lone. A Militant group called Al Mansurin claimed responsibility for the attack. Abdul Ghani Lone, a prominent All Party Hurriyat Conference leader, was assassinated by unidentified gunmen during a memorial rally in Srinagar. The assassination resulted in widespread demonstrations against the Indian forces for failing to provide enough security cover for Mr. Lone.

On May 3, 2006 militants massacred 35 Hindus in Doda and Udhampur districts in Jammu and Kashmir. On June 12, 2006 one person was killed and 31 were wounded when terrorists hurled three grenades on Vaishno devi shrine bound buses at the general bus stand in the morning.

India's Northwest Borders have also become a headache due to Pakistan militant groups exploiting sectarian clashes in Burma. India and Bangladesh, both of which have significant population of *Rohingya* Muslim refugee communities, have exchanged notes on the stepped up operation by Pakistan's Inter-Services Intelligence and the Lashkar. They also believe that there has been activity by Jaish-e-Mohammed (JeM) in Bangladesh's *Chittagong* hill tract especially in the area from *Cox's Bazaar* to the *Teknaf* sub-division along the border with Myanmar. After *Rakhine's* sectarian riots the Lashkar and its parent organisation the Jammat-ud-Damma (JUD) formed a new forum *Dita Arkam Burma* conference (Defence of Muslims) in Myanmar in order to materialize supporters for a campaign against the ruling military Junta of Myanmar. The Lashkar and Junnar deputed a two member team comprising Jannar spokesperson *Nadeem Awari* and *Shaid Mehboob Rahim Atullah* in August 2012 with the task of forging links with senior representatives of Islamic institutions in Bangladesh and Myanmar. Indian Government sources said that senior Lashkar leaders including the terrorist organisation's leader Hafeez Saeed have been discussing plans to target Myanmar for possible recruitment and militant activism. The Lashkar blames the reformist *Thein Sein* government of Myanmar for the plight of *Rakhine* Muslims. Pakistani terrorist organisations like LeT are already in contact with Huji, J-e-m, Jammaat-ul-Mujahideen Bangladesh (JMB) to build relations with the Rohingya Solidarity Organisation in a bid to extend activity and setup new bases on India's eastern fringes said a senior official. India's internal security agencies have informed the Manmohan Singh Government about the formation of a new front called Jammat-ul-Arkam (JUA) with elements from JMB and other extremist *Rohingaya* entities. Report indicates that the JMB could also be involved in running militant training camps in remote areas of *Banderban* district of Bangladesh. They may have plans to undertake action in Myanmar, said the official. The expanding ISI footprints in *Rohingya* Belt were revealed following the arrest of one *Noo-ul-Amin* from the *Idgama Madrassa* in *Cox's Bazar Chittagong*, in September 2013. A cleric recognized from *Dar-ul-Uloom Islamiya Madrassa* in Karachi, *Noor-ul-Amin* had served as a militant talent spotter and a recruiter of *Rohingya* cadres in the past. During his interrogation, *Amin* confirmed his association with the ISI and also the Karachi based *Maulana Abdul Qudus Burains*, the so called Chief of Huji (Arakam). He also confirmed that the Pakistan military intelligence agency was involved in running the Rohingya Refugee Belt. Subsequently, *Noor-ul-Amin's* close associate *Ali Ahmed Alka abu Jibral* was also picked up by Bangladesh Security Agencies on October 8, 2012. He was involved in money transactions between the ISI and the Karachi *Islamiya Madrassa*. During interrogation *Jibral* described his days in Afghanistan as a Jihadist soldier and his association with the Taliban during his stay in *Miran Shah* North Waziristan, from 1985 to 1999. An active member of Huji, Jibral was caught with Pakistani documents and a Bangladeshi Passport. While alerting Dhaka and *Naypyidan* to the emerging *Rohingya* terror threat, India is worried about the growing ISI interest in Muslim Refugees in the passive *Rakhine* state. Through terror groups like Lashkar, Jaish, Huji, SIMI and the Telerik-e-azadi Arakam (TAA) trained extremists could be used to rake mayhem in India's North Eastern states. There is evidence that Pakistan based explosion experts are teaching militant refugees to manufacture improvised explosive devices to fight Myanmar security forces.

India's long standing concerns that a U.S. military withdrawal from Afghanistan could lead to an increase in terrorist activity by Lash-e-Taiba is consolidated by the reports of LeT cadres moving towards *Kunar* and Nuristan provinces in eastern Afghanistan looking for bases that would provide them an independent base for training and collection. Pakistan militant groups had a similar strategy of being based in Afghanistan and attacking Indian Kashmir from there when the Taliban Government ruled Kabul in the 1980's.

"Pakistan's Role in the Kashmir Insurgency", a report from the American RAND Corporation reveals the truth, "The nature of the Kashmir conflict has been transformed from what was originally a secular, locally based struggle (conducted via the Jammu Kashmir Liberation Front—JKLF) to one that is now largely carried out by foreign militants and rationalized on pan-Islamic religious terms." Most of the militant organizations are composed of foreign mercenaries, mostly from the Pakistani Punjab.

LINE OF CONTROL (LOC)

In the second week of January 2013 a violation of ceasefire occurred along the Line of Control. The entire nation rose in shock and anger. The media had a lot of debates about the role of Pakistan in this big tragedy and its incapability to restrict fundamentalist operations being deployed from its soil. According to intelligence sources an ISI operative led border Action Team (BAT) of terrorists drawn from outfits like *Lashkhar-e-Tayeiba* and *Jeyish-e-Muhammad* was utilized by Pakistan. On January 8, 2013 the BAT was rewarded for mutilating the bodies of Lance Naik Hemraj and Lance Naik Sudhakar Singh which were later discovered in *Mendhar* sector of Jammu, beheaded. Though Pakistan had steadfastly denied its role in the incident, Indian officials believe that the operation was carried out by the Pakistani Army. In absence of any corroboration we are not giving much credence to it, said a Pakistan official. The security establishment also argues that all these BATs act in coordination with the army. Pakistan Army provides cover to the lands from where BATs operate across border. Most of the times, the BATs have Pakistan army regulars masquerading as independent terrorist groups. These BATs are nothing but strategic instruments of Pakistan army.

Recently a letter sent by Imtiaz Ahmed from Islamabad (Pakistan) disclosed that General Parvez Musharraf, former President of Pakistan, crossed the Line of Control in 1999 and spent a night within Indian Territory. Pakistani authorities downplayed this news. A former aide of General Musharraf who was the Chief of Pakistan Army at that time said that weeks before hostilities escaped between Indian and Pakistani troops in the Kargil sector, General Musharraf crossed the LoC in a helicopter and spent a night at a location 11 km inside Indian Territory.

"We cannot compromise, confirm or deny this", said an official of foreign office on Friday 25th January 2013. Colonel (retired) Ashfaq Husain, who was a senior officer in Inter Services Public Relations which is the Pakistan Army's media liaison, claimed in a TV show that General Musharraf flew across the LoC on March 28, 1999 and trenched 11 km into the Indian side. This is not the first time Husain made this claim. He also revealed this in a book that was published in 2008.

The army official claimed that General Musharraf who was accompanied by Brigadier Masood Aslam, the then commander of 80 Brigade, spent the night at a spot called Zikria Mustaqar where Pakistan troops commanded by Colonel Amjad Shabbir were present. Saud Rafique a spokesman of the Pakistan Muslim League (Nawaz) however told media on Friday that claims made by Ashfaq Hussain were highly exaggerated. Rafiq said that an army chief on such an adventure should have been in the knowledge of the then Prime Minister Mian Nawaz Shariff. *"This was not the case so I can say that this is in all possibility a myth,"* he said.

This evidence confirms that the enemy is always active on the LoC and is prowling for the slightest sign of weakness to mount an assault. Pakistan is jealous of the prosperity and integrity of incredible India which is imparting peace, love, education and a secular culture to all its citizens and in the process educating the entire world about the practise of nonviolence and harmony.

The perspective of the armed forces is not only limited to the purview of a war or a military conflict. Any political decision which regulates the organizational, operational or tactical facet of the armed forces demands due consideration and involvement of the prominent officers of the armed forces, including the three Chiefs of staff. However this is not the case in India. For instance, in the initial aftermath of the eruption along the LoC it was not clear whether the government and the army were on the same page or not. The gap in their understanding is partially because of the fact that almost none of our politicians have a military background. Moreover there isn't a regular interaction between these politicians and the soldiers who fight for the country.

Vasudev Kutamb means that people of all regions, religions and races are our family. In other words we respect, love and invite people from all over the world to visit our country and our culture permits us to welcome them to live with us like our dear family. Whole world is our family and we are in this world to create respect, love, peace, education, prosperity and nonviolence. We must protect our family against all evils.

While concluding I only pray to my countrymen to see that there is a big burden on our soldiers. The Government must look into their problems. Whether it is the procurement of latest defence equipment or the release of pension funds, no amount of delay or default is permissible. We not only owe our sovereignty and autonomy to their valour, but the Indian way of life evolves peacefully only because there are soldiers who are defending our borders.

The security ramifications of the U.S. pullout from Afghanistan for India and the South Asian region were debated during a brainstorming session at the highest levels of UPA Government. Indian Prime Minister Dr. Manmohan Singh was particularly concerned about the fallout on country's internal Security, especially the situation in Kashmir. Multipronged strategies were worked out to firewall India from Pan-Islamic Jihadists that would rise once the pressure from the American precision drone attacks and Special Forces raids subsides along the Durand line.

In October, 2010 during his official visit the then CIA director Leon Pannetta had for the first time communicated to New Delhi about the movement of L-e-T cadres towards Southern and Eastern Afghanistan.

At that time, the input was noted but not considered actionable due to the lack of any substantive evidence. India also believed that there were serious ideological differences between L-e-T and Taliban with the former ascribing to *Ahle-e-Hadith* school of Islam and the later being a *Deobandi*. LeT Terrorist David Coleman Headley, the Scout for the 26/11 Mumbai Attack, disclosed that the ISI did not want Hafiz Saeed's group to be involved in Afghan operations against US troops. Headley gave specific examples of Syed Abdur Rehmani Hashim, the father of the so called Karachi Project that was aimed at India. The Khuram brothers, who were thrown out of the LeT after they tried to shift the terrorist organizations target from the Radcliffe Line to those across the Durand. A part of the internal security establishment still believes that there can be no operational unity between LeT, Tehreek-e-Taliban (Pakistan) and the Afghan Taliban due to serious ideological differences between the Punjabi and Afghan groups. But there is now evidence that some 600 LeT cadres are seeking shelter and setting up bases just across from the Pakistan border well inside the Taliban territory. After analysing electronic and spatial evidence, Indian counter terrorism experts have concluded that the pressure from the ISI combined with generous funding have led the warring sides to override their theological differences for the time being. The assessment of India's intelligence agencies is that the LeT will once again try to target Kashmir as the US walks out of Afghanistan next year. This move will give Pakistan the much needed respite as well as strategic alternatives to their handlers and then they might push towards Kabul in order to destabilize the government or hit India. After the foreign forces have left, these groups will only fight to implement *Shariat* law in Afghanistan.

New Delhi has already sensitized key players like the US, Afghanistan, Russia, Iran, Saudi Arabia and Tajikistan about its concern. Western countries are again softening their stance against Pakistan's sponsorship of terror groups, presumably in return for support of the attempts and preachments between the Taliban and the Hamid Karzai government. China is also worried about Jihadists crossing into its Xingjian-Uighur region through Afghanistan's Wakhom Corridor.

India has asked Saudi Arabia to make efforts to delegitimize violence in the name of Islam. As a custodian of the two Holiest places of Islam—the *Kaaba*, Mecca and *Al-Masjid-an-Nawabi* (Mosque of the Prophet)—Saudi Arabian government should take steps to stop radicalization of youth and engage them in the correct interpretation of Islam through either a website or dialogue with the clerics, or else every suicide bomber would destroy not only his own but hundreds of other lives dreaming about the virgins in heaven. India is using its new found closeness with Riyadh to pitch for peace in Kabul and weed out radicalization in the region.

India worries that the peace in Kashmir will be short lived and the state of affairs will return to pre-2001 condition. The U.S. Afghan pullout will take place at the same time as the Jammu and Kashmir assembly elections in 2014. With U.S. soldiers no longer on the ground, militants could return to their traditional battleground—Kashmir and the Line of Control. With less than a year to go before the pull out, New Delhi plans to push for a new political initiative in the valley and has ordered the Indian Army to keep temperaments along the LoC at a low level.

In an interview to New York Times, Hafiz Saeed recently revealed that as U.S. troops prepare to leave Afghanistan next year Lashkar is unsure of its next move—whether to join the Jihadist fight against the West in numbers never seen before or take up the battle in Kashmir. It will depend largely on Saeed. His security is manned by the Pakistan Government as he fearlessly addresses large public meetings, makes appearances on Primetime and now even gives interviews to the Western media. During the interview with New York Times Saeed insisted that his name has been cleared by Pakistani Courts. Why does the U.S. not respect our Judicial System? He says he has nothing against the Americans and fondly remembers the visit he made to U.S. in 1994 during which he spoke at Islamic centres in Houston, Chicago and Boston. During that stretch his group had focused on attacking Indian soldiers in Kashmir—the fight that led the ISI Directorate's decision to establish L-e-T in 1989. But that battle died down over the past decade and Lashkar began projecting itself through its charity wing *Jamaat-ud-Dawa*, which runs a tightly organized network of hospitals and schools across Pakistan. One possibility is a return to Lashkar's traditional battle ground of Kashmir risking fresh conflict between nuclear armed Pakistan and India. The past actions give substantial evidence to the fact that Pakistan has the capacity to unsettle peace by sponsoring terrorism.

It is no secret that Pakistan is a fake and failed nation and unofficially a terrorist state. In Pakistan, the Army and Civilian Government seems to be pulling in different directions. Its shadowy intelligence agencies—the Inter

Services Intelligence (ISI) and Federal Investigation Agency (FIA)—have long supported the so called non-state actors. Its leading intellectuals (or at least those we see on television) appear to have a visceral hatred for India and a very narrow vision for the future. The prolonged subject of resolving the Kashmir conflict is trotted out in relation to every issue including that of Afzal Guru's hanging. Currently experts recommend continual vigilance of Islamabad's troublemaking propensities as well as their other foreign policy initiatives. No doubt peace with Pakistan would be a prized legacy for the UPA-2 Government. But we might end up neglecting other South Asian Countries or even China in our obsession to hammer out a peace agreement with Pakistan. Peace with India would take away Pakistan's only trump card. It is already facing trouble from the so called Jihadists it has nurtured. They are no longer obeying the Pakistani Government, in fact the recent activities hint towards an upheaval which might see the Jihadists seizing control of the entire country and thereby their nuclear arsenal. The whole of the South Asian Association for Regional Co-operation (SAARC) has been held hostage by the bilateral dispute between India and Pakistan. India really needs to move on. Given India's growth trajectory and the aspirations of its youth, Pakistan cannot take centre stage in our policies. Pakistan may be trying very hard to point out the speck in India's eye. But we must firmly set our sights on the relationships with other countries which will prove constructive and beneficial to our well being as a nation.

As per an estimate nearly a million people were killed and more than 10 million people were made refugees by the cataclysmic partition of India in 1947. My family was just among these millions uprooted, from their village near Campbellpur, Tehsil Pindi Gheb Villlage Eklas. I was only seven when we crossed over to Atari the first Railway station of India. I saw naked dance of death and unbelievable brutality that led to an unbearable loss of human values. What is extraordinary about these accounts, passed down from generation to generation, is that the partition is also a collective memory. I can only recall what happened to us in the cruelty—the rapes, abductions, the wells full of human bodies, the desecration of shrines, and the betrayals. Pakistan came into being on the basis of communal rage against Hindus, Sikhs, Christians, Jews, Zoroastrians and Shias now indifferently referred as "*Kaafir*" (Infidels).

I am 75 years old now and the carnage of 1947 is still afresh. Why were we forced out from our homes? Why all our properties were taken over by

Pakistan Muslims? I ask another question from myself—if the proponents of purification violence, instigators of innumerable communal riots, planners of terrorist attacks, evictors of religious exoduses, and the perpetrators of heinous crimes like rape and murder are ultimately to find closure and healing, then we need to urgently find public spaces for both justice and forgiveness. Justice is critical but Indian leaders and Hindus have compromised justice with compassion over the last fifty years. In the same period, Pakistan has become the granary of terror and hate. They want to destabilize the Indian Republic by their nefarious design.

Our P.M. Dr. Manmohan Singh wanted to have breakfast at Amritsar, lunch at Lahore and dinner at Kabul; Atal ji rode on a bus all the way to Pakistan, in return we got the Kargil War. History is a testimony to India's attempts at peace and Pakistan's refusal to budge from its hostile stance. India is very keen to play cricket, give Pakistanis free visa and open gates of free trade across the border. The media houses and Bollywood production companies welcome their singers, actors and literary persons to our country so that they are able to execute more 26/11 style attacks in not only Mumbai but in the entire country. Their citizens are invited to get free treatment in our hospitals. The history tells that India has always respected Islam and Muslims because Hindu culture not only preaches but also practices its age old scriptures which condemn violence. Hindus have equal respect for all religions of the world and more so for human life in general. But it is about time to forget Pakistan and Pakistanis and give importance to Nepal Bhutan, Sri Lanka, Bangladesh, China, UAE, Japan, Thailand, Taiwan, Myanmar, Malaysia, Indonesia, Qatar, Saudi Arabia, Israel and Egypt. We should write-off Pakistan and no importance should be given to them in any field.

The state Government also demands the withdrawal of Security forces as the civilians in valley are not interested to keep them anymore. This is the most complex situation and the public in general should back the reason of law and order and we should not appease the Muslims for votes. Defence of the country as a whole is to be taken into account. We should always support our Jawans (soldiers) who are on duty 24 hours for the safety and security of the nation and the people of this incredible India. Security Forces are being targeted constantly in the valley and Srinagar. In the month of March (2013) several cases of stone pelting against the Security Forces were reported. Strikes, curfews and violent protesting in the streets are happening almost daily. The Security personnel have not been provided with proper equipment to fight. They have only *Lathies* (wooden baton) to protect themselves from the unruly and hostile crowd. In spite of great provocation and a sizeable number of wounded and casualties, the Indian Jawans are doing their duty. State Government and Central Government say that even in most difficult situations they cannot use arms and ammunition to protect them.

JAWAN: THE SOLDIER

Today is 26th Jan 2013, the 64th Republic day of Partitioned India. Parade has been held as usual and the King of Bhutan, who also happens to be the youngest ruling monarch of the world, is the Chief Guest this time. I saw the parade on television today and some thoughts stuck with me. My mind made a journey to the *Poonch* district of Jammu and Kashmir where a Tragedy occurred across the Line of Control (LoC). Two Indian soldiers (Jawans) Hemraj and Sudhakar were killed. Their bodies had been mutilated. One was beheaded and the head was taken away by ferrymen to claim their reward from the Pakistan Government. This has sent waves of shock and anger in the whole nation. This is how Pakistan's Islamic forces wish "A Happy New Year" to India's Sovereign Socialist Secular Democratic Republic.

It is not only Hemraj and Sudhakar, there are a host of other soldiers who have been deployed along the LoC for different Jobs. Indian Army is one of the best armies in the whole world. Most of our countrymen, political parties and our ministers including the Premiere of the country have no knowledge of their lives at the border. These politicians neither have a military background nor are they interested in understanding its harsh realities. It is not an uphill task to create and sustain respect for our Armed Forces. This is merely a consequence of apathetic politicians who are unfortunately elected by a naïve populace.

Every year millions of young men and women apply to get recruited as officers in armed forces, however, only a few make it to the forces. It is because the quality is never compromised. Besides offering honour, prestige, and self respect, it provides a quality life, which makes them even more dedicated to their job. The high morale and motivation of the armed forces is rock solid despite the shortage of officers and paucity of hi-tech equipment. They provide the youth of today a level of dynamism and adventure that few professions can match. The traditions, camaraderie, impeccable etiquettes and glamour of the men in uniform are the envy of many. Apart from the three main facets of Indian Defence forces we also have various paramilitary forces which guard our nation. These include key organizations such as Central reserve Police Force (CRPF), Border Security Force (BSF), Indo-Tibetan Border Police (ITBP), Central Industrial Security Force (CISF), Sashastra Seema Bal (SSB), Border Road Organisation (BRO), Assam Rifles, National Security Guard (N.S.G.) So if an individual is looking for a career that cultivates his full potential then the armed forces is not for you; Indian soldiers outperform human limitations.

However the big question here is about India. Do we as a country deeply respect and care for our soldiers? Are Army traditions seamlessly woven into the fabric of our politics? If that is not the case then we have mercilessly thrashed upon the youngsters a war. I only wish, we were evolved enough to build a serious and genuine culture of respect for our soldiers. After a few days the debates vanished from news channels, social media resumed its tweets about the latest crash diet and the print media became silent. This is because Indians specifically, and humans generically, slip into a complacent space where they are too eager to put their past behind. This might be a good thing in most cases, but not at the actual Line of Control where nothing is back to normal. The actual line of control is marred by loneliness of mourning Army families and the unimaginable burden that an obligatory stoicism places on them when everyone else has moved on with their lives. It is then that the honour and a rightful place in the collective consciousness of the country can help. Brave are the martyrs and even braver are their families. The entire country is indebted to them, a debt which cannot be repaid by making hollow speeches and false promises.

Barkha Dutt (NDTV) writes, "I owe my life to a soldier who pulled me away from a hail storm of ammunition into the safety of an underground bunker in 1999. Since then, more often than I can count, I have seen the warmth, generosity, humility and valour of our men in uniform. They did not complain when they fought to reclaim Indian Territory without snow boots, night vision goggles or even bulletproof jackets. They did not complain when their days work was only to spend hours searching never ending stretches of road in militancy lit areas for explosives and mines to declare it open for safe travel. And they don't complain when they are called upon to do the work of the civil administration—build bridges during floods, rescue toddlers from open manholes and lead flag marches to calm hostilities in riot hit neighbourhoods. They don't even complain that they are barely remembered in peace time."

A lot can be said about the indifferent and ungrateful Indian public, but nothing puts it better than the desperation of a martyr's mother who had to go on a hunger strike to get political attention for the plight of her family. And while media focus was intense on this grief ridden mother, there were more than 90 other army funerals last year that remained out of public attention. The emotional disconnect between the military and civilian life is a result of the structural faults in the organization of decision making process and a depleting political will. Nothing offends army men more than the fact, that bureaucrats who have never been to a conflict zone long enough to see a bullet fly, have the final say in different aspects of military life—from procurement to pensions. This is despite sustained street agitation by ex-servicemen demanding, "One Rank One Pension".

The gap in their understanding is partially because of the fact that almost none of our politicians have a military background. Moreover there isn't a regular interaction between these politicians and the soldiers who fight for the country. Contrastingly in the United States of America, twenty four Presidents have roots in the Army; U.S President Barack Obama will rush to the ground in Iraq or Afghanistan to meet U.S. troops; where every family who loses some one in battle receives a personal letter from the President to honour the martyrs. Even something as basic as a national memorial for soldiers—a perfect way to make a nation's relationship with the idea of valour more organic—has been tangled and crippled by years of nepotism. First mooted in 1960, the proposal never got off the ground because of political wrangling. At present it is stuck because of a disagreement over its construction site, (India Gate which was built by the British in the memory of Indian soldiers who died in World War I is being considered) ensuring more delays to an embarrassingly overdue debt. We have failed to make military a part of the popular imagination or our history. There isn't a single state-of-art multimedia museum, where we can take our children to reconstruct for example, the battle of tiger Hill. It is far too easy to sit back in the safety of our homes and talk loosely about conflict. Before the 2003 ceasefire along the LoC as many as 100 lives were lost every year.

Men in uniform have become common fodder while doing their duty in the absence of negotiated solutions whether in Jammu and Kashmir or the Naxal infected States. Right since 1947, insurgency is prevalent and the common man has become a silent spectator, angry at heart but incapable of stopping all this.

Recently when the caskets of martyrs were brought back from the border, there was no throng of cameras. There were very few politicians attending the funerals. But as soon as the news of the slain soldiers got primetime focus a dramatic surge in the number of people, who wanted to hog the limelight, was noticed. But more often than not, the story of their death is told in the language of sorry little statistics that neither appreciates nor humanizes the martyr. And the image of a silent silhouette draped in a tricolour box barely registers in the transit memory of Indian masses.

So you know that five Jawans (soldiers) were killed in a militant strike in Srinagar. But can you recall their names? Did the tragic account of their violent deaths make them actual persons in the public imagination and not mere numbers? The leading Indian National Conference (INC) was quick to issue a passionate and angry public statement when the paramilitary forces shot a party supporter in the city. For a valley caught in the vortex of Islamic fundamentalism the disquiet in the Omar Abdullah Government is understandable. And so is the absolute condemnation of misuse of force on civilians. Yet there were no similar words of rage or grief expressed for the killing of the five Jawans. Nor did any major politician attend their funerals. The State's main opposition party, Mehbooba Mufti's PDP, has led an aggressive debate inside the assembly over how the execution of Afzal Guru (a convicted terrorist mastermind) has the capacity to rupture a fragile peace. Once again no politician shot back at the illegitimacy of this concern. Can't the otherwise stormy assembly find any space to debate the first *Fidayeen* (suicide) attack in the past three years? These politicians are incapable of formulating a robust and effective procedure for security operations. They have neither received the training nor have they showcased the intellect required for maintaining peace in a state where daily life is marred by violent protests and bombings. Only one-third of the deployed forces in Jammu and Kashmir are armed. While the Pakistan sponsored militia is endowed with latest weapons and intelligence information fed by our unfriendly neighbour.

Every life lost to the relentless cycle of violence in the valley must be accounted for by the civilians as well as the soldiers. Our outrage must be borne by both the civilians and soldiers. Our outrage cannot be ideologically selective like the polarized politics of Jammu and Kashmir. Yet, it was only after the enraged CRPF soldiers went public and issued the statement that—they felt orphaned by the absence of any significant political presence at the funerals of their comrades—that the martyrs got national attention. The Jammu and Kashmir Chief Minister then placed a wreath on the coffins before they were flown out from Srinagar airport and parliament finally found the time to discuss the militant strike, but only after the home minister had fulfilled and tripped over his ritualistic tribute (reading his prepared text twice by mistake).

This time the steady media attention ensured that the soldier's story was not pushed to the margins of political and public attention. But while violence in Kashmir valley draws in the energies of the mainstream media, it is the interiors of India's Maoist dominated belt that have become the major theatre of instinctive urban elitism. Media does not give adequate space to either the stories of exploited tribes or the plight of the Jawans in the forests of Central and Western India. Not so long ago the massacre of 76 CRPF Jawans in Dantewada forced us to look at their dismal living conditions. Torn tents that allowed in both—the heat and the rain, dilapidated police stations still unrepaired from previous Maoist strikes and 800 structures indentified in an official report as tactically unsafe. Add to these the paltry salaries (equivalent to those of a Government clerk. With a couple of thousand rupees added for hardships) a depleting moral and you have an alarmingly high number of men seeking voluntary retirement from the seven lakh strong paramilitary forces. Government data released right after the Dantewada massacre showed that 14,422 men applied for premature retirement in 2009, up 112% from 2007. Interestingly though, the CRPF and BSF don't enjoy the stature that is accorded to the three main wings of the armed forces, in recent years their attribution and losses in action have been significantly higher than the army, air force or the navy.

Over the years, the uniformed Jawans in India have not just safeguarded our nation against the interior and exterior threats but have also exemplified National Integration. Establishing the twin principles of unity and discipline the Defence forces of India are a source of pride, reinforced by trial and sacrifice. Since India achieved Independence the men in Uniform have been guarding the nation's frontiers. These forces outlast the enemy in every environment possible so that their countrymen live safely.

The tragedy is that between flawed policy making and public complacency not much is likely to change anytime soon. The absence of sustainable negotiated solutions and a decisive dialogue initiation, whether in Jammu and Kashmir or in India's Naxal tracts, means that the Jawans will continue to be cannon fodder for political failures. And it will take the next crisis or the next militant strike to bring back the focus on the soldiers. One of the cornerstones of our book is that there is no official authority or policy to blame for placing on emotional distance between us and the plight of our soldiers. It is just us and them.

TODAY'S KASHMIR

Indian people as a nation face an overbearing question mark. Is there a national policy in place regarding the Kashmir Conflict? Or Are there so many policies that we do not know which one to enforce? And in case we do have a policy (or a set of policies), who has the responsibility to enforce it (or them)? Does it come under the purview of the Home Ministry? Is the State government permitted to have a sovereign stand? Or a national committee for solving the Kashmir Conflict will effectuate the Central Government's big plan? Before you interpret our book as a series of never ending questions, try to answer any of the aforesaid questions. The circumstantial evidence paints a very clear picture of the missing political will.

COMMUNICATION SKILLS

A militant is arrested by the Delhi Police, who have apparently thwarted his plan to rake havoc during the forthcoming Holi festival. The Jammu and Kashmir Government resents the pre-emptive action of security personnel. According to the chief minister of Jammu and Kashmir, the hapless man was actually a surrendered militant enroute to a rehabilitation centre. To counteract the state government's accusations, the Home Minister has said that he will employ services of the National Intelligence Agency to unearth the truth. The debate to establish the legitimacy of this arrest will take some time to settle.

However, this incident exposes the lack of communication between the police force of the two states. In fact the home ministry and the state government seem to have buried any conduits of information exchange amongst the various national security agencies. On face of it, the Chief Minister of Jammu and Kashmir seems to have a point—Would a militant come to India with family on a terror mission? Not likely, but then again stranger things like suicidal attacks by women and children have surfaced in the past. The Home Minister seems least bothered by this incident which if nothing else, shows India's inept coordination. The Government now plans to review the policy on the surrender and rehabilitation of militants. A proxy war like the one Pakistan is engaged in (on Indian soil) justifies all Machiavellian tactics to take full advantage of the weakness of this deceitful adversary. It is a well established fact that Jihadists are coming from Pakistan. We also know that the current chaos within Pakistan is a direct consequence of the uncontrollable nature of violence and terrorism.

Off and on they made forays into India. But in recent times the collateral damage was contained by India's defence forces and hence the semblance of peace returning to the valley of Kashmir. But now once again, India seems to be the preferred target of those political parties that want to use the anti-India sentiment (instead of economic or social development) as their one point propaganda.

During the time when marauders from across the border were reduced to occasional trespassing violations, India should have ideally fortified its security apparatus. But unsurprisingly the short sighted political parties at the centre were busy rubbing shoulders in different directions. And to the joy of militants, Indian Government was unable to capitalize on the interim anarchist reign that weakened Pakistan's ability to retaliate. Today, as a result of all the cloth-eared responses to the challenges, Jammu and Kashmir has a Chief Minister seemingly at odds with the centre. Miscreants are ruling the street once again and Pakistan is blathering about the so-called 'Core Issue' that needs to be addressed. In other words little has changed. As the government goes into the penultimate year of its term, it retracts to a risk-averse policy. But since the ineffectiveness of UPA-2 has already been exposed on multiple accounts, may be it could find the time to at least streamline the communication system between various security agencies on issues relating to Kashmir, so that we do not look any more incompetent than we already do. Political stalwarts in India are either concentrating their energies on regional conflicts like Kashmir, Telengana and the Red-corridor or battling the doldrums of stock exchange brought upon by a falling Rupee and declining interest of foreign investors. However Indian government always falls flat on minor housekeeping issues which need to be tackled before even suggesting a solution.

LEADERSHIP

If ever a competition were to be held in the discipline of intellectual bankruptcy, then the Governments and secessionists of Kashmir would invariably end up on the podium. The Government is jolted out of its stupor to do something constructive only when it's time to appease the voters (before elections) or in case of a militant coup which opposes their authority in the valley. Moreover their boorish counterparts (the secessionists) seem intellectually incapable of facilitating peaceful negotiations, leave alone reaching an amicable solution.

The Separatist

Hurriyat Leader Ali Shah Gilani, came up with a brilliantly retarded solution recently and haplessly we quote him to expose the pitiful intentions of local Kashmiri leaders, "Don't rent your homes to non-Kashmiri labourers." He also adds that, "It is highly shameful for Kashmiris to send girls to army organized tours and functions." In the same speech he also dissuaded the general public to not cast votes and refrain from participating in the democratic process. Evidently these organizations (Hurriyat) are not political unions, but are in fact the marketing agents of authoritarian regimes who seek power. They have effectively brainwashed a huge fraction of the Kashmiri public and convinced them to submit to their regressive policies. A very recent incident brings to light this totalitarian tendency. The official high priest of Kashmir, Grand Mufti Basheer-ud-din Ahmad, who had issued a Fatwa (Islamic dictatorial order) against the all woman Kashmiri rock band *"Pragaash"*, branded music functions as Un-Islamic. Interestingly a video of the cleric—showing him enjoying a musical performance in the company of former Doordarshan director Shehzadi Simon in a houseboat on the Dal Lake—went viral on the social networking sites. Thus hypocrisy is a prominent feature of Muslim fundamentalists, who forbid every means of social interaction in a bid to maintain their dominance over the unaware public. They know that if Muslim youth from Kashmir gets a chance to participate in the process of national development through numerous schemes of the central government it well spell doom for their depraved power game. Once in a while these secessionists turn up in Delhi like bad pennies to show their support for Pakistan. The Indian union replies with an official statement that reiterates the fact that Kashmir is an inseparable part of India. The secessionists have also been known to take a trip around Pakistan every once in a while. There they get an opportunity to observe "Democracy" up close. Their hurried return from such field trips is credited to the freedom and rights that the Indian union offers its citizens. The politicians who make anti national statements, especially against the military or the *Madrasas*, in Pakistan usually end up on their death bed within days. We can safely assume that even the Hurriyat wants peace in the Kashmir valley, although it seems to have run out of means to achieve the end. Since these separatists have nothing positive to contribute, they should do a favour and keep their admonishments and poverty of ideas to themselves. The rest of Kashmir wants to get a life.

The Government

The Centre and State Governments are not far behind the Hurriyat leaders in this race to prove their own incompetence. Complete lack of earnestness is apparent in all their efforts. Amidst great fanfare the Centre had appointed a three member non-political team of interlocutors—journalist Dilip Padgaonkar, academician Radha Kumar and government official M. M. Ansari—to defuse the simmering anger in the disputed Kashmir region. The announcement received widespread anger, hostility and even ridicule. Amitabh Mattoo, Professor of International Studies at Delhi's Jawaharlal Nehru University commented that the three interlocutors chosen were undoubtedly professionals who have excelled in their respective fields, but give an impression that the panel had been finalised without due diligence or a serious application of mind by those who were quite oblivious to the complexities of the problems in the state and consequently were insensitive to the sentiments of the people living there. Nevertheless, the doughty trio, which was by then squabbling with each other, did come up with a report recommending amongst other things, greater autonomy for the State. And after thanking them heartily, Indian government flung the report into a cupboard which has not been opened since. Clueless Indian citizens still hope that maybe the next committee or panel will be more conclusive in resolving the issue and wait for the government to repeat the same routine.

Both the government and the Hurriyat have failed to provide a dynamic leadership to the people of Kashmir. At times they come up with statements just for the sake of contentiousness. They live in considerable luxury far from the ugly realities of daily life in Kashmir, and come with their often preposterous demands especially when TV Cameras are around. Both the Hurriyat and the government should end their zero sum game. The excitement over the young cricketer from Kashmir, the I.A.S. Topper, and the all-women rock band hints that the youth of Kashmir valley is not interested in the steroids of either the Hurriyat or the Government. They are not particularly interested in outdated shibboleths spouted by both sides. They want to make a mark in life, take advantage of the opportunities that for the moment India and the secular world can give them. Hence it is imperative that they stop their petty game of allegations and counter allegations.

NAWAZ SHARIF

The resurgent Prime Minister of Pakistan Mia Nawaz Sharif joined office amidst sky high public expectations. The people of Pakistan gave him a clear mandate to counter the rampant multiple insurgencies (including the Pakistani Taliban), take concrete measures to save the sinking economy and somehow restore a peace initiative with neighbours. In an interview to a Turkish media network he laid emphasis on the fact that "Serious sustained and constructive engagement with India must include the issue of Jammu and Kashmir". Describing the recent tension along the Line of Control, he expressed his concern and affirmed that Pakistan army would respond with "restraint and responsibility". However the army and Nawaz Sharif have not reached any formidable conclusion.

The United Nations General Assembly Meet in September 2013 was sidelined by a special tête-à-tête between Mr. Nawaz Sharif and his Indian counterpart Dr. Manmohan Singh. Indian Foreign Minister Salman Khurshid stated before the meet that—"We need some satisfaction, we need some deliverables". In response to Pakistan's helplessness Indian intellectuals came up with a three point approach to set the ball rolling in the right direction:—

1. Pakistan should reciprocate the Most Favoured Nation status to India because India has already given this privilege to Pakistan for quite some time now. This will go a long way in improving trade relations between the two countries.

2. The trial of seven Lashkar-e-Taiba militants accused of involvement in the 2008 Mumbai massacre has been in the lurch for more than half a decade. Justice must be delivered by a speedy fast track verdict.

3. Lashkar-e-Taiba, a globally banned terrorist outfit, must not be allowed to operate from Pakistani soil and its leader, Hafiz Saeed should be arrested, interrogated and cross examined to extract crucial information regarding future militant threats.

While addressing the U.N. Mr. Sharif was expected to spell out his country's commitment in addressing various concerns of India regarding terrorism and world security. But instead Pakistan government sought old means of prolonging the peace process by avoiding action. He said drone strikes by the U.S. not only violated their sovereignty but were counterproductive and caused further radicalization. The clueless Pakistani tacticians also came up with a toothless strategy to counter the Pakistani Taliban which all the political parties endorsed. According to this policy the government would open unconditional talks with the Taliban, declaring them stakeholders rather than terrorists and a government-run all-Parties Conference blamed the US and NATO for causing terrorism in Pakistan. The Taliban issued a list of more than 30 demands, including the imposition of *Sharia* (Islamic law) and the military's withdrawal from the tribal regions. Hafiz Saeed, who has remained under a tight control of the intelligence agencies, was allowed to lead a large anti-India rally in the capital Islamabad in early September. Pakistan fails to distinguish and stand by its decision of dismantling terror outfits. Moreover, after a 10-year hiatus there has been repeated firing between Indian and Pakistani forces along the Line of Control in Kashmir, killing a dozen soldiers and civilians on both sides this year. When Mr. Nawaz Sharif spoke of better ties with India and his determination to combat terror, he incurred the wrath of numerous militant groups. Hence the soil of Pakistan and now even India witnessed numerous bloodbaths. Whether a civilian government is in place in Pakistan or not, it makes little or no difference to the proactive militant groups. They make their own laws. The fact that a so called "social wing" of the Lashkar-e-Taiba has got state funding in Pakistan's Punjab province shows how well the militants are entrenched in that country. Consequently there will be no lack of resources or logistical support for attacks on India.

If Pakistan even under Nawaz Sharif's Government is unwilling to deal with the issue of cross border terrorism, then it is unlikely that the conflict between the two South Asian nuclear powers will be resolved. The Indian Prime Minister Dr. Manmohan Singh seemed confounded at the prospects of a meeting with his Pakistani counterpart Nawaz Sharif in New York on the sidelines of the United Nations General Assembly. While a proper political campaign was organized to dissuade him from the dialogue, some muted voices were in favour of such a meeting. This is a symptomatic course of action which cripples our approach to India-Pakistan relations. The politicians are preoccupied with shaking hands in public while ignoring matters of national concern. From past experience it can be concluded that Indo-Pak meetings rarely yield results that shape Pakistani responses to Indian concerns, particularly when Indians have consistently pursued peacetime negotiations.

There needs to be careful assessment of the current political and economic dynamics unfolding in Pakistan internally. India might gain valuable insights into the challenges it is likely to face along the western frontier. The question then would be not whether the proposed meeting in New York should take place or not, but rather what could be its substantive agenda aligned with Indian interests.

The Prime Minister's Visit

Dr. Manmohan Singh is the Prime Minister of India. He was scheduled to visit the state of Jammu and Kashmir in the last week of June 2013. This visit was strategically scheduled amid peace overtures of the P.M. designate of Pakistan Nawaz Sharif. Less than a day before his arrival, militants attacked an Army vehicle near *Bemina* on the outskirts of Srinagar. Eight soldiers were killed, seven critically wounded and another 6 injured. The vehicle, a senior CRPF officer said, was riddled with bullets, the armed men reportedly fired from both sides of the arterial road which leads to the Srinagar airport.

But Dr. Manmohan Singh's plan remained unchanged because this was the first high profile political visit to the valley post the hanging of parliament attack convict Afzal Guru. He kicked off the two-day visit with a public rally in *Kishtwar* in Jammu on Tuesday 25th June 2013. He was accompanied by UPA 2 Chairperson Sonia Gandhi and Chief Minister of Jammu and Kashmir

Umar Abdullah. Dr. Singh commissioned an 850 M.W. Ratyle Hydro Power Project in Ishtar. He later reached the valley amid high security to release a five rupee postal stamp in the memory of Kashmir's' famous poet *Ghulam Ahmed Mehjoor*. He said Kashmir was a valley of great cultural history which needs to be taken to rest of the country. The Prime Minister further extended an 'Olive Branch' to Kashmir valley by inaugurating the 17.7 K.M. railway line from *Banihal* to *Quazigund*. This rail link, which realized a century old dream of the people of Jammu and Kashmir, connects Kashmir valley with Jammu through the countries longest transportation tunnel called the Peer Punjab Tunnel. It was late Maharaja Pratap Singh, who in 1898 had first toyed with the idea of connecting Jammu with the Kashmir Valley. This infrastructure program is a part of the Udhampur Srinagar Baramula Railway Link (USBRL) and is utilizing the new Austrian Tunnel Method (NATM) for the first time in India.

Meanwhile, life had come to a standstill in the valley. Separatist leaders called for a shutdown to protest against the visit. Much of Srinagar was put under curfew-like restrictions. Vehicular traffic was restricted to some parts of the old city. Police and paramilitary forces had been deployed in huge numbers across the region with additional checkpoints along major highways. Officials however claimed, there were no restrictions in place. "People are not coming out of their homes due to the separatist shut down call." said Inspector General of Kashmir Range A.G. Mir. The outrage in Kashmir as well as the surge in terror attacks in Afghanistan and Pakistan suggests that the South Asian region has become more volatile and dangerous than ever. For tackling this hail storm of bullets, blood and counteraccusations the Pakistan Government has to take concrete steps instead of mute lip-service.

The development projects initiated by the Indian Union in Kashmir Valley will not bear fruits unless the source of this terror is dealt with. The attacks on the convoy of Indian soldiers suggests that the militants were well aware of the route and were able to get pass the security and carry out the audacious attacks. It is easy to be wise in hindsight, but the devastation of these eight families could perhaps have been averted with better intelligence. While it is also easy to blame intelligence failure for such incidents, it does not seem that the number of terror attacks in recent times have imparted any sense of urgency to the securities and intelligence agencies. Despite the situation on the ground being very fragile and fraught, we have not seen any initiative by the Home Ministry or the State Government. What we do see is another series of diplomatic conventions in the offering. In his speech following the militant attack in the heart of Srinagar that killed eight army Jawans, Prime Minister Manmohan Singh said such attacks would not deter the peace process in Kashmir. "We are ready to take-in everybody who shuns the gun." The Prime Minister of India assured that the centre was ready for a dialogue with all sections of Kashmiri society. "The dialogue process will be an all inclusive process", he told a select group of media persons.

Past Dialogues

There is now an established pattern in of our relations with Pakistan—"Dialogue—disruption—dialogue". Given this pattern and India's submissive attitude towards territorial offenders, it is not a surprise that even a failed nation like Pakistan takes India for granted. The sooner India abandons this bankrupt policy, the better chances it has of focusing on substantive issues in its relationship with Pakistan. India should determine its approach towards Pakistan on the basis of a careful assessment of the current global geo-political environment and its likely evolution over the next few months.

Pakistan is most likely to persist with its hostile policies towards India which are bound to escalate with the withdrawal of U.S. troops from Afghanistan in 2014. It may then suit India to maintain a formal engagement with Pakistan, even though means to constrain Pakistan's adversarial proclivities would be much sought after. Alternatively, the emergence of a democratically elected civilian government in Pakistan and the altered perception of its elite towards an India which is neither an existential threat nor a regional competitor would provide the much needed diplomatic nudge to Pakistan in a direction that addresses India's major security concerns.

Assessment of Political Dynamics of Pakistan

The third period of military dictatorship in Pakistan succumbed to the pressures of coalition parties towards the end of the last decade. Thereafter Pakistan has been successful in reviving a democratically elected civilian government which commands a Parliamentary majority, enjoys constitutional legitimacy and acknowledges the major challenges confronting the country. It has committed itself to better the relations with neighbouring countries (including India) and appears keen to promote bilateral economic relations. India recognizes and welcomes this constructive transformation. However, there is little evidence to indicate any change in the state policy regarding cross border terrorism. Moreover it has been verified that the jihadist and fundamentalist groups enjoy state sponsorship within Pakistan. Unless India notices a visible change in Pakistan's stand with regards to proxy war, a nationwide scepticism would persist despite of repeated efforts on either side of the border.

Even if Indo-Pak relations were to improve in the months leading up to the withdrawal of US led peace forces in Afghanistan, the impending and likely disruptive change may cause a serious setback. One way to avoid such a crisis would be an India-Pakistan dialogue on Afghanistan, wherein the two countries would focus on ensuring political stability and trilateral economic prosperity with Afghanistan rather than engaging in competitive hostilities. So far there is no evidence that Pakistan's new leadership is ready to give up its claim on a virtual veto over Afghanistan's political dispensation. There is more evidence to suggest that Pakistan considers post 2014 Afghanistan as an opportunity to restore its territorial superiority using its Taliban assets in the bordering states of Afghanistan. In such a scenario, India may have no alternative but to device means in tandem with other regional actors to thwart the oppressive plans of Pakistan. If that fails, then Kabul would become a jihadist breeding whorehouse for Pakistan. Containing such a fundamentalist terror generating machine in Kabul would be possible only by a direct confrontation on the battle field.

In fact the United States of America recently acknowledged Pakistan's "indispensable" role in facilitating an honourable for its forces from Afghanistan. There is every possibility that Pakistani politicians might misinterpret this courteousness as an international carte blanche and further exploit it to revive the Kashmir Issue. To dissuade Pakistan from pursuing such a policy, it must be shown the gargantuan costs of such an operation in contrast to the minuscule benefits that the politicians hope to reap. India needs to seriously consider a potential plan of action taking into account Pakistan's major vulnerabilities. The same holds true for coping up with Pakistan's despotic aspirations in Afghanistan. In between its policy of appeasement and war, India must avoid getting caught between a rock and a hard place while dealing with Pakistan. In fact there are a lot of positive and negative levers available to influence the strategic calculus in Islamabad. Knowing what these are and a willingness to use them is what would make a summit between the Prime Ministers of the two countries meaningful. If Pakistan, even under its democratic civilian Government, is unable or unwilling to deal with the issue of cross border terrorism, then it is unlikely that the Kashmir conflict will be resolved through a dialogue.

Challenges Ahead

Dr. Abdul Qadeer Khan 77, revered at home as a hero for building the Muslim worlds' first atomic bomb, formed his party Tehreek-e-Tahafuz Pakistan (TTP) in July 2012. His party fielded 111 candidates in the national as well as provisional assemblies but failed to win even a single seat. Khan said his party will keep monitoring the government performance and would become active again if the government failed to deliver.

It can be easily concluded that the Pakistani populace has put in immense faith in the leadership of Mr. Nawaz Sharif. Unsurprisingly his pro-India comments during state's latest media release were largely welcomed by the press and the people of Pakistan. Mr. Talat Mehmood, a defence analyst said, "A shift is taking place inside the power structure of Pakistan. The army is yielding a lot of the elected leaders. Possibly foreign policy will now change for better." He suggested that this would be the apt time for bringing the army on board. "The shift, however, would be slow and painful", added Mr. Ali Ehsan, another defence expert. Ehsan said while it was difficult to arrive at a consensus over the relations with India. And that Sharif was best placed in moving ahead, given that he had the mandate of the Punjab province.

Many neutral observers wonder how the civil leadership in Pakistan would differ from its military counterpart in terms of policy and practice. The visit of Indian Prime Minister Mr. Atal Bihari Vajpayee and the almost simultaneous military transgression in Kargil are still a fresh memory. Similarly questions have also been raised regarding the activities of terror mastermind Hafiz Saeed. Does the elected government have enough influence and political will to bring to justice one of their own. So the issue at hand actually pertains to controllability of government machinery within Pakistan. If Sharif was able to take charge of Pakistan Intelligence Agencies and also the non-state actors, only then can a peace initiative be sincere and durable. Mujib-ur-Rehman Shami, a senior Pakistani journalist, argued that no progress can be made with India until Nawaz sharif moves beyond Kashmir.

ZUBIN MEHTA

"Hum bahut khush hain, hum bahut khush hain (I am very happy). I have waited and dreamt of this moment for years", setting the tone for the concert, the 77-year-old music maestro continued by saying in Hindi, "*Agli baar se to yeh sab muft hona chahiye.* Music *sabke liye hona chahiye* (the next time, this should be free for everyone. Music should be for everyone) and it should not be for a select few."

"We only want to do some good. Music must go out from here to all our friends everywhere . . . To all Kashmiris."

This is a glimpse of the world of Zubin Mehta, an Indian Parsi conductor of Western classical music. He is the Music Director for "Life of Israel"

Philharmonic Orchestra and the Main Conductor for Valencia's Opera House. Zubin Mehta is also the chief conductor of Italy's Maggio Musicale festival. On 7th September 2013, he earned the unique distinction of conducting the first ever Western Classical concert in the Kashmir Valley. The magnificent *Chinar* trees, aesthetically landscaped in the 400-year old Shalimar Gardens along the banks of Dal Lake, swayed to the melodies of Mehta and his Bavarian State Orchestra as they played a full cast of works by Ludwig Van Beethoven, Franz Joseph Haydn and Pyotr Ilyich Tchaikovsky in front of an invited audience of 1,500 guests.

BEFORE THE CONCERT

The separatist in Jammu and Kashmir found a brand new cause—the 'danger' of organizing a Zubin Mehta concert in the state—which demonstrates their desperation to remain relevant and a lack of exploitable causes which they can espouse.

The first one to cry foul was Kashmir's Grand Mufti Azam Bashiru-ud-din. According to him such a concert would send a wrong signal that the people of Jammu and Kashmir are prosperous and have the leisure time to participate in such high profile events. However Mufti Sahib found plenty of time to attend a similar musical soiree not long ago. In fact the video of his hypocritical demeanour went viral on the internet, following his controversial allegations of blasphemy against an all-girl Kashmiri band called "*Pragaash*". The separatist leader Syed-Ali-Shah-Gilani and Mir-Waiz-Umar-Farooq have also joined the chorus opposing the concert.

What are they so afraid of? It beggars the imagination to comprehend how a classical music concert can harm the interests of Kashmiri people. The separatists fear that any possible projection of Kashmir as a place where people have individual pursuits, other than their pernicious ideology, will render them expendable. Apparently the separatists lack conviction in their own devilish schemes. Such a scenario sprouts up only when a person knows that his means do not justify the end. This is also indicative of the declining influence of fundamentalists. The bizarre reactions exposed their instinctually oppressive character and the underlining insecurities which motivated them to assume that the fate of Kashmir would change after the concert. And above all else, it shows sheer lack of any positive contribution from their side to improve the quality of ordinary Kashmiri life.

The separatist may be able to spark off street protest with the aid of their friends in Pakistan but they have fallen woefully short of conjuring any substantial influence in the state elections. Trapped between the army and the separatist (along with their Pakistani masters) the Kashmiri people have not been able to realize their immense potential. What is more worrying is the silence of political parties and the state government. If the despicable attempts of these retrograde elements succeed in preventing such concerts, it would certainly strike a discordant note among the Indians, most of all those in Kashmir.

EURPEAN UNION

Of late, the European Union (EU) has taken a keen interest in the Kashmir problem. It helped in setting up of a special task group called the "*All party group of Kashmir*" which frequently holds sessions to further the cause of human rights in the valley. The EU is also in touch with separatists like Jammu and Kashmir Liberation Front (JKLF) Chief Yasin Malik and moderate Hurriyat Chairman Mir-Waiz-Umar-Farooq, who has praised the EU in the past for debating human right issues. A special group mandated by the EU even described Kashmir as a "*Beautiful Prison*". A critical section of the Kashmiri people sees the EU as the global representative of democracy, federalism, liberty and the right to self-determination.

To many of them the Zubin Mehta concert came as a shock, and they interpreted it as a possible U-turn in the policy of the EU. Moreover Zubin Mehta's concert was viewed in such dismal political light because it was sponsored by Germany, which commands great influence within the EU. It was naive on the part of German Ambassador Michel Steiner, who sent invitations in his own name, to organize such an event without assuaging the fear of all stake holders. Steiner's frequent visits to the valley (more than six times) show he was well aware of this challenge. Besides, Steiner's role as the head of the United Nations Mission in Kosovo (UNMIK) makes him a highly controversial leader, who cannot afford to host a political concert in a place like Kashmir without raising a few eyebrows.

In the past also when a Pakistan based musical group *Junoon* visited Kashmir, a large section of the population was up in disgruntlement. People's agitation was centred on the "disputed" status of the valley. The proposed Harud Literary Festival was cancelled in 2011 on similar lines.

Therefore it was expected that India and Germany would ultimately have to justify the purpose of organizing a cultural program in the Kashmir valley.

Simultaneously the EU has implemented policies to enforce a background check of all those lobbying in Kashmir after America based Kashmiri separatist and lobbyist Gulam Nabi Fai came under the scanner for getting funds from Pakistan.

Whether Mehta's concert is an indication of a new, more neutral, stance of the European Union in the Kashmir region or just a reflection of the evolving bilateral relations between India and Germany is yet unclear. It will continue to be an open-ended question until the EU comes clean on any change in its stand on the Kashmir issue.

Decreasing Relevance of Separatists

The recent choking of the separatist politics reveals another side of the story. Hardliner Hurriat Chairman Syed Ali Shah Gilani, who had called for a shutdown on September 7 against the Zubin Mehta concert, had remained mostly under house arrest since the execution of Parliament attack convict Afzal Guru. For twenty six Fridays he was not allowed to offer congregational prayers because of his unsolicited antinational speeches at such gatherings. Umar Farooq was even banned from attending Eid prayers because of similar provocative statements. Malik was bundled out of Jammu twice to ensure civil life remained unaffected in the region.

The shrinking political spaces of separatists forced them to hog the event out of desperation. Moreover, they feared that such an event would send out a message of "Normalcy gaining ground in the Kashmir valley" to at least 50 countries where the show was telecasted simultaneously. This is also seen as the first International convention in Kashmir by a foreign country since the 1989 armed rebellion. The separatist must have felt that this normalcy balloon would be easy to prick and provide the much needed political mileage. These self-proclaimed baton holders of a crisis ridden Kashmir society must not be allowed to control the public (global) perception of the state of Jammu and Kashmir.

Unfortunately, Kashmir has witnessed politicization of every otherwise apolitical space. Students going to school, voters queuing up for development and kiosks promoting tourism have been targeted of and on. The security agencies were the first to use the space of culture, art and music to either dissuade the youth from toeing the line of a particular ideology or insulate them from the politically charged atmosphere of the state. Hundreds of talent shows have been organized by the police and the army in Kashmir. Even sporting events are being held with a political agenda.

HAQEET-E-KASHMIR

Civil society groups are joining hands to reclaim public space of narratives. In fact the protesters went to extent of organizing a rival concert called Haqeet-e-Kashmir, being held against Zubin Mehta's concert. On Saturday, when Zubin performed at the Shalimar Garden, a local Civil Society Group also invited local artists to hold a show at Lal Chowk's municipal park. They opposed Mehta's concert because it portrayed peace and normalcy in the valley.

The civil society was afraid that foreign countries might decide to assist India in maintaining an active vibrancy of cultural conventions in Kashmir through similar initiatives in the future. It is not easy for them to digest a future wherein the global focus might shift from political aspirations of the elite to the individual enterprise of local youth. The leaders of such civil societies accuse the government of India for their plight and persist on presenting Kashmir as a region devoid of prosperity. Their narrow mindedness actually imposes a false sense of aloofness amongst the Kashmiris. The populace is gullible and the local politicians exploit them to spread unrest in the state.

A Tribute to Kashmir

Kashmiri opposition to the Bavarian concert came as a complete surprise to the German organizers, who wished to honour the peace loving Kashmiris. Two days before the concert German Ambassador Michael Steiner tried reaching out to local population again saying the September 7 event was not an alternative, but a mobilizer for more engagement in Kashmir. Kashmir and Civil Society and separatist contend that the concert glosses over the situation in Kashmir and Germany endorses it.

"This is purely a cultural event and does not alter the political position of Germany and EU", said Steiner in a message to the local media. "This concert has the potential to make the world look at the complex realities of Kashmir. Germany's commitment to Kashmir goes well beyond music".

Steiner reminded people, "We fund a health camp for underprivileged people in Matti-Poora near Baramoola. We foster academic exchange. And there is more to come—a mechanical engineering centre for young Kashmiris by a German Company and German-know-how for conserving Dal Lake."

However protestors marched into the streets with stones in their hands. They refused to call off the city-wide strikes. Consequently the security agencies had to enforce curfews in some areas. Islamic jihadists threatened the organizers with dire consequences. The past few weeks had witnessed a verbal volleyball match between the various stakeholders. Arguments were intense, insensitive and often reflected short sightedness. Notwithstanding such threats Zubin Mehta reached the city a day before the concert.

The Concert

Can music provide an answer to tragedies of life? Renowned Indian born music conductor Zubin Mehta certainly thinks so, "Kashmir is beautiful, I am happy to be here . . . My music will provide the answer, let the music play".

Zubin Mehta titled his concert Ehsaas-e-Kashmir. On the very same day protesters organized in the same city another concert of local artists called Haqeeqat-e-Kashmir. The debate between Ehsaas (feeling) and Haqeeqat (reality) is nothing new for a place where the prolonged territorial conflict has turned mundane events like attending marriage functions or funerals highly political. Mehta's explanation as to why he wanted to organize a concert in the valley was unapologetic, "It began as a dream, as a lifelong ambition to do something in Kashmir, a part of the country that I love so much", he said in an interview.

On the eve of the concert, the warring parties did not share the conviction. The separatists were ready with detailed plans of protests and shut downs. Moreover the civil society groups had received a green signal for their parallel protest concert. The government had their hands full with the security arrangements. Shalimar Garden, the venue of *Ehsaas-e-Kashmir*, had been sealed. Vehicles were being thoroughly checked, people frisked and even the movements of boats in Dal Lake had been severely curtailed. The protests meanwhile, picked up pace. Practically overnight "GO ZUBIN GO" graffiti mushroomed across the city. Even students joined the protest with demonstrations at Kashmir University. Asiya Andrabi, chief of separatist organization Dukhtaran-e-Milat, went a step ahead to motivate the local Kashmiris on communal grounds. Her argument was that, "Mehta is the director of the Israel philharmonic orchestra and Israel is the country responsible for the killings of innocent Muslims."Andrabi further requested the locals to raise anti-India slogans on loudspeakers. The mainstream political parties conspicuously maintained their silence. The two main parties—National Conference and PDP—refused to comment, saying they had no wish to "Politicize the issue".

Bollywood actress Gulpanag, who would be hosting the show, had words of hope, "Music transcends disputes, goes beyond political and ideological boundaries, and encourages hope. This concert will get Kashmir into the limelight for something positive. Let the music play."

Diplomats, corporate magnates, film stars, lawmakers, civil servants and politicians were on the list of 1500 invitees. A wonderful depiction of love and beauty amazed the listeners. The evening started with Beethoven, Mehta having picked Leonora overture No.3 from the German composer's only opera, Fidelio, with its theme of abuse of power and liberty. Beethoven and birds in one voice were audible to the whole world. After Zubin Mehta's performance at Shalimar Bagh the whole world recognizes the fact that there is much more to Kashmir than just hatred. As the evening progressed Mehta, with his eyes closed, guided the second movements gently through the middle all the way up to reach its crescendo, the birds joined in perfect conjunction. It was nothing short of magic. The vigorous notes of passionate musicians sounded heavenly as they were carried by one hundred and twenty microphones across the country by Doordarshan. The world listened intently to music as it transcended opinions. The third movements of Joseph Haydem's trumpet concert in E-Flat Major followed. Soloist Andreos Ottl made his trumpet talk with the orchestra joining in as conversation. Mehta not so much conducted the musicians on the stage as much as librated them in the Srinagar outdoors. Nothing underlined the function more than Lithuanian born violinist Julian Rachlin as he burned up the September air with his solo rendition of Russian master Pyotr Tehaikosky's violin concert. The sight and sound of Rachlin was palpable even to those not at Shalimar. As he flung himself back to hurl the last note, only the growing "Allegro Vivcasissmo" of the birds remained along with the aftershock of rapture. The climax took the listeners into a world of demonic lust with Beethoven's Fifth. Encores of Johann Strauss' Thunderous polkas had not even subsided when Abhay Rustom Sopori and Mehta's orchestra brought the evening to a happy end, with a melding of Kashmiri folk melodies, although the birds continued their concert well into the dying light.

Allah Rakha Rehman

On 23rd October, 2013 A.R. Rehman, India's only popular music composer to be decorated with the Oscar award by the Academy of Motion Picture Arts and Sciences (USA), announced, "The Zubin Mehta's concert was good, something different from all usual negative news, failed peace talks . . . I would perform there if an opportunity arose but only if Kashmiri people want me too, not at the cost of controversy."

Islamic clerics condemn music in Kashmir as blasphemy. Separatists are obsessed with their portrayal of a sadistic Kashmir with regular bouts of stone pelting and strikes. Civil society is competing with its own schedule of cultural programs. Are any of these controversies supported by the common man of Kashmir? Do they reflect a progressive attitude which is the signature of human evolution? Will clutching to any of these policies help the youth of Kashmir?

Zubin's music has the aroma of a modern Kashmir which is no more a prisoner of such mindsets. It represents a generation which is yearning for acceptance, inclusion and India. It is the music of a people whose voices go unheard amidst the blaring loudspeakers of fundamentalism, their opinions and aspirations oppressed by political agents of dogma. And after this concert the entire world has heard this voice. A proud voice not only heard but also resonated by peace lovers across the globe. Injustice anywhere requires action everywhere and the whole world believes that Kashmir still has hope. The whole world is willing to take action because this concert touched their hearts.

The Global Problem

On Saturday, 21st September 2013, terrorists targeted the West Gate Mall in Nairobi, Kenya. Most of the shopkeepers were Gujarati businessmen of Indian origin. This is not a secluded event. It reminds us how localized militancy can suddenly take the shape of an organized international militia. When it comes to terrorism no continent, country, community or class is safe. *Al-Shabab*, the Somali militant outfit that took responsibility of the "Black Saturday" in Kenya, has been trading blows with the neighbouring Governments for over half a decade now. The terrorists described the recent target as "An Israeli owned mall frequented by foreign tourist and diplomats." Such attacks are tiny off-shoots of the sapling called pan-Islamism. Somalia's militant problem has metamorphosed into an International open Islamic Threat to the secular world. U.S. claim has proved false.

U.S. thought seeking and killing terror mastermind Osama-bin-Laden would cripple Al-Qaida and they would be forced to vacate Kabul. Moreover they were hoping to strike fear in the hearts of fundamentalists by this decade long manhunt. However, once the United States of America began the sequential withdrawal of its peace keeping forces from Central Asia, the dormant blood-seeking power-hungry Islamic institutions resumed their fist fights for territorial supremacy. In Iraq alone 1000 lives are claimed by sectarian clashes every month. Similar localized wars are being fought in Yemen, Nigeria and Pakistan. All of these are either Islamic sectarians or tribes that have been taken over by Islamic terror groups. Tehreek-e-Taliban is leading the anti minority violence in Pakistan. Al-Qaeda showed the way to all these extremists, a path that cannot be erased from a terrorists' imagination. Hence transnational cooperation against terror needs to be developed further.

Black September

September proved to be the most unfortunate month for India this year. Every day was headlined by bad news from the border. On one hand Pakistan is externally provoking India by violating ceasefire in various sector of Jammu and Kashmir, while on the other hand there is internal opposition in the form of frequent strikes and curfews. On 26th September, three men in uniform (possibly belonging to the Pakistan Army) conducted twin strikes in Jammu. This unfortunate incident is a result of intelligence failure and lack of coordination between the Border Security Force, Police and Army. Indian Prime Minister Dr. Man Mohan Singh got this news while he was celebrating his 81st birthday on board a flight to Washington. He did not cut the cake as a mark of respect to those killed—4 policemen, 4 army personnel and 2 civilians. This deadly attack jeopardized the tentative meeting between the Prime Ministers of India and Pakistan in New York.

Dr. Man Mohan Singh said that India was resolved to defeat the terrorist menace that continues to receive encouragement and reinforcement from across the border. He dismissed the barbaric attacks as one more in the series of provocative actions by enemies of peace. Singh also conveyed condolences to the families of brave army officers and innocent civilians "Martyred in this cowardly attack". Chief Minister Omar Abdullah added, "The history, timing and location, the aim is to derail the proposed meeting between Prime Minister Man Mohan Singh and his Pakistani Counterpart".

The terrorists, in army fatigue, crossed International borders in a vegetable truck at Gunpoint to reach Hiranagar Police Station in Kathua district at 6:45 A.M. Zonal officials informed in their statements that the militants shot and killed a shopkeeper and sentry before barging in. "Inside they killed four police personnel", said Inspector General Rajesh Kumar. The three men then killed the truck cleaner and drove to the heavily fortified army camp in Samba, 40 Kilometres from Jammu. In the officers' mess they shot dead Lt. Col. Vikramjit Singh and three Jawans. As a fire fight broke out, the army employed choppers to locate the terrorist and arrest them. "At 5 p.m. all three terrorists were shot dead", said an officer.

Shohada brigade, a little known front of Hizbul Mujahideen, has claimed responsibility. Denying the hand of Pakistan state agents, its high commissioner to India, Salman Bashir said such a senseless act of violence does not deter us from pursuing the path to a better future for our people.

Finally on 29th September Dr. Man Mohan Singh, the prime minister of India, met the Prime Minister of Pakistan in spite of dissuasive national sentiment. The twin attacks of 26th September added to the already grim state of affairs along the LOC. The rising graph of bloodshed in the state of Jammu and Kashmir is a direct consequence of encouragement by the Pakistan Army. One of the lessons that can be deduced from the years of authoritarian rule under General Pervez Musharraf is that Pakistan's army has the ability to turn off militant infiltration at will, in a manner not dissimilar from a person turning off a tap.

Nine Indians were killed in Kashmir last year. This year the death toll has already reached 38. In the present volatile political environment India needs to tackle political summits in a cautious way, wary of Pakistan's hypocrisy. Even the Indian public seems tolerant of diplomacy, in the backdrop of terror attacks, as long as the talks lead to some tangible gains. The agenda of the meeting in New York was never finalized. And although in principle such a dialogue is progressive, but a true summit, with full agenda and a bouquet of accomplishments is bulletproof against any sort of violence by the enemies of peace.

Nothing drains India's treasury more than the beautiful valley of Kashmir. Nothing besmirches its democracy more than the blood spilled in the valley of Kashmir. Nothing vetoes its claims to "Equal Rights for all citizens" and mars the International reputation of the Socialist Secular Democratic Republic of India more than the beautiful blood valley of Kashmir. Since 1989, at least 50,000 people have been killed (mostly civilians) in the valley. Hundreds of thousands of Non-Muslims have been either forced to discard their religion or flee for their lives. The valley has sparked three full-blown wars between India and Pakistan. It is the single largest issue over which Pakistan foments Islamic terrorism in India. Jihadist groups originally setup to "liberate" Kashmir have become the insolvable itch of putrefying Pakistan. Solving the problems of Kashmir, it appears, would make the subcontinent a safer, happier, more righteous and prosperous place.

Is Kashmir Worth It?

Strategically, politically and egoistically, the answer is a huge "Yes", shouted emphatically from both sides of the border. Kashmir is located on cartographic crossroads of several mountain passes. If these mountains were not to be patrolled than infiltrators would get a free pass to march-in from any side they chose North, East or West. The national resources which would then be required to engage in battles along the porous borders would be manifold of the billions of dollars spent presently by India. The political dilemma doesn't stop there, secession by India in Jammu and Kashmir would greatly encourage dormant desires for independence elsewhere viz. Naxal-belt, Punjab, North-eastern states etc. In principle Kashmir is also contested on the grounds of being a Muslim majority region in a secular nation.

Jammu and Kashmir is an imagined place, an artificial political entity created by the British in 1846. Christopher Snedden, an Australian strategist, adds, "Throughout its hundred and one years of existence, little held this diverse and disunited state together except autocratic rule by Dogra Maharajas". It was not unexceptional that Hindu Maharaja kept their Muslim majority subjugated. The opposite was true elsewhere.

Histories' fault lines tend to endure. That is why Yugoslavia splintered into ethnic components 73 years after achieving statehood. This is also why Turkey, Iraq, Iran and Syria agree that an independent Kurdistan must never emerge, much as India and Pakistan now tacitly agree on the infeasibility of Kashmiri Independence.

The word "Kashmir" refers to the valley, where the desire to separate from India is the strongest. The erstwhile princely state of Jammu and Kashmir was almost 14 times as large and more diverse. Jammu now a Hindu-majority will be ever Indian, as will Buddhist—majority Ladakh. Kashmir's traditional Islamic character itself has changed from inclusive Sufism to hardliner *Salafism*.

Independent Kashmir

What we call Pakistan Occupied Kashmir (POK) or Azad Kashmir, is now firmly under Pakistani control. The pretentious façade of independence has gradually disappeared from this region. The last component of former princely state of Jammu and Kashmir is the remote North-Eastern region of *Gigit-Baltistan*, whose people were once unequivocal about being Pakistani. New material has surfaced which refutes the widely held belief that Maharaja Hari Singh's accession and India's intervention in Kashmir were sparked by a Pakistan backed Oct 1947 invasion of the state by warlike Pashto or Pathan tribesmen. By the time this happened three major actions had already divided the princely state of Jammu and Kashmir.

Firstly, a Muslim uprising in Poonch (Western Jammu) driven largely by former Indian army soldiers who had a host of grievances against Maharaja

Hari Singh's regime. The uprising saw large parts of Jammu rising in mutiny. The second action, overshadowed by the carnage in Punjab, was a massacre in Eastern Jammu. Nearly 70,000 people were killed. A similar massacre raising the death toll by another 25,000 occurred in Western Jammu. Hindus and Sikhs appear to have been specifically targeted in both these secluded incidents of manslaughter. Lastly, the creation of a provisional government by the rebels in the insubordinate areas of Poonch sealed the fate of an entire future generation.

All these events unfolded in the 10 weeks following the creation of Pakistan on 15th August 1947. Hari Singh accessioned to India on October 26 that same year. But by then thousands had already died, the state had been divided, and an everlasting bitterness had been born.

They have since been competing and compounding reasons for Kashmir imbroglio, all of these have been dealt with in great detail previously in the book. It will suffice to say here that India lost the hearts of Kashmiri Muslims in 1987, two years before the start of armed rebellion and the Pundit's exodus. The birth of an Independent Islamic narrative, no matter how tokenised it sounds, harks back to the 8th century. "Same old dream, passed to us at our birth" raps Kashmiri singer M.C. Kash, in his latest song. The plebiscite, promise by Pundit Jawaharlal Nehru and Mahatma Gandhi is a political suicide for any Indian government. But if India and Pakistan want to plug a bottomless drain of ever descending morals, money, lives and stability, they could consider something that both countries abhor a third party solution.

The third party should be the people of Jammu and Kashmir. Hindu, Muslim, Buddhist and Sikh, from both sides of the border. Let them pick their representatives and start talking about their anger, sorrows, and solutions, anything and everything. Groups happy with the current status quo can opt out, implying that their reason will stay where it is. Possible solutions could be tested through a series of polls. It could also lead, we believe, to things that people really want: open borders, trade and trust. How long might this take? It could take anything from 20-30 years to 50 years or even more. Time is not a factor. Indeed, what has anyone got to lose?

Kashmir: An Integral Part of India

Kashmir is indeed at the core of a very divergent, eclectic and plural India. That message has been constant during the political discourses in the Valley, where separatists clog the airwaves between two elections at the expense of a national narrative. Political parties must set aside their differences and their partisan electoral impulses to dominate the discourse in the troubled state. They must devise special opportunities for Kashmiri youth to give them a stake in the survival and prosperity of the country. The challenge is to link India's destiny with that of the alienated province. For that to happen, the political class will have to work together for a bright future for the very people they profess to support, more so because they are residents of a state whose territory is so often violated by the enemies of peace.

The Kashmiri pundits who have been chased out of their homes should be called back and facilities should be provided for their proper rehabilitation. As the rightful owners of their movable and immovable property they should also be given financial assistance to settle down once again in their own land. That will be the Kashmiriyat and the pride of incredible India. This will solve almost all the internal problems of Kashmir and the Kashmiri people. In times of cultural disorientation and confusion the voices of liberalism grow stronger. Sadly there is no leadership to provide the much needed constructive vision. There is no leadership—political or intellectual—confident enough to assert the virtues of modernism in a society that is still in the grip of superstition and backward traditions. In a society becoming increasingly dogmatic and jingoist, there is no leadership to assert the values of progressiveness and pluralism.

The need of the hour is a rooted cosmopolitanism. Without sounding disconnected, leaders must speak the language of reform at every level of society. The story of Hyper-nationalism, hurt sentiments, constant outrage at artistic expressions is dominant today. There is no objection to daily incidents of individuals upholding there religious, nationalist and regional credentials above the national interest. Unless a robust alternative emerges both in politics and in society, the future generation will continue to tear down paintings, burn novels and send out bloodthirsty war-cry against "Infidels" and "Traitors". They have no knowledge of a better course of action. Not long ago an elderly gentleman in a modest loincloth, who lived like a naked Mahatma (*Fakeer*), challenged every shibboleth that disgraced the human society in the form of caste, religion or region. He is called the Father of India.

Peace-Meet

On 29th September, the Prime Minister of India Dr. Man Mohan Singh and Mr. Nawaz Sarif (the Prime Minister of Pakistan) met in New York for an hour long meeting. Both the Prime Ministers agreed and described the meeting as "Useful". They concluded that restoring and sustaining the cease fire along the line of control (LoC) was mandatory if any progress was to be expected in bilateral relations. The Director Generals of Military Operations (DGMO) of both countries have been tasked to ensure that peace and tranquillity returns to the LoC. While briefing the Media on the first interaction between the two Prime ministers of India and Pakistan the National Security Advisor of India Mr. Shiv Shankar Menon said, "There is no timeline, but we expect results as soon as possible". Menon counted punishing the culprits of 26/11 Mumbai Terror Attacks—"along with terrorism in general" among the immediate issues. After the meeting the two Prime Ministers, which came in the backdrop of recurring violations of the ceasefire along the LoC, arrived at some understanding on how to move forward. But Menon was cagey while responding to questions pertaining to the revival of bilateral relations between the two countries. All such high level interactions indicate a new stage. The situation is better than it was one and a half hours ago.

Although, Prime Ministers of both the countries have met, but warmth is still missing in Indo-Pak bilateral ties. People from both the countries say that this meeting is meaningless. From past experiences it is obvious that Pakistan will bring up the antiquated Kashmir issue, while India maintains that there is no dispute with Pakistan. Jammu and Kashmir is an integral part of India. Pakistan will have to vacate the illegitimately occupied regions with in Kashmir either today or tomorrow. For many this meeting is a waste of time and energy. In fact the protestors have succeeded in radicalization of the army and civilians in Pakistan. On the day of the meeting there was a bomb blast in Peshawar which killed 40 people and injured another hundred and thirty. The Prime Ministers of both countries were in a cordial summit to better the relations when another unfortunate incident took the tribal region of Pakistan by surprise—a US drone.

Pakistan media accused India for these tragedies without any evidence or investigation. Before the summit, it was Pakistan's twin attacks in Jammu on a police station at Hira Nagar and army camp in Samba. The pressure was on the Indian Prime Minister to make Indo-Pak summit more realistic than rhetorical, more pragmatic than passionate because three terrorists cannot be allowed to set the terms for a nation. Equal credit needs to be given to Mr. Nawaz Sharif who is Pakistan's first Prime Minister to challenge the might of his army chief. Opting out of this peace process would have only weakened the Premiers and in fact strengthened those who utilize proxy war as a strategic asset in their arsenal against India.

But now that Dr. Man Mohan Singh has taken the plunge, he needs to avoid the vicious cycle of fruitless argumentation. It is usually the greed for an outcome and the haste over a consensual press statement that ends up being the ruin of such summits. From Agra to Sharm-El-Sheikh; from Musharraf to Yusuf Gilani, it is the headline hunting instinct of subcontinent politicians that converts such meetings into dysfunctional melodramatic misadventures. This schizophrenia of the India-Pakistan equation is to be blamed for the disequilibrium in their bilateral relationship. In other words, while the PM may feel braver about taking a risk with his foreign policy in the final few months of his term, he cannot overload the Sharif meeting with his own longstanding and unfulfilled desire to make a lasting breakthrough with Pakistan. The Indian Prime Minister Dr. Man Mohan Singh had vowed that he would definitely meet Sharif in the US and he had a meeting as planned. Dr. Man Mohan Singh, before the meeting, made it clear that this particular summit was to put an end to the violation of cease fire along the LOC. He refused to include Kashmir (as Jammu and Kashmir is an integral part of India) on the agenda and declared that peace should prevail between both the countries and attackers of 26/11 must be punished.

Although the meeting concluded with a cordial media conference, it sent across a stern message to Pakistan, who needs to tighten the reins of its irrepressible brainchild—Jihad. Such photo-op meetings expand political capital for minimal gain. However the citizens of both countries, overwhelmed by a sense of déjà-vu upon glancing at the pictures of their leaders shaking hands, truly wish that this time round peace will prevail.

WHERE TO DRAW?

I would like to share an intriguing fact—the last few pages of this book were finally penned down on 2ⁿᵈ of October, 2013. The nation was celebrating Gandhi Jayanti, 144ᵗʰ birth anniversary of their Mahatma, by observing a national holiday while the world commemorated the life of Mr. Mohandas Karamchand Gandhi as the International Day of Non-Violence. In India, Gandhi might be revered as the Father of the Nation, but elsewhere he is known as a man who walked the talk. His teachings are an integral part of not only Indian but world history.

Today is also the birth anniversary of Lal Bahadur Shastri, the Prime Minister who led India to victory in the war of 1965, who died in Russia during the summit that brought an end to the second war between India and Pakistan. He gave the slogan *"Jai Javan Jai Kisan"*—Hail the Youth, Hail the Labour. Communal, provincial and linguistic conflicts weaken a country therefore it is imperative to forge a sense of unity in diversity.

Gandhi in the Valley

In the context of Jammu and Kashmir Mr. Mohandas Karamchand Gandhi is a great source of inspiration for the people of the State, especially the youth. In 1947 when the state was burning in the fire of communal frenzy, Pt. Jawaharlal Nehru, the then Prime Minister of India, resolved the territorial dispute on the behest of Mr. Gandhi thereby putting an end to the bloodshed. It was the will of a frail dhoti-clad man who spent most of his time spinning cotton on a wooden wheel. His un-compromised ideals have sailed far away from us. His wise words are inaudible in the backdrop of our loud music; his lustre has been dimmed by the twinkling of cell phones and we are running out of patience in the rat race to keep India shining.

Youth of 21st Century

India is the land of the young. According to national demographics, 50 percent of the total population is in the age group of 18 to 40. And this youth is inspired by cricketers, movie stars, rock bands and in general anything that is cosmetically lofted. Such a generation does not have the ability to fathom the significance of Mr. Gandhi or understand why he was revered as a Mahatma.

We spoke to the people of Jammu and Kashmir, particularly students, about relevance of learning the Gandhi philosophy. Their reply was that—He is very much a part of their lives. His teachings are still accessible to them through his books and stories of his life. Gandhi is an indomitable spirit, filled with compassion for humanity and never appearing, in the least bit, intimidated by any opposition. He epitomizes the fact that living truthfully is the highest achievement of all living beings. His non-violent philosophy, his stupor and his general demeanour are what set him apart from other revolutionary thinkers and visionaries. Above all, he proved that words are not important and what matters are actions and one's belief in the truth of one's conviction. The Gandhi factor for younger India is not merely a history lesson. What makes Mahatma's legacy so wonderful is that young people in this world continue to be inspired by him. Gandhi's twin ideals of honesty and non-violence form the basis for understanding the notions of morality in present world. Gandhi's teachings are now a part of academic curriculum in schools, colleges and universities. Gandhi's ideas and experiences act as a lighthouse for the misguided youth in frenzied ocean of materialism, his philosophy of "simple living and high thinking" can pave the way for a better future.

Since the youth today is engulfed in a wave of violent, aggressive and intolerant machismos, they should take the teachings of the Father of Nation seriously and should practice honesty, compassion, live in harmony and the act of forgiving everyone. One should eternally pursue *Satyagraha* and let the people of the world know that the change they wish for must come from within. Gandhi also taught people that fighting against the odds is difficult but not impossible, this stirs up a sense of patriotism in today's youth, which seems lost somewhere. We have the power to change the nation and not let the sacrifices of our freedom fighters go waste.

Trial and Tribulations of the Mahatma

We find Gandhi's autobiography a testimony to his truthfulness and honesty in which he reveals every single detail of his life, including mistakes. It is written with stark honesty, urging the reader to be honest and forthcoming as well. Gandhi's written words imply that at the end of the day what matters is inner peace and one can only achieve it through the truth. His vision of India was not just a dream. He had pragmatic solutions to make that happen.

Gandhi's life was exemplary and full of qualities for which we admire him. He showed the path of self-sufficiency, one of the most arduous tasks for human beings. Despite hurdles he persisted with his acts of *Sarvodaya* (welfare for all). His positive, practically viable and sincere approach along with the determination to follow his heart was exceptional and inspiring. Irrespective of whether anyone would adopt his methods or not, he had full conviction in his ideals. It is fascinating to see how determined he was even in the face of adversity. He never budged from his commitment to the cause or lost his moral ground. The Whole world is in admiration of this great man due to his resilience and dignity. He was a man who rose above all the negativity and faced adversaries with a calm dignity, a true patriot who readily gave up everything to save his country. He generated patriotism, and fanned the flames of passion for a cause. He awakened us to our inner selves, and if we all learn to be self-reliant, then all the evils of the world would automatically clear away.

A South African historian and author of *Gandhi before India* writes, "You sent us a lawyer and we gave you back a Mahatma". This is true. In 1893, Gandhi sailed for Durban to mediate in a dispute between two Gujarati Merchants. He stayed there for more than two decades serving the Indian community as a lawyer, friend, mentor and a leader. Based first in Natal and then in Transvaal, he developed a moral and political philosophy that he then sought to apply on a far wider scale. Had he practiced law after returning to India in 1915, which was his original plan, Gandhi would have scarcely grown out of the insular and conventional mercantile world that he grew up in. It was by going overseas that he learnt to appreciate the social and cultural heterogeneity of his homeland. Gandhi travelled to South Africa to represent Muslim merchants. But when the guarantor who had originally supported his Satyagraha backed out, both his movement and morale were kept alive by Tamil activists, especially Mr. Thambi Naidoo, whose wife and sons were also arrested along with Mr. Gandhi.

Gandhi's social consciousness was also deepened by his encounters with European radicals. Gandhi and his wife, Kasturbha, shared a house in Johannesburg with a British couple named Henry and Millie Polka. Henry was a Jew with a natural empathy for the underdogs. He assisted Gandhi in his law practice, helped run his journal, the "Indian opinion" and made several trips to the subcontinent to raise awareness about sufferings of Indians in South Africa. Millie was a Christian socialist with strong feminist leanings. She pushed Gandhi to take women rights more seriously while encouraging Kasturba Gandhi to be less submissive to her often overbearing husband.

South Africa also served as the incubation centre for Satyagraha, the technique of non-violent resistance that is Gandhi's legacy to India and the world. Between 1906 and 1909, and again 1913, he led his compatriots in movements against discriminatory laws and practices. Several thousand Indians courted imprisonment. Gandhi himself underwent four jail terms. In the course of the struggle, he closely interacted with Indians of low caste and Dalit backgrounds. It was there in the four walls of the State prison, that Gandhi established the core elements of his ideology: the promotion of Hindu-Muslim harmony, the respect for linguistic diversity, the mitigation of caste and gender inequalities, the eschewing of violent method to resist oppression. These were the methods and beliefs he brought home to India, applying them, with uneven success in his lifetime.

He has been one of the pioneers in the practice of spirituality in modern Indian History. The ideal spirituality is sacred beyond contamination and at the same time it is dynamic enough to face rejection, fear and violence with fairness, courage and self control. His amiable and religious mother *Putlibai* and his equally devote nurse Rambha were key spiritual influences around young Gandhi. He was also greatly enthused by noted Jain Philosopher and scholar, *Shrimad Rajchandra*. Reading the Bhagwat Gita, one of the ancient Vedic scriptures, and the Bible introduced him to the ideas like—"love thy enemy" and "turn the other cheek". Tolstoy's "The kingdom of God is with you" and Henry David Thoreau's essay "Civil Disobedience" encouraged Gandhi to initiate a non-violent movement against the pitiless government of South Africa. He later used the same tools to oppose racism and ethnic injustice being done against the dark skinned people. Tolstoy's book, "A letter to a Hindu" had a profound effect on Gandhi and his organization. Later, Mr. Gandhi sent a letter to Tolstoy looking for approval to republish his book as "A letter to Hindu Gujarati". Tolstoy approved the request and the two were in regular touch until the former's death in 1910. Satyagraha extended the same concept by showing that love as the weapon of choice could even bring down a mighty colonial empire like Britain. Spirituality being the epicentre of Gandhi's philosophy gave him immense conviction in the power of non-violence.

Gandhi rejected the Noble Peace Prize repeatedly after being first recommended in 1937. The Noble Peace Prize was awarded to no one in the year 1948, as the Noble Committee had intended to award the prize to Gandhi who was unfortunately assassinated that year.

The whole world says, "We miss you today, Bapu".

Pakistan's Surrogate father

Today, India has become a powerful, free and secular nation by virtue of a Gandhian philosophy. While India adopted a progressive policy that promoted peaceful endeavours of economic and social elevation, Pakistan refused to accept Mahatma Gandhi as the Father of a common lineage. They preferred an Islamic way of rule which is laced with hatred and violence. An entire country has been fed on fundamentalist notions targeting India through a network of *Madrasas*, Schools and Colleges. However the fact of the matter is that India is home to more Muslims than the entire population of Pakistan.

The Muslims who left India at the time of partition in 1947 still continue to partake in an existential battle, whereas the Indian society has evolved over the same period of time into a fertile intellectual ground for vibrant individual aspirations, which are duly sponsored and promoted by the state. Pakistani citizens categorize Indian migrants as *Mujaheir*, a racial slang based on their refugee status. Contrary to what was promised at the time of partition, these migrants are denied equal political rights and social status within the native cultural circuit of Pakistan. Nobody had envisaged the sectarian clashes that surfaced within the Muslim community of Pakistan. Numerous bombings, targeting areas with dense migrant population are reported by media every month. All this hostility has made the social order in Pakistan very fragile with chances of a civil war in the near future. Moreover Pakistani population is facing an economic crisis due to non-receipt of aid from a recession hit US. Ultimately we get a time bomb full of fidgety, aggravated, and contumacious fractions contesting for regional supremacy at the cost of sanity and human life called Islamic Republic of Pakistan.

Why the Mahatma Is Even More Relevant Today?

Sixty six years after Gandhi's death should we still remember him? Endless atrocities in the name of Jihad, frequent violations of cease fire along the LoC, rampant Naxal guerrillas in the tribal belts, riots in Uttar Pradesh, bomb strikes in metropolises, brutalization of women, political corruption—the exemplary life of Mohandas Karamchand Gandhi remains completely relevant.

A lot of has changed after the death of this great man. In every sphere of our life the soul of *Bapu* (father) has been giving us strength through his twin principles of truth and nonviolence. These ideals are responsible for the progress India has made in the last 66 years. Since 1947, India's spasmodic journey has been widely publicized and envied. Our leaders have taken Gandhi's words as the guiding force to run the biggest democracy of the whole world. Peace brings positivity and development and that was the mantra of the Father of the Nation. We need Gandhi and Gandhi's.

Domestic woes of Pakistan

The leadership in Pakistan has alternated between authoritative military domination and a puppet civilian government. The recent winds of change blessed Pakistan with two successive democratic elections and for the first time ever an elected political party completed a full term in office. The senior army leadership has been able to recognize the changing civil society pulse in Pakistan, though it may still be unwilling to relinquish control over three or four vital areas of security and foreign policy especially those pertaining to India, Afghanistan, US and nuclear issues.

In a surprisingly scathing indictment, the Abbottabad Commission of Enquiry report, leaked to the media in July, concluded that Pakistan's military and political leaders collectively displayed an exceptional degree of incompetence and irresponsibility which was historically unrivalled. Moreover their inability to detect Osama-bin-Laden's presence in Abbottabad was condemned as its worst intelligence failure since 1971. It cautioned the army against its pervasive role in the future. Furthermore it recommended an honest, competent and consultative leadership to democratically enunciate a national security policy. It also advocated dismantling Pakistan's state sponsored terrorist infrastructure which had deleterious blowback effects on the security establishment within the country. The new civilian executive body must display courage, dexterity and commitment as it perseveres to bridle the military. The entire world is observing how soon or how effectively the Pakistan Government accomplishes the task at hand.

One of the foremost problems confronting Pakistan would be their own illegitimate brainchild—Taliban. Nawaz Sharif's main political opponent during the election campaign, former cricketer Imran Khan talked of extending an olive branch to the militants. Similarly Sharif's own political party, the Pakistan Muslim League (Nawaz), has many closet fundamentalist in its rank who favour talks with Tehreek-e-Taliban Pakistan (TTP).

The All Party Conference (APC) held on September 9th 2013, agreed on an inclusive dialogue with all stakeholders to restore peace in the region. General Kayani confirmed, "The army will follow whatever decision is taken by the government". Political commentators in Pakistan initially commended this rare partnership between the army and the civilian population but the recent killing of General Sanaullah Niazi in Upper Dir forced Gen. Kayani to caution that the army's rectitude should not be interpreted as a sign of weakness. However the attacks on Christians in a Peshawar church and the continuing bomb blasts do not augur well.

Since it began fighting the Taliban, the Pakistan army has suffered 12,829 casualties in the war against terror, including 3097 killed. Total army officers killed were estimated to be 196 an unusually high ratio of officers, one for every 16 soldiers killed. This dilemma continues to haunt the senior army leadership. On one hand it remains conscious of the need to maintain army's image as the defender of Islam while on the other hand firm military action is compulsory to counteract the aggression of its fraternal coreligionists.

Because the P.M.L. (N) was soft on Punjabi sectarian radical groups like the Lashkar-e-Jhangvi, an impression persists that the civilian leadership, both in Islamabad and in Khyber Pakhtunkhwa, may be at cross purposes with the security forces. In the recent past when even the elite sections of the society were not spared by sectarian violence, the state apparatus did lumber into a retaliatory mode but failed to engage beyond short lived palliatives. The difficulty is that many discerning analysts in Pakistan detect a spreading reluctance within the army ranks to sustainably fight with hardened militants and wonder whether this Munich Chamberlain style appeasement will lead to any different outcome this time round.

Against this back drop, Nawaz's choice of the next army chief will be vital. Before the elections, Sharif promised to go by seniority. Lt. Gen. Haroon Aslam, who headed the elite Special Services Group (SSG) and took part in anti-terror operations in Swat, is the senior most in the batch of eligible candidates. But instead Gen. Kayani who was the Director General of logistics and staff (considered a backwater post) got Sharif's affection. He was also one of the junior officers sent out by Gen. Musharraf to disarm Lt. Gen. Ziauddin when Nawaz Sharif was deposed in the October 1999 coup. The next in line is Lt. Gen. Rashad Mahmood, former GOC-IV Corps Lahore. He seems to be Gen. Kayani's choice, having previously served as his deputy in the ISI. Presently he is the Chief of General Staff, a key staff position. He has also served as the military secretary to President Rafique Tarar, friend of the Late Mian Mohammad Sharif. Another Senior General of the same batch is Raheel Sharif, brother of a Martyred war hero whose case is being pushed by one of Sharif's Ministers. Lt. Gen. (Retired) Abdul Qadir Baloch. General Kayani appointed him as the Director General, Inspectorate of Weapons Evaluation and Training (IWET), another sinecure post. The other two generals in this cohort are Tariq Khan, GOC I Corps Mangla, highly rated professionally because of his stint as IG Frontier Corps during the Swat Operations in 2009, and Zahirul Islam, current DG,ISI.

Sharif would have to make a choice not only on the basis of consensual perceptions within the army, but also among key external and internal power brokers. A key deciding factor would also be the chosen officer's personal opinion about sensitive issues like Islamic radicalism and civil-military relations. Any discord between the army's choice and the PM's political decision could carry the seeds of future upheaval.

Asked recently to compare his present stint as Pakistan's PM with his previous two terms, Nawaz replied that this tenure was the most difficult. Despite his landslide electoral victory his first 100 days in office saw him already boxed-in by domestic challenges. The first challenge is law and order. More than 1000 people have already died at the hands of Islamic militants since his election. His attempts to hold talks with the Tehrik-e-Taliban Pakistan (TTP) are yet to materialize, despite his unconditional invitation to all stake holders. Terror incidents in Karachi and other important cities have skyrocketed and the military has come out strongly against the talks. The army insists only a military solution is possible. The Baluchistan insurgency refuses to die down.

Secondly the economy has been crippled by extended terms of ineffective governance. The foreign investment has dried up in the midst of all this internal violence. Attempts to jumpstart the economy have had a mixed reaction. The Pakistani Rupee has been constantly sliding down against the American Dollar. All major Industries have been hit by an acute power shortage in the country. Many factories in Faisalabad and the neighbouring Industrial belt in Punjab have shut shop, affecting exports. His attempts to oblige India with the "Most Favourable Nation" status were thwarted again, this time by the Commerce Ministry which did not meet the deadline for formalities.

Pakistan's trinity of challenges is completed by unstable and unyielding state executive machinery. Nawaz has had limited success in trying to assert control over the military and its Intelligence Agencies. His desire to choose a pliant new army chief has led to delays in the selection process. Fearing their authority will be trimmed. The Corp commanders have ganged-up against the elected Government. One of the ways in which the army is getting back at Nawaz is by sabotaging his peace overtures to India. In fact Prime Minister Nawaz Sharif's other confidence building measures also fail to garner any military support. Surprisingly the control of the Foreign office remains with the ISI leaving de-facto foreign Minister Sartaj Aziz in an ambiguous executive capacity. The Interior Minister of Pakistan, Choudhary Nisaar Ali Khan on 30th September 2013, rejected the allegations made by Indian External Affair Minister Salman Khurshid against the Pakistan Army. In a strongly worded statement issued through the Press Information Department, Chaudhary said that the remarks made by Khurshid were unnecessary and against diplomatic norms.

The Line of Control (LoC) has almost become the new litmus test of the India-Pakistan relationship. Prime Minister Man Mohan Singh repeatedly emphasized upon the towering tension along the LoC and the problem of cross-border terrorism before the United Nations General Assembly, at his meeting with President Barack Obama and during his confabulations with Pakistan's Prime Minister Nawaz Sharif. Of course cross-border terrorism has been a red thread throughout India's dialogue with Pakistan. However, the present tensions along the LoC are more important to the bilateral relationship than they have been in the past. To begin with the LoC ceasefire meant that militant infiltration across the border fell from a few hundred to some isolated instances here and there. Additionally the ceasefire made it possible to monitor the militant infiltration across the border more extensively and with relatively less distraction. Most importantly, the end of the endless artillery exchanges between the two armies and the drop in militant activity helped bring about a degree of stability in Kashmir that is still being enjoyed by the locals. Internationally, a quieter LoC reduced concerns about Indo-Pak relations being further strained to the extent of inviting possible nuclear war. Finally, the normalization of the activities along the LoC was seen as an indication of a de facto acceptance that this would eventually be the International boundary. The relative equanimity along the LoC has been one of the primary accomplishments of the peace process carried out between President Pervez Musharraf and two Indian prime ministers, Mr. Atal Bihari Vajpayee and Dr. Singh. The recent violence along the LoC and the definite spike in militant activity inside Kashmir threaten to annul these gains. The LoC is important because it encapsulates the hope of Indo-Pak peace process. That process may be moribund, but it is much easier to revive it if a legacy of previous generation's diplomatic efforts endures the test of time.

Pakistan's outgoing army chief may be looking to set an Anti-India agenda for the next general to come. There is also a possibility that Kayani might become the joint chief of military operations of Pakistan and go on to head the entire army establishment of the country. Incursion along the LoC are a part and parcel of life in the Sub-Continent, but the recent hyperactivity incurred due to infiltrators from Pakistan has raised questions about whether the November 2003 ceasefire needs to be reviewed. The Pakistani army seems to be on an overdrive to push in as many infiltrators as it can to stir things up in Jammu and Kashmir ahead of the winter months. The outgoing Pakistani army chief General Ashfaq Parvez Kayani could be looking at setting the agenda for his yet-to-be named successor. This is perhaps his way of consolidating his legacy of waging covert war against India. He may also be sending out strong signal to Pakistani Prime Minister Nawaz Sharif that it is not civilian leadership but the military that has and will continue to dictate the Kashmir agenda. Mr. Sharif's peace overtures will amount to nothing if Pakistani army refuses to cooperate. Indian army Chief General Bikram Singh has ordered his commanders to launch retaliatory strikes with artillery guns and mortars if provoked by Pakistan. But fortunately for Pakistan, the Indian army has exercised utmost restraint in the face of repeated and grave provocation.

Despite stiff domestic opposition, Prime Minister Man Mohan Singh walked the extra mile in New York when he met Mr. Sharif. His magnanimity was returned with one of the biggest infiltration bids in the *Keran* sector of *Kupwara* district. The two PM's declared that their respective Director Generals of Military Operations would be asked to set up a mechanism to stabilize the LoC. But clearly Mr. Sharif is either unable or unwilling to deliver on promises. He has huge reservoirs of political acumen but if he can't prevail upon the Pakistani army to give peace a chance, there is little point in humouring his whims.

The only formidable course of action for India is to ensure that further infiltration is stopped decisively and those who have already entered the Indian Territory are dealt with swiftly and ruthlessly. As the situation unfolds along the LoC in the coming months, it would be interesting to see who actually gets to call the shots in Pakistan. But there is little hope that better times are in the offering. This is bound to be a personal disappointment to Dr. Singh, whose political ambitions were to be materialized in the form of a lasting peace accord with Pakistan.

India's President Parnab Mukherjee has taken a very tough stance against Pakistan for ceasefire violation in Jammu and Kashmir. According to him it is easy for the Government to point fingers at Non-State actors and escape the blame. Pakistan should refrain from providing shelter and training to the so called Non-State actors in Pakistan occupied territory of Kashmir. Otherwise the relation between the two countries cannot be normalized.

The context of 2013 and the back drop of 1998 are certainly different. The military in Pakistan has lost control of many civilian institutions including the Presidency and the Judiciary. This means, the General cannot stage a constitutional coup. In Pakistan power still flows from the barrel of a gun and there is no guarantee that senior army leaders would abstain from ordering a bullet-headed political seizure. Nawaz is one man who has learnt his lessons from two run-ins with military. Negotiating with Taliban as well as guardedly criticizing the U.S. drones attacks have nothing in them that would remotely trouble Rawalpindi. Military in Pakistan has divine rights which constitute the basis for military's special place in Pakistani society. Therefore no peace loving citizen in either country should count on Sharif and talk of a "Lahore Peace Process 2.0". Kayani has been in the present seat for five years which means most of the senior army commanders are close to him. Even when he retires his shadow will persist.

The army has chosen Imran Khan to be their clandestine poster boy. One of the candidates from his political party, Tehreek-e-Insaaf, has been caught on tape proudly admitting this. The line and length of Tehreek-E-Insaaf is decided by its veiled captain Kayani and not the former swing bowler.

General's Retirement Plan

Pakistan army chief Kayani announced on 6th of September, 2013 that he would retire and step down from his position by the end of November, dispelling rumours that he is being considered for a new position in the military. According to a press release issued by the army, Kayani will step down on November 29 as army chief after serving for more than twice the normal tenure. The choice for his replacement has not been announced. "It is too early to say who will replace him but my bet is on General Haroon", commented Ayaz Khan, a senior editor. Kayani, in the army press release, said that he has no intention of extending his tenure as the chief of army staff. "For quite some time, my current responsibilities and likely future planes have been debated in the media, with all sorts of rumours and speculations doing the rounds. The subject of being entrusted with new duties has also come up in several reports. I am grateful to the politico leadership and the nation for reposing their trust in me and the Pakistan army at this important juncture of our national history. However, I share the general opinion that institutions and traditions are stronger than individuals and one must take precedence", said the army chief in his statement. Kayani had earlier said that Prime Minister Nawaz Sharif wanted to make him Head of a revamped and more powerful Joint Chiefs of Staff Committee (JCSC), but the army chief has declined this position, officials confirmed. Express News, a local TV Channel said that Sharif planned to overhaul the JCSC, a largely ceremonial office in to a "Central Defence Body" by restoring its command over the entire military establishment and giving it additional powers. It said that the new JCSC Chief would be in charge of the nuclear arsenal, would decide on action against terrorists, and exercise the right to promote, post and transfer key military officers. In the press release, Gen. Kayani added, "As I complete my tenure, the will of the people has taken root and a constitutional order is in place. The armed forces of Pakistan fully support and want to strengthen this democratic order." Is this the end of Kayani's services? Only time will tell whether Haroon becomes the next army chief of Pakistan or somebody else will take the centre stage.

Moment of Truth

Right from the outset of 2013 the situation on the border has been volatile and it has further deteriorated in the recent months. Now how to solve this problem? Where to draw a line? This is a very complicated issue. Whether the Indian Polity should take a decision on the path shown by Mahatma Gandhi i.e. Gandhigiri or solve it via a more direct military confrontation is yet to be decided.

As per the democratic and secular standards conceived by the founding fathers of India—Pt. Jawaharlal Nehru, Mahatma Gandhi, Lal Bahadur Shastri—as well as the prominent contemporary leaders like Mr. Atal Bihari Vajpayee and Dr. Man Mohan Singh, the thought of a war with Pakistan never crosses any Indians heart because of the simple fact that we are the same people and before 1947 both the countries together formed the golden goose called "Bharat".

Since 1947 Pakistan has been waging a misguided war in the name of Islam against India and has repeatedly tasted dirt at the hands of righteous Indian soldiers. Therefore Indians are never intimidated by the Pakistani aggression. In fact, it is not in the nature of peace loving Indians to be vexed, irate or spiteful even in the presence of pestering neighbours like Pakistan. We have evolved a culture of tolerance which spreads far beyond the petty territorial ambitions of Pakistan. India served as the think tank for several progressive policies and movements including Non-Aligned Movement, Green Revolution and Chipko movement. Being the big brother, India fully supports Pakistan in all peaceful endeavours, so that it can develop its agriculture, industry, healthcare, infrastructure and the unique way of Islamic existence, the very reason for its inception.

India has cordial relations with all Muslim countries because of a long standing tradition of trade and cultural exchange. Islamic institutes receive special government aid under the various schemes for minorities. The country is also home to one of the biggest seminaries of Asia in Deoband, which imparts training to Muslim scholars from all over the world in *Dini* Education. Muslims have a large political representation and occupy important offices including the Presidency. A much larger number of Muslims address India as their home than the entire population of Pakistan. Special importance is given to legitimate tourists from across the border including free medical treatment and preferential visa regimes. Our policy towards the visitors to our nation is "Atithi Devo Bhava" which means, "Guest should be served like a representative of God".

It is rationally incomprehensible to understand why Pakistanis are eating Kashmir, drinking Kashmir, thinking Kashmir and dreaming Kashmir. Political parties are elected on the basis of propaganda to annex Kashmir. The proprietors of a "failed" Muslim Pakistan mislead the youth from both sides of the border into believing that a Muslim Kashmir is desirable. They have already shown how fundamentalist Islam can cripple social, economic, educational and scientific progress of a country. And to top it all they preach that such a dream is achievable by terrorism alone. Muslims in Kashmir have forcibly thrown out all other communities from the valley. These atrocities were carried out by the clandestine Pakistan army itself at many places. To make matters worse Pakistan tutored the youth of Kashmir in the false doctrine of "Mujahedeen". These naive boys and girls have been waging a war against their own elected government. Pakistan doesn't plan on vacating Pak occupied Kashmir (PoK). Instead it wants to annex the entire Kashmir region. It has continually failed to succeed in direct military confrontation. Hence it creates unrest in the valley and then channels the frustration of the masses into its terror machinery. The truth is that in 1947 Pakistan sent some tribes to annex the whole Jammu and Kashmir region when Maharaja Hari Singh joined India and merged the state with the Indian Union and rejected Pakistan.

Since then generations of Pakistani polity have been singing the same song—"We will gift Kashmir to the people of Pakistan after snatching it from India through army action." Every Pakistani believes that one day or the other their rulers would come clean on this promise. Overcome by a desire to live in "Paradise" Pakistanis are willing to sacrifice their life which would otherwise flourish in the plentiful valley of Indus. To justify their insatiability, the unrighteous quote Islamic texts consenting a crusade or "Jihad" for achieving their unholy goal. The extent of this reckless approach can easily be estimated by their slander past—26/11, attack on parliament; beheading of Indian soldiers; Kashmiri Pundit exodus of 1990; Sheltering Osama-bin-Laden and the recent twin attacks just before the visit of Indian Premier.

Indians from all communities come together to constitute a peaceful and progressive modern society whose goodwill spreads uniformly throughout the world. There is unrestricted freedom of speech and thought in the national media. Pakistan is taking undue advantage of India's cultural "weakness". The fountain-head of terrorism is situated in Pakistan due to the blinkered *Dini* Education of Islamic culture propagated through a vast network of *Madrasas*, Schools and colleges in the country. The height of radicalization had attracted Bin Laden, the most wanted man in the world, to seek refuge in Pakistan's province of Abottabad. Pakistani army has been recruiting terrorists from Afghanistan (Taliban), Somalia, Libya, Tunisia, Yemen, Kazakhstan, Bosnia, Syria, Palestine and other Islamic countries to wage a war in Kashmir. The recent attack on Samba and Hiranagar in Jammu is an eye opener for India.

Junta Party President Subramanian Swami (now BJP) whose party is a constituent of the National Democratic Alliance of India, said, "We are not ready to compromise on an inch of land in Kashmir. The only thing to be done is to get back the Pakistan occupied part of Kashmir. Kashmir is an integral part of India and there is nothing to be resolved." On 22nd May 2013 in Srinagar he added, "Plebiscite was not promised by the Indian Government to the people of Kashmir."

Hurriyat Leader Umar Pharooq, while offering Friday prayers in Kashmir, said, "Kashmir would have naturally gone to Pakistan given its religious and political affinities." Such statements strengthen the Home Ministry's claim that Mir Waiz is no different from fellow separatist leader Sayed Ali Shah Gellani and thus he should not be allowed to travel abroad. Seen internationally as a face of Kashmir, the Awami Action Committee Chairman had applied for a passport on January 3, 2013. "There are communication intercepts that clearly show Mir Waiz was in touch with his Pakistani masters. There is no difference between Mir Waiz and Sayed Ali Shah Gellani for us," a senior officer said. Mir Waiz was not given the permission to travel abroad for UN Human Right Conference in March this year and Home Ministry was in no hurry to grant him a passport either. When contacted by journalists, Mir Waiz Farooq said that he had simply reacted to legal expert A.G. Noorani's statement that it was Mohammad Ali Jinnah who did not support right of self determination for Kashmir. "I was just putting things in a historical context." he explained. However, senior JKLF Leader on condition of anonymity said: "We were on the streets in

Pakistan. Demonstrations against Shahid's killing were led by our leader and chairman Amanullah Khan."

The Home Ministry's stance on Mir Waiz reveals a new strategy of not allowing hardliner separatists leader to box above their political weight. The Government feels that Kashmiri separatists like Yasin Malik should not be pampered, because Jammu and Kashmir Liberation Front (JKLF) was a part of the united Jihad council and received operational funding from Pakistan in the past. Malik turned conspicuously silent after the All Parties National Alliance (APNA) leader Arif Shahid, a PoK based staunch advocate of independent Kashmir, was gunned down by unidentified men in Rawalpindi on May 13. He might slowly understand that Pakistan has no plans of establishing a sovereign Kashmir, thus a fear is accumulating in all hard-lined leaders who might be deemed obsolete if Kashmir were to be separated from India. Just like Arif Shahid, many more leaders fear that their expiry date might be near.

JOINT ANTI-TERRORISM MECHANISM

The first meeting of India-Pakistan Joint Anti-Terrorism Mechanism was held in Islamabad in March 2007. A senior Home Ministry Official, part of the delegation from Delhi, bitterly complained about Islamabad's support to cross border terrorism. The head of the Pakistani delegation apparently told the delegate that all terrorism would end if India left Kashmir. Six years later the joint mechanism is dead, but Pakistan supported terrorism is rampant in Kashmir and the rest of Indian Hinterland. The recent increase in violence—suicide attacks, the killing of Indian Troops along the line of control (LoC), infiltration and cease fire violation—indicate that Jammu and Kashmir is taking a turn for the worse and the passive Pakistan Army chooses to look away. Prime Minister Man Mohan Singh put it very succinctly to his Pakistani counterpart Nawaz Sharif in New York last month. He emphasized the dominant influence of Pakistani Army on his government's policies towards India.

The escalation of violence in Kashmir is directly linked to the upcoming assembly elections in India and the US troop withdrawal from Afghanistan, scheduled for 2014. "Since 9/11 the Afghan-Pak Region has received the much needed light of constant vigilance thanks to the NATO forces which constantly monitor terrorist movements and communication.

US withdrawal will mean that this restive region will descend again into darkness, with India alone not having the capability to match the terror forces breeding in the region", says an Indian counter-terrorism official. While India has every reason and enough evidence to point the finger at the whorehouse of world terrorism, Pakistan, the Nawaz Sharif government is too weak to internally fight this menace. This became quite evident after his government indefinitely postponed the August 23 hangings of the Tehreek-e-Taliban Pakistan (TTP) terrorists accused of the 2009 attacks on Pak Army Headquarter in Rawalpindi. The reason being a threat from TTP to retaliate by executing high profile citizens whom they have kidnapped and continue to hold hostage—including Al Haider Gillani, son of former Pak PM Yusuf Raza Gilani, Shahbaz Taseer, son of former Punjab Governor Salman Taseer and Former ISI Brigadier Tahir Masoor. While New Delhi does not face a direct threat from the TTP, it is seriously concerned about the ISI controlled LeT groups' focus on India and the movement of its cadres to the Kunark and Nuristan provinces for strategic depth. Lashkar Chief Hafiz Saeed, who has personal links with Nawaz Sharif's party in Punjab has already publically promised full scale Jihad against India after the 2014 US pull out. "Until the Pak Army seals the LoC from its side, suicide attacks in civilian areas and renewed sabotage activities in the state will remain a distinct reality," says a senior Home Ministry Official.

The situation on the eastern front would take a turn for the worse too if Bangladesh Prime Minister Shekh Hasina loses the upcoming elections, which is again a probable prospect. Since the Awami league swept to power in 2009, Dhaka has been responsive to Indian security concerns and has cracked down on terrorist groups. With the Jamat-e-Islami and the *Disband* joining hands against Hasina, her electoral prospects are less than ideal. The rise of Jamat in Dhaka will lead to more radicalization and create more space for Rohingya Solidarity Organization and LeT joint ventures against the entire South Asia, including India. Nepal has taken decisive steps in positive direction towards Indo-Nepal relations, with Kathmandu going out of its way to root out terror directed against India. The arrest of LeT's Abdul Karim Tunda and IM's Yaseen Bhatkal and Asadullah Akhtar from Nepal bear testimony to the close bilateral counter terror operation. The same can be attributed to Sri Lanka which is opposed to any anti-India activity on its territory.

This leads us to the only unanswered question—Is India prepared to handle an onslaught on the western front in 2014?

The answer is a clear "No", because the Afghan-Pak region is an epicentre of terror and must be tackled jointly by major world powers or else the September 21, Nairobi mall attack and the Peshawar church attack will be repeated with sickening frequency.

As a frontline state against terror, India must improve its pre-emption capabilities and intelligence coverage of the region. It is time to shake off our lethargy and make decisive moves.

Soviets Invasion and Kashmir

Recalling 11 years of Jihad in Kashmir, a Lashkar-e-Tayyeba bulletin in 2001 spoke of a young man named Abu Waleed Zaki-ur-Rehman who fought the Soviet invasion alongside the mujahedeen for three years between 1987 and 1990. Once the Soviets left Afghanistan, young Abu Waleed and Pakistani clerics like Hafiz Mohammad Sayeed laid the foundation of Markaz-e-Taiba (Urdu for Centre for the Pure) in the Kunar province of Afghanistan on February 22 1990. At the same time, Kashmiri militants decided to take a leaf out of Afghan's book and lit the torch of Jihad in that state.

The Bulletin further claims that Mujahedeen began pouring in Kashmir. Later, another training centre, Baitul Mujahedeen (House of Mujahedeen), was established in Muzaffarabad, the capital of Pakistan occupied Kashmir, to facilitate Jihad in Jammu and Kashmir. "Either in the end of 1990 or at the start of 1991, the first group of Mujahedeen reached Baitul Mujahedeen in Muzaffarabad," the Bulletin stated. That was the beginning of the Jihad in India, linked intrinsically with Soviet withdrawal from Afghanistan. Over the past 23 years Mujahedeen have not only entrenched themselves in Kashmir but have penetrated the Indian hinterland.

Young Abu Waleed is now better known as Zaki-ur-Rehman Lakhvi, operations chief of LeT, the terror outfit responsible for 26/11 terror siege in Mumbai five years ago. Lakhvi is currently in Pakistan's high security Adiala Prison, facing trial for his involvement in those attacks. But Zabiuddin Ansari alias Abu Jundal, one of the Indian Handlers, told Indian Investigator that his arrest was a sham. He is guarded by Lashkar men in jail and his operatives can still meet him there. He also alleged that Lakhvi has been provided with a satellite phone in jail so that he can talk to his men in the field.

With the bulk of US forces set to leave Afghanistan by 2014, the Indian Security Establishment is waiting with bated breath to see if history will repeat itself. "The situation is uncertain. We will have to see how many troops the US leaves behind. Another major factor will be the drones. If the US continues its drone strikes after the withdrawal, the Taliban will most likely not be able to capture and hold fresh territory. And Pakistan would not risk getting overtly involved in any Taliban offensive as the US retribution for such involvement would be swift. As long as Pakistan is not comfortable in Afghanistan it will not be able to escalate terror operations in India," says a security expert and Director of institute for conflict management.

Alleged Indian Mujahedeen (IM) operative Yaseen Bhatkal, arrested on 29th August 2013 by Indian Counter Terror Squad, during his interrogation allegedly gave significant insights into Pakistan's current strategy against India. "According to Yaseen, at the moment Pakistani spy Agency ISI is not in favour of a large scale operation like 26/11 for the international pressure it might spark, but wants the IM to continue exploding improvised explosive devices to keep the terror pot simmering," said a counter Terror Official. But Yaseen has also revealed that the IM is seeking a tie-up with Al-Qaeda, since it is fed up with the dictates of the ISI. "At the time of Yaseens' arrest the modalities of such a tie-up were being finalized," added the counter terror official. "Yaseen claims that a senior aide of Al-Qaeda Chief Ayman-Al-Zawahiri directed IM operatives to target Buddhist sites in India in order to allure Rohingya insurgents of Myanmar". The recent Nairobi attacks show how the scale of operations goes up once the ideology of Al-Qaeda penetrates a group like Al-Shabab.

India is playing its diplomatic cards very carefully to ensure that Afghanistan does not fall into the hands of Pakistan in post 2014 scenario. We must first see how many US soldiers stay behind, and in what capacity. As many as 12,000 could stay back either as training coordinators or Special Forces Personnel. Escalating terror activities in Kashmir are essentially linked with the US withdrawal. There is a need to study in detail the reports of a tie-up between IM and Al-Qaeda including any visible factionalism within these groups. We need to study the extent to which IM, LeT and Jaish-e-Muhammad can be independent of ISI. There is factionalism and infighting within the Taliban. This could alter the course of events in unpredictable ways and the ISI might then find itself incapable of controlling them. Al-Shabab leader Abdi Godane, responsible for the Nairobi attack, was ousted from leadership but refused to relinquish his position and tried to sensationalize the recent attack as a means to re-establish his leadership credential, using Kenyan recruits and the Somali settlers of Kenya. Parallels could be expected in India.

India is in constant discussions with China, Russia, Iran and other Central Asian Republics for a common strategy to deal with the issue of terrorism in order to ensure that it's National Security Concern are taken care of. The Indo-Pak equation may be entering one of its worst phases. The simmering tension at the LoC is a barometer of that impending fever. There are constant ceasefire violations and the border has become a hot bed of terror and bloodshed. For a country the size of India, It has become cumbersome to be constantly engaged in territorial disputes along its border. The fact that Pakistani top brass is completely radicalized also adds to India's woes. The present Prime Minister of Pakistan Mr. Nawaz Sharif is battling his own army after his decision to open talks with Pakistani Taliban. The outgoing army chief has already made it clear that Terrorist will not be allowed to set the terms. But the Pakistan security establishment shows no such allergy to Lashkar-e-Taiba or its founder and ideological patron Hafiz Saeed, who lives with impunity despite a $10 million U.S. bounty for information resulting in his arrest. In early September, Saeed was allowed to lead an inflammatory anti-India rally right in the heart of Pakistan's Capital and not too far from its National Assembly. The Pakistani-Punjab Government, led by the brother of Prime Minister Nawaz Sharif, has been repeatedly accused of looking the other way as Saeed mocks Indian concerns regarding the Mumbai attacks. Reports have also confirmed that the brother of Nawaz Sharif has donated a hefty sum to Jamat-ul-Dawa. These funds are to be utilized by Saeed for fanning fire across the LoC and the recent incidents of terrorism add weight to this report.

The Pakistani Leader who believes in peace with India does not do so for love of India. He believes the cost of hostility is too high a price to afford. The best thing can be said about the handshake in New York was that it was a non-event. In fact India-Pakistan equation cannot be set in order as long as the people of Pakistan are hungry for Jammu and Kashmir. They risk everything to attain this piece of "Paradise". The leaders are also singing the same song and all the areas of civil society like state policy, Judiciary and army are radicalized. They don't want a pluralistic society in Pakistan and only the Jihadists or Sunni Muslims have a say in the day to day running of the Government.

Solution

This book itself serves as a part of the solution proposed to neutralize the clout of Islamic terrorism. In fact we have been able to compile a plan of action for uniting the peace loving citizens of the world by empowering them with facts and figures which form the rock solid foundation of a vision to improve the abysmal state of affairs.

By means of this book we aim to spread awareness amongst Indians, including our political parties, parliament and Judiciary about Jammu and Kashmir. It is an integral part of India and people of that state have chosen this destiny for themselves. In 1947, Pakistan annexed a large part of the Indian state of Jammu and Kashmir by sending tribal people to plunder the Valley of Kashmir and intimidate the innocent masses of the neighbouring area to surrender. At that time a U.N. resolution was made that directed Pakistan to take back the tribesmen as well as its army which invaded the state, they should vacate and handover the Pakistan occupied Kashmir to India. Therefore it becomes the prerogative of the Indian Government to take back what rightfully belongs to the people of India from Pakistan and China.

For such a dream to materialize we require all the political parties (in power or opposition) and all the stakeholders to be brought on the same page. Every common man in India should understand that this task needs to be completed otherwise India as a whole nation would be a failure.

India epitomizes peace and communal harmony. Pakistan is considered a neighbour and Indians "Love Thy Neighbour". India has always helped Pakistan, but Pakistan has become a fountainhead of terrorism. In the absence of a true democracy, jihadist and radicalized Muslims have become leaders of the country and they are running a parallel Government in Pakistan. In other words we can say that the religion of Pakistan has

271

become Islamic fundamentalism and only a singular society can exist in Pakistan today. In today's world Pakistan is the ultimate sanctuary for terrorists as was made public by the assassination of 9/11 master mind, Bin Laden, who was tracked down in Pakistan's Abbotabad province and killed by U.S. navy seals.

India and Pakistan Unite

We respect all the religions of the world and the entire world considers India as a peaceful, progressive and highly educated people who are friends to one and all. This problem should be solved peacefully with Pakistan. We should have political discussions on the matter and appeal to the Pakistani people, the jihadist and the army top brass that they should settle this matter peacefully, for Pakistan before 1947 was India and they are our brothers, although they have a different philosophy of life and they have became too rigid mentally in solving the territorial matters. There should be people to people contact and cultural exchange between civilians. If Indians visit Pakistan they should be respected and allowed to pay respects to their temples, Dargahs, Shrines and Gurudwaras. We should encourage sports and facilitate maximum number of games being played in Pakistan itself to send out a strong message of fearlessness and unity to extremists. We should have long term respectful and amicable relations with Pakistan in order to ensure that Pakistan progresses in a modern way and attracts respect from the whole world as a part of the Incredible Indian Subcontinent. India's chairman Justice Markandey Katju said in a press conference on 5th February 2013, "Pakistan is a fake country; artificially created by the British who started the bogus two-nation theory." The former Supreme Court judge said that he was confident that India and Pakistan could reunite during the next 15-20 years into a strong, powerful, secular and modern country.

We have been trying to sort out differences with Pakistan on all the matters that divide us yet they have waged three wars against us. They have not attained even a single grass of blade with this mayhem, but lost Muslim Bengal forever. During Indira Gandhi's era about a lakh of Pakistani army was captured by India and they were respectfully returned to Pakistan without any harm, on the other hand we have seen that Pakistan has exploited even small matters like Sarabjeet Singh's trial in jail, killing him there itself.

The Pakistani nuclear scientist (Abdul Kadir Khan) says that he has developed the Great Islamic bomb to safe guard Pakistan but India is also a nuclear power. However we are using the same energy for peaceful purposes. In case the dirty bomb produced by Dr. Khan goes in the hands of Islamic terrorists, that will be the end of the world as we know it.

Pundits

All the seven lakh Kashmiri Pundits who have become refugees in their own country need to be pacified. For the last 25 years they have been rotting in migrant camps of Jammu. Nobody is helping them and our political parties have turned a deaf ear to their plight. They are living in miserable conditions. They should be brought back to their homeland and their safety, security and employment should be insured. Only then can they feel pride in being a part of secular India. According to official figures 15 to 20 lakh tourists visited the Kashmir valley during the last tourist season and yet not even a single Pundit could enter his home. Justice must be served along with adequate remuneration for their loss.

Local Population

The separatist leader like Ali-shah Gilani, Mir Waiz Umar Farook, Yaseem Malik and others should be not allowed to visit Pakistan or the embassy of Pakistan in the interest of peace in the valley. The Kashmiri Muslims should not listen to the separatists. They must forgo all public provocations to indulge in strikes, stone pelting or demonstrations against the security forces which are stationed there to counter any offensive by Pakistan. They should live in peace and harmony with Pundits in the valley because peace is also the teaching of Islam.

Most importantly they should respect the fact that they live in a secular, democratic and peaceful country which provides all the amenities to the people without any vested interests. Kashmir has been given special status under article 370 for their progress and prosperity. They should not give any donations to Pakistanis for purchasing arms and ammunition. They should not believe the hollow promises of Pakistan. No terrorist should be sheltered in their houses, mosques or village.

In case they do so, their *Kashmiriyat* for which they are known as the residents of paradise gets eroded. What is left; only a battle spanning their entire life for mere survival? Terrorism will eat away all their peace and prosperity, which they have attained as Indians.

REQUEST TO WORLD CONSCIENCE
BY THE WRITER

The saga of Kashmir valley may well be called World's Greatest Hamletian Dilemma. Kashmir doesn't belong to a handful of quarrelsome stakeholders. It has been bestowed upon this Earth by God himself. Therefore we appeal to all peace loving people of the world to come forward and play their crucial role in deliverance of justice. Injustice anywhere requires action everywhere.

"Agar firdaus bar roo-e-zameen ast,
Hameen ast . . . . hameen ast . . . hameen ast . . ."

"If at all paradise occurs anywhere on this Earth, It is here and here alone."

Paradise is believed to be the abode of God and based on the present state of affairs it is impossible to bestow such a title upon Kashmir. The fanatic Muslim activists operate from the backyard of the Omnipotent, Omniscient, Omnipresent and Omnificent Maker of the World. So the authors of this book have no reservations while titling this book *"Is God Dead? And Islamic terriorist are condemned to be free in Kashmir."*

It is high time that the conscience of mankind awakened to the reality of Kashmir. The so-called freedom struggle is merely an escalation of the ongoing offensive against the small, yet ancient and distinct ethnic and religious community, which has been turned into a minority—the Kashmiri Pundits (Hindu). They are being exterminated under a diabolical plan masterminded by religious zealots-turned-terrorists with the direction, support and connivance of their mentors from across the border in Pakistan; we appeal therefore to all the nations of the world; to all peace-loving, secular and democratic countries which value and recognise the rights, realities, and aspirations of minorities round the globe; To all organisations that monitor and report on human rights' violations against ethnic religious communities and to all individuals, groups and institutions that stand for justice, equality, tolerance and human dignity. We must break this silence and speak out to save these descendants of the oldest human civilization of the world, which has been thrown out of its homeland and made a refugee in its own country.

Presently every other day the common Man of Kashmir protests against the incompetence of Indian Governance. Fuelled by provocative speeches of separatist leaders the common man refuses to cooperate with the security forces, the elected legislature and the rest of India. Their demand is a Kashmir left alone.

They ask, *"Is God dead?"* They ask for a day when the only noise on the streets is not from a gun. They ask for an age where the youth is not in rebellion. They ask for a time when no child is orphaned, no sister is raped and no mother is widowed. They ask for a Kashmir separate from the rest of India. They ask for a *"Paradise"* on earth.

And while they wish for all this,

They forget that happiness is true only when it is shared. They forget that they have to take the responsibility for their actions. They forget that millions of Kashmiri pundits were forced out of their homes. They forget that the only comparison that history allows us to make is the Jewish exodus of Nazi Germany. They forget that God was not dead when they orphaned a child, raped a sister, and widowed a mother. They forget that they fired a gunshot in the *"Paradise"* on Earth.

Being the embodied soul of love that India aspires to become,

We pray that Islamic radicalism steps down and offers peace a chance. We pray that the Kashmiri Muslims listen to their heart instead of a Mullah issuing orders on a microphone. We pray that the Kashmiri pundits get their long denied constitutional right to live in India and settle down in any part of the country they deem fit to be their home. We pray that Muslims welcome Hindus with open hearts in the valley, just as Muslims were received by the local Hindus several generations ago. We pray that all bad blood is forgotten. If Muslims, Buddhists, Christians, Zoroastrians, Sikhs,

Jews and other Animist faiths along with their multitude of sects, castes and creeds can prosper in an India where 80 percent of the population follows Hindu culture, then why can't the Kashmiri Muslims tolerate a mere 4 percent of humans sharing their valley. We pray that the next jihad in the valley is in the name of Love and Peace.

BIBLIOGRAPHY

- Yang, Qinye; Zheng, Du (2004). *Himalayan Mountain System.* ISBN 9787508506654.
- Bishop, Barry. "Himalayas (mountains, Asia)". Encyclopaedia Britannica.
- Imperial Gazetteer2 of India, Volume 15, page 99—Imperial Gazetteer of India—Digital South Asia Library
- Hutchinson, J. & J. PH Vogel (1933).
- Aggarwal, J. and Agrawal, S. Modern History of Jammu and Kashmir: Ancient times to Shimla Agreement
- Nalwa, V., 2009. Hari Singh Nalwa-Champion of the Khalsaji.
- Allan, Nigel J. R. 1995 Karakorum Himalaya: Sourcebook for a Protected Area.
- Zeisler, Bettina. (2010).
- Hussain, Ijaz. 1998. "Kashmir Dispute: An International Law Perspective", National Institute of Pakistan Studies.
- Khan, L. Ali The Kashmir Dispute: A Plan for Regional Cooperation
- Irfani, Suroosh, ed "Fifty Years of the Kashmir Dispute": Based on the proceedings of the International Seminar held at Muzaffarabad, Azad Jammu and Kashmir 24-25 August 1997: University of Azad Jammu and Kashmir, Muzaffarabad, AJK, 1997.
- Peerzada, Ashiq (December 27, 2012). "'90 Srinagar massacre: SHRC orders fresh probe". *Hindustan Times.*
- The Earthtimes (2007-09-24).
- 2011 census of India. Retrieved 7 December 2012.
- *Official Web Site of Jammu and Kashmir Tourism.*
- The Holy Himalayas By Shantha N. Nair
- Economic blockade affects life in Kashmir (4 August 2008).
- Bose, Sumantra (2005).
- Bakshi, S.R. (1997). *Kashmir: History & People.* Sarup & Sons. p. 103. ISBN 8185431965.

- Essa, Assad (2 August 2011). "Kashmiri Pandits: Why we never fled Kashmir". aljazeera.com.
- Radhakrishnan, Sarvepalli (1973). *The Hindu view of life.* Pennsylvania State University: Macmillan.
- Sivaraman, Krishna (1997). *Hindu spirituality: an encyclopedic history of the religious quest. Postclassical and modern, Volume 2.* The Crossroad Publishing Co.
- D. S. Sarma, Kenneth W. Morgan, *The Religion of the Hindus,* 1953.
- The Vedas / Puranas.
- Abdul-Haqq, Abdiyah Akbar (1980). *Sharing Your Faith with a Muslim.* Minneapolis: Bethany House Publishers. *N.B.* Presents the genuine doctrines and concepts of Islam and of the Holy Qur'an, and this religion's affinities with Christianity and its Sacred Scriptures, in order to "dialogue" on the basis of what both faiths really teach. ISBN 0-89123-553-6
- Khanbaghi (2006). *The Fire, the Star and the Cross: Minority Religions in Medieval and Early Modern Iran.* I. B. Tauris.
- Najeebabadi, Akbar Shah (2001). *History of Islam.* Dar-us-Salam Publications. ISBN 978-1-59144-034-5.
- Buddhism". (2009). In Encyclopædia Britannica. Retrieved November 26, 2009, from Encyclopædia Britannica Online Library Edition.
- Padmasambhava, Jamgon Kongtrul, Erik Pema Kunsang (2004). *Light of Wisdom.* Rangjung Yeshe Publications.ISBN 978-962-7341-37-6
- *The Bodhisattva Vow: A Practical Guide to Helping Others,* pages 4-12, Tharpa Publications (2nd. ed., 1995) ISBN 978-0-948006-50-0
- For Gupta Dynasty (c. 320—500 CE) and Puranic religion as important to the spread across the subcontinent, see: Flood (1996)
- Flood, Gavin. D. 1996. An Introduction to Hinduism.
- Sastri, K.A. Nilakanta. "A Historical Sketch of Saivism", in: Bhattacharyya (1956), Volume IV
- Singh, Khushwant (2006). *The Illustrated History of the Sikhs.* India: Oxford University Press. p. 15. ISBN 978-0-19-567747-8.
- Chahal, Devinder (July-December 2006). "Understanding Sikhism in the Science Age". *Understanding Sikhism.*
- Chanchreek, Jain (2007). *Encyclopaedia of Great Festivals.* Shree Publishers & Distributors.
- Shree Guru Granth Sahib. (Adi Granth)

- Ambedkar, B.R. (1946). *Pakistan, or Partition of India* (2 ed.). AMS Press Inc.
- Pakistan: The Indo-Pakistani War of 1965". *Library of Congress Country Studies, United States of America.* April 1994. Retrieved 2 October 2010.
- APP and Pakistan Television (PTV), Prime Minister Secretariat Press Release (18 May 1974).

ABOUT THE AUTHORS

Shri Raghubir Lal Anand was born in a middle class family on October 28, 1939 in a village named *Eklas* in *Tehsil Pindigheb* of District *Campbellpur* near Rawalpindi (now in Pakistan). After the partition of India in 1947, his parents migrated to India as refugees. Though his early education was in India, he graduated from Tribhuvan University (Nepal). His wide portfolio of employers includes Military Engineering Services, Department of Atomic Energy Government of India, headed by Dr Jehangir Bhabha, Birla Group of Industries, Ashoka Hotel, India Tourism Development Corporation in various senior positions. His pioneering concept about the use of solar energy is being applied throughout the country and abroad due to paucity of electric power. In 1974, a book for MBA titled *"New Horizons in Purchasing"* was authored by Mr. Anand and was published by Thompson Press. The book turned out to be a grand success. He has written the book "Is God Dead???" on a concept given by *Shri Tirath Raj Bhanot* whom the author considers his "Preceptor". Mr. Bhanot has written more than one thousand books in the field of education.

"It was my preceptor who inspired me to write the present book when I was bedridden due to cancer. This book "Is God Dead" deals with the miserable plight of the innocent Kashmiri Pundits who were almost exterminated from their homeland by Islamic Jihadists and terrorists. The total genocide was prevented only due to the brave Jawans (soldiers) of India.

Abhilash is a young Vaishnava monk residing in New Delhi, India. He studied Mass communication at Xavier's college Mumbai. After graduation he developed an interactive learning module for National Handloom and Handicrafts Museum (NHHM). A recipient of the prestigious Jawaharlal Nehru Yuva Dhara Youth internship and Gandhi Fellowship Program, he has previously collaborated with United Nations Educational and Cultural Organization (UNESCO). He is one of the co-founders of "7 Ways Through Sunday" Project. In his leisure time he conducts creative writing workshops for underprivileged children.

Follow your Favourite Author on Twitter @TheReaderWriter